THE EXTRAORDINARY IN THE ORDINARY

THE EXTRAORDINARY IN THE ORDINARY

The Aesthetics of Everyday Life

Thomas Leddy

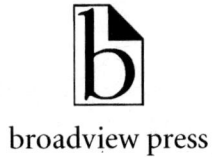

broadview press

© 2012 Thomas Leddy

All rights reserved. The use of any part of this publication reproduced, transmitted in any form or by any means, electronic, mechanical, photocopying, recording, or otherwise, or stored in a retrieval system, without prior written consent of the publisher—or in the case of photocopying, a licence from Access Copyright (Canadian Copyright Licensing Agency), One Yonge Street, Suite 1900, Toronto, Ontario M5E 1E5—is an infringement of the copyright law.

Library and Archives Canada Cataloguing in Publication

Leddy, Thomas
    The extraordinary in the ordinary : the aesthetics of everyday life / Thomas Leddy.

Includes bibliographical references and index.
ISBN 978-1-55111-478-1

    1. Aesthetics. I. Title.
BH39.L43 2012   111'.85   C2011-908309-4

Broadview Press is an independent, international publishing house, incorporated in 1985.

We welcome comments and suggestions regarding any aspect of our publications—please feel free to contact us at the addresses below or at broadview@broadviewpress.com.

North America
PO Box 1243, Peterborough, Ontario, Canada K9J 7H5
2215 Kenmore Ave., Buffalo, New York, USA 14207
Tel: (705) 743-8990; Fax: (705) 743-8353
email: customerservice@broadviewpress.com

UK, Europe, Central Asia, Middle East, Africa, India, and Southeast Asia
Eurospan Group, 3 Henrietta St., London WC2E 8LU, United Kingdom
Tel: 44 (0) 1767 604972; Fax: 44 (0) 1767 601640
email: eurospan@turpin-distribution.com

Australia and New Zealand
NewSouth Books
c/o TL Distribution, 15-23 Helles Ave., Moorebank, NSW, Australia 2170
Tel: (02) 8778 9999; Fax: (02) 8778 9944
email: orders@tldistribution.com.au

www.broadviewpress.com

Copy-edited by Robert M. Martin

This book is printed on paper containing 100% post-consumer fibre.

 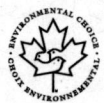

PRINTED IN CANADA

Contents

Acknowledgements • 7

Introduction • 9

Part I: The Domain of Everyday Aesthetics • 15

Chapter 1: The Nature of Everyday Aesthetics • 17
Chapter 2: Aesthetic Experience and Aesthetic Properties • 57
Chapter 3: Everyday Aesthetics and the Environment • 93

Part II: A Theory of Everyday Aesthetics • 125

Chapter 4: Aesthetic Experience as Experience of Objects with Aura • 127
Chapter 5: A Bestiary of Aesthetic Terms for Everyday Contexts • 151
Chapter 6: Criticisms Actual and Possible • 187
Chapter 7: Everyday Surface Aesthetic Qualities • 217
Chapter 8: Everyday Aesthetics and the Sublime • 237

Conclusion • 259

Index • 263

Acknowledgements

I would first like to thank the following for permission to include parts of my previously published writings. *The Journal of Aesthetics and Art Criticism*: "Everyday Surface Aesthetic Qualities: 'Neat,' 'Messy,' 'Clean,' 'Dirty,'" 53, no. 3 (1995): 259-68; *British Journal of Aesthetics*: "Sparkle and Shine," 37, no. 3 (1997): 259-73; Columbia University Press: "The Nature of Everyday Aesthetics," *The Aesthetics of Everyday Life*, ed. Andrew Light and Jonathan M. Smith (2005), 3-22; *Notre Dame Philosophical Reviews*: "Yuriko Saito. Everyday Aesthetics," review, 2/15/09 http://ndpr.nd.edu/review.cfm?id=15188; and *Aesthetic Pathways*: "Everday Aesthetics and the Sublime," 1, no. 2 (2011), 21-46.

A number of philosophers have assisted me with comments and encouragement along the way. Russell Quacchia wrote at length in reply to an early draft. Stan Godlovitch has always been a good friend and a trenchant critic. Yuriko Saito deserves special thanks for being a constant and early supporter and for carefully reviewing the entire text as philosopher critic for Broadview Press. Robert Martin of Broadview Press provided valuable editorial help. Others include in alphabetical order: Arnold Berleant, Allen Carlson, Theodore Gracyk, Sherri Irvin, JoEllen Jacobs, Carolyn Korsmeyer, Sheila Lintott, Stephanie Ross, Cynthia Rostankowski, Barbara Sandrisser, Larry Shiner, Richard Shusterman, and Robert Stecker. I want to thank my colleagues at San Jose State University for many comments on ideas in their early stages, and just for being great people to work with. I wish to thank San Jose State University for a sabbatical and a release time grant dedicated to completing this book, and Arto Haapala and the University of Helsinki for an invitation and a travel grant to give "Everyday Aesthetics and the Sublime" at the International Institute of Applied Aesthetics Summer School on Everyday Aesthetics. I also want to thank my students in a variety of classes ranging from Introduction to Aesthetics to two graduate seminars on aesthetics. Ahmad Mohmand deserves special thanks for going over an entire early draft. Dave Cellers has assisted by way of many years of stimulating conversation. Finally, my wife, Karen Haas, has probably been the strongest influence in my work. As a painter, she has made me constantly aware of the role of the artist in our perception of everyday life. I dedicate this book to her.

Introduction

I first became interested in everyday aesthetics when I found myself wondering about lists of aesthetic properties and why some properties which I would consider to be aesthetic did not appear on the lists commonly offered. This led to my writing an essay on the properties of neatness and messiness. From there I found that these neglected properties, and others like them, were often associated with an entire field of phenomena that had been ignored in aesthetics. Although these properties are often found in the aesthetics of art they were neglected largely because they were associated more with the everyday. At first, I thought that I was alone in doing this kind of research, but gradually I came to recognize that others were doing related work. I also discovered many affinities between what I was doing in everyday aesthetics and the rise of the aesthetics of nature. The aesthetics of nature had largely been neglected in the twentieth century until the 1970s. When I was a graduate student, aesthetics was largely limited to the aesthetics of art, and to fine art at that. However, in the 1970s and 1980s nature aesthetics grew, largely under the influence of such figures as Allen Carlson and Arnold Berleant, to become a major part of contemporary aesthetic theory. During the same period, there was an increasing interest in the popular arts. For example, discussions of jazz, rock and rap took their place alongside more traditional discussions of classical music. This interest in the popular arts contributed to expanding the notion of what aesthetics could cover, opening the door for the everyday. Also, as feminism and feminist theory grew, so did feminist aesthetics, and feminists were more likely than other aestheticians to attend to things of everyday life, for example quilts and cooking. The rise of multiculturalism was another factor insofar as philosophers became aware that non-Western cultures often had aesthetic interests that did not correspond to our Western concept of art. In considering these matters the boundaries between art and non-art began, if not to disintegrate, at least to become softer and more complex. This opened up aesthetic interest in what would be considered from a Western perspective to be non-art phenomena. Another contributing factor to the birth of everyday aesthetics was the rise of applied philosophy. Just as ethicists were getting interested in such topics as the ethics of business and sports in the 1970s and 1980s, a small number of philosophers in aesthetics found themselves involved in such topics as gardens, sports and clothing.

Increasing interest in interdisciplinary studies contributed to this new field in yet another way. Aestheticians gradually discovered that scholars in other disciplines were doing work that could lend fresh insight into their subject-matter. The human sciences in particular had much to say, at least tangentially, about aesthetics, and what they had to say was not necessarily limited to the arts. Anthropologists, for example, have increasingly taken interest in both art and non-art aesthetic issues in the societies they study, and although folklorists have long been interested in everyday life they have come recently to theorize their field in ways that should be of interest to aestheticians. Meanwhile, art history and art criticism have moved away from exclusive interest in the fine arts, and have embraced a new emphasis on the wider domain of visual culture, a domain that includes such things as advertising and amateur photography.

In addition, the revival of pragmatism due to the work of Richard Rorty and specialists in American Philosophy encouraged new approaches to aesthetics. Within aesthetics itself, Joseph Margolis and Richard Shusterman were particularly associated with the new pragmatism. This tendency quickly gained adherents among philosophers who, although disillusioned with aspects of analytic aesthetics, also found themselves confused by, or unenthusiastic about, recent trends in continental philosophy. The rediscovery of John Dewey's pragmatist aesthetics, which had been buried under the onslaught of the analytic revolution in aesthetics that took place in the 1950s, paved the way for everyday aesthetics through its emphasis on the human as a live creature interacting with its environment and on the continuity between art aesthetics and everyday life. Finally, the rise of cognitive science, along with an increasing interest in the evolutionary roots of aesthetic experience, has lent to a broader science-based understanding of aesthetics which, in turn, has pointed to a wider domain of aesthetic experience than that covered by the arts alone or even by the arts plus nature.

My own training in philosophy was diverse. I had teachers from various traditions: analytic, phenomenological, existentialist, and Marxist. Over the last fifteen years I have been strongly influenced by Deweyan pragmatism, partly due to an NEH summer seminar on Culture and Pragmatism led by Richard Shusterman and John Stuhr at Penn State in 2001. Nor did I come to aesthetics directly from philosophy. My first graduate degree was in Interdisciplinary Humanities from San Francisco State University. There I was encouraged to think about philosophy and the arts together. This gave me a broad perspective that I have attempted to maintain throughout my career. My PhD Dissertation was on theory of metaphor, a central issue in philosophical aesthetics. My advisors were Marx Wartofsky, who combined American pragmatism with epistemological insights derived from Marxism, and Erazim Kohák, who gave me a new appreciation of phenomenology. As a graduate student I became involved in the American Society for Aesthetics, becoming co-editor of their newsletter with Hilde Hein, who was an important mentor. I have been active in that organization ever since, including one stint as a Board of Trustees member.

Most of my professional career has been in the world of analytic aesthetics as this is the dominant mode of aesthetic thought in the English-speaking world. I enjoy reading in this tradition, discussing the papers, and interacting with my colleagues at conferences. However, it has constantly seemed to me that analytic aesthetics has a significant blind spot in what it has to say about the creative process and about the relationship between everyday phenomena and the arts. Analytic aesthetics everywhere sees disconnection between creative process and product and between everyday aesthetics and fine art. John Dewey, by contrast, saw the continuity that analytic aesthetics denies. He has inspired my own conviction that the bridge between everyday aesthetics and the arts, and thus the unity of aesthetics itself, is through understanding how artists perceive the world in their daily practice. This blindness to continuity can be found in the attempt to explain aesthetic experience in terms of something non-aesthetic, to see aesthetic properties as dependent on non-aesthetic properties. I shall argue that this is a mistake comparable to the attempt by ethicists to derive moral statements from statements of fact.

I have my own theory of aesthetic experience which I will develop in this book. This is a phenomenological approach to aesthetics. It emphasizes the way in which an object can take on a quality when it is perceived aesthetically, a quality I call "aura." Think about the way that you experience things when you are in love: the world seems transformed, and everything has a new significance; a certain aura seems to emanate not only from the person loved but from other objects in one's environment. Admittedly the experience of aura is subjective, or is shared only by similarly situated subjects. However, aura also has an object side. That is, it is objects and events that have aura in our experience of them.

Admittedly, also, this approach raises the danger of relativism. However, as I shall argue, this danger may be alleviated by understanding evaluation as a social process that draws from a number of legitimate sources. I will pursue this issue in relation to evaluation of objects of everyday aesthetics. In most matters, an approach derived from David Hume's theory of taste as guided by the good judge can overcome this problem. At times, however Hume's approach needs to be supplemented by a strategy closer to that of Kant, whose notion of taste does not require Hume's idea of delicacy of sentiment, but only the kind of free play of imagination and understanding that is available to anyone. At times, other approaches to evaluation are more relevant. In the end I will advocate eclecticism in evaluation of everyday aesthetic phenomena.

What is everyday aesthetics? It would be a mistake to take the term "everyday" too literally.[1] A musician who practices and plays every day can justly say that her everyday aesthetic experience is mainly connected with music. A naturalist could similarly say that his is of nature. Yet when we talk about everyday aesthetic experience, we are thinking of aesthetic issues that are not connected closely with the fine arts or with the natural environment, or with other areas that have their own restricted aesthetic domains, for example the aesthetics of mathematics or physics. We are thinking instead of the home, the daily commute, the workplace, the shopping centre and places of amusement, including now, increasingly, online "places" of experience.[2] That is, we are thinking of these things in the context of the world-wide city-based culture within which most of us live.

Of course there will also be a distinctive everyday aesthetics for other cultures, for example, seventeenth-century English aristocratic culture, or twenty-first-century indigenous culture in the Amazon. Data from these

---

1   Chapters I, II, and III are revised from material I first discussed in "The Nature of Everyday Aesthetics," Chapter 1 in *The Aesthetics of Everyday Life*, ed. Andrew Light and Jonathan M. Smith (New York: Columbia University Press, 2005), 3-22.
2   I owe this point to my student Esuebio Lozano who has reminded me that the Internet virtual world "Second Life" contains entire environments and communities, and that online experiences have become part of the everyday life for "residents."

societies should not be excluded from the study of everyday aesthetics.[3] An aesthetic of everyday life, as also aesthetics in general, needs to avoid making universal judgments based solely on the cultural lives of the writer and his or her likely readers. We should even consider whether the aesthetics of everyday life should also extend to the lives of non-human animals, particularly those that are relatively intelligent.[4]

Many readers may wonder why we should bother with everyday aesthetics since the places to find the most intense aesthetic experiences are the domains of art and pristine nature. I would like to make four points in reply. First, if we are going to have a discipline of aesthetics we must study the whole field, not just the high points. We also need to look at the experiences of all human types, not just those of people typically found in departments of philosophy. For example, we need to look at the experiences of children and we need to overcome a long-standing neglect of feminine experience. We also need to look at the experiences of people in other cultures. Second, the aesthetics of art depends in many ways on everyday aesthetics. Unlike most philosophers, artists are constant and close observers of everyday life. Failing to study the aesthetics of everyday life is failing to study the basis for the practice of art itself. Third, everyday aesthetics is immensely important for our lives. Right attention to aesthetic properties can contribute to our well-being; wrong attention can be harmful. Efforts to improve society should take into account the role that aesthetics plays in everyday choices. Finally, as we shall see, the aesthetics of everyday life poses significant challenges to assumptions within aesthetics generally and perhaps even within philosophy itself.

---

3   On Amazonian culture, see Joanna Overing and Alan Passes, eds., *The Anthropology of Love and Anger: The Aesthetics of Conviviality in Native Amazonia* (New York: Routledge, 2000). For Himalayan everyday aesthetics see Robert R. Desjarlais, *Body and Emotion: The Aesthetics of Illness and Healing in the Nepal Himalayas* (Philadelphia: University of Pennsylvania Press, 1992).
4   Thanks to my student Jesse Tieu for drawing this to my attention. See Wolfgang Welsch, "Animal Aesthetics," *Contemporary Aesthetics* 2 (2004), accessed July 13, 2010, http://www.contempaesthetics.org/newvolume/pages/article.php?articleID=243.

Part I: The Domain of Everyday Aesthetics

CHAPTER 1
The Nature of Everyday Aesthetics

A NEW FIELD IN AESTHETICS

I began my Introduction with the question "What is everyday aesthetics?" Answering that question requires carving out a new field of inquiry from an area that seems to many to be covered already. Many writers assume the domains of nature and art cover the entire field of aesthetics. Yet, both are too narrow to cover the aesthetics of everyday life. The aesthetics of nature is usually limited to pristine nature, or something close to it. The beauty of a garden or a flower arrangement would not normally be discussed in a book on the aesthetics of nature. Nor would the way a sunset enhances the beauty of a city street. Similarly, the aesthetics of art has largely been limited to the fine arts, and although many writers have recently sought to expand it to include the popular arts, few have considered expansion to, for example, the arts of conversation or car repair. So aesthetics of nature and the aesthetics of art have failed to cover the entire field of aesthetics despite efforts to extend the reaches of each.

But, someone might ask, isn't aesthetics just another name for the philosophy of art? If so there is no room for the aesthetics of everyday life. It is rare to find this view actually argued by a philosopher, although perhaps Hegel held it. However it is a popular one. I have even found "aesthetics" defined in a well-known dictionary as "1. the branch of philosophy dealing with such notions as the beautiful, the ugly, the sublime, the comic, etc., as applicable to the fine arts, with a view to establishing the meaning and validity of critical judgments concerning works of art, and the principles underlying or justifying such judgments. 2. the study of the mind and emotions in relation to the sense of beauty."[1] The first meaning clearly limits aesthetics to the arts and, although the second allows for non-art aesthetics, someone coming to the concept for the first time through this definition would probably conclude that there can be no such thing. Yet when the term "aesthetics" was coined in 1735 by the German philosopher Alexander Baumgarten, he defined it more broadly as "the science of how things are to be cognized by means of the senses."[2] Although Baumgarten was mainly interested in the arts there is no reason why this science (or "study" as we would call it today) would need to be limited to the arts or to the arts plus nature.

There has been growing recognition of the importance of extending aesthetics to non-art, non-nature objects. Robert Stecker, for instance, in his recent introduction to aesthetics, notes that many things possess aesthetic value that are neither artworks nor natural objects: "many everyday things, such as our clothes and other adornments, the decoration of our living spaces, everyday artifacts from toasters to automobiles, packaging, the appearance of our faces and bodies, the artificial environments we create, the food we eat...."[3] This is a nice list, although it fails to mention events such as weddings and festivals, and it talks more in terms of objects than of the experiences that might contain them. Unfortunately, Stecker does not pursue everyday aesthetics in this book beyond a brief discussion of restaurant meals.[4]

Drawing from Stecker's list, and others like it, we may say that everyday aesthetics considers such things as personal appearance, interior decoration, the workplace environment, sexual experience, appliance design, cooking, gardening, hobbies, and play. Of course the boundaries between the aesthetics of art, nature and everyday life are not clearly drawn, nor is it clear that they

---

1 Dictionary.com, accessed April 14, 2011, http://dictionary.reference.com/browse/aesthetics.
2 Paul Guyer, "Baumgarten, Alexander Gottlieb," in *Encyclopedia of Aesthetics*, ed. Michael Kelly, Vol. 1 (New York: Oxford University Press, 1998), 227-28.
3 Robert Stecker, *Aesthetics and the Philosophy of Art: An Introduction* 2nd ed. (Lanham: Rowman and Littlefield, 2010), 4.
4 Stecker, 4-5.

can be definitively. (Are sports art-forms? If so, then the aesthetics of sports is part of the aesthetics of art. If not, then it is part of everyday aesthetics.) This would especially be the case if we were required to define "everyday aesthetics" in terms of necessary and sufficient conditions. A definition in terms of necessary and sufficient conditions (also called a "real definition") is often considered to be the gold standard of definition for philosophical terms. It is generally supposed to describe the essence of the thing under consideration. Most agree that such a definition can be accomplished with some mathematical concepts. For example, "triangle" can be defined in such a way as to cover all triangles and exclude all things that are not triangles. Some believe that it can also be accomplished in the hard sciences: for example "Water is H_2O" is such a definition. Being H_2O is both necessary for something to be water and sufficient for something to be water.

However, not being able to define "everyday aesthetics" in these strict terms would not put it in any worse shape than many other philosophical concepts. For example, the attempt to define "art" in terms of necessary and sufficient conditions came up against the powerful criticism raised by Morris Weitz in the 1950s under the influence of Ludwig Wittgenstein, and although Weitz's view has had many critics, it continues to have a strong influence.[5] I bring up this issue since the ideal of definition in terms of necessary and sufficient conditions continues to be popular amongst contemporary aestheticians and an attempt to give such a definition might be expected here. This expectation would be disappointed. What I hope to do instead is give some idea of the scope of inquiry into the aesthetics of everyday life as well as of implications that such inquiry might have for aesthetics in general.

Although a "real definition" of everyday aesthetics is unlikely, it is worthwhile to say something more about how the field might be limited. One commentator on an earlier draft of this book has asked whether it is to be distinguished from ordinary aesthetics?[6] The answer is, not at all! Everyday aesthetics is a *branch* of aesthetics. It is not distinguished from ordinary aesthetics unless one sees "ordinary aesthetics" as the way aesthetics is done when it does not recognize the importance of everyday aesthetics. The other two main branches of aesthetics are aesthetics of art and aesthetics of nature. (Aesthetics of mathematics might be considered a fourth area.) Some however will think

---

5 Morris Weitz, "The Role of Theory in Aesthetics," *The Journal of Aesthetics and Art Criticism* 15, no. 1 (1956): 27-35.
6 Robert M. Martin raised the question.

that "aesthetics" and related terms are necessarily tied to art, or even more specifically, to high art. Richard Shusterman has observed a similar problem in relation to his defence of the aesthetics of popular art.[7] To the objection that the term "aesthetic" tends to be exclusively appropriated to high art, he replies that this is no longer true outside of intellectual circles and that the practice needs to be changed within those circles. He argues further that, although the term "aesthetic" originated in an intellectual context, and has been most often limited to high art and to refined appreciation of nature, it is no longer so constrained. He also observes that such aesthetic terms as "grace" and "elegance" are applied to popular art every bit as much as to fine art. Although my concern here is not with popular art, the point I would make is similar to Shusterman's, for example that such terms as "grace" and "elegance" may also be applied to such everyday phenomena as human movement, arrangement of tableware for a party, and conversation between friends.

Nothing I am saying here is to deny the distinction between art (both high and popular) and non-art aesthetic phenomena. The objects of everyday aesthetics are not works of art. Although some works of art, both high and popular, are experienced every day by someone, as I mentioned in the Introduction, everyday aesthetics is not defined by what is experienced literally every day but by what is not art or nature. Moreover, there is a commonly accepted domain of everyday objects and experiences. People generally recognize what is meant by "everyday life": that it refers less, for example, to the part of a concert pianist's life that involves performing as an artist than to what happens when she goes to the grocery store.

So where is the dividing line that marks the limits of everyday aesthetics? This is a matter that is relative to social, cultural and historical context. It is doubtful that the Navajo, for example, make a clear distinction between the aesthetics of everyday life and that of art. It is said that they do not have a word for art, and the closest word they have to our "beauty," *hózhó*, seems to be applicable in every aspect of their lives. In Western culture the distinction between everyday life and art is often made clear simply by location: concerts happen mainly in concert halls and visual art is found mainly in museums and galleries. However, the distinction between everyday aesthetics and the aesthetics of popular art is more difficult in that the two are closer together and

---

[7] Richard Shusterman, "The Aesthetic Challenge of Popular Art," *British Journal of Aesthetics* 31, no. 2 (1991): 203-11.

often overlap. Many of the phenomena discussed by everyday aestheticians have been in the domain of what have been called the minor arts (for example textiles, jewellery), and these are often associated with popular art. Although the appreciation of one's clean-shaven face in a mirror is never seen to be a matter of appreciating art, whether fine or popular, it could be argued that barbering is a minor art, and that this is just the home version of it. The quick and easy solution to this problem is to gladly accept the minor arts as part of everyday aesthetics. They certainly have not been readily accepted into the aesthetics of art. A typical example of such an art is cooking. Although sometimes some food is given the status of high art, home cooking is generally seen to be a minor art at best. Everyday aesthetics is the natural home of such arts.[8]

Of course much of the question concerning the relationship between everyday aesthetic phenomena and the arts depends on how we are to define art. For example, if art is defined as "whatever is designed for aesthetic experience," this would allow the minor arts to be included within the realm of art, thus narrowing the remaining field of everyday aesthetics to things that look or sound aesthetically interesting but are not designed to be so. If, however, art is defined as "whatever is designated as art by a member of the art world," then this would exclude some of the minor arts (for example, home cooking) and thus would leave the realm of everyday aesthetics quite broad.

The debate over the definition of art has been long and difficult and is ongoing. We cannot, for example, assume that "made for aesthetic appreciation" delimits the world of art since much is made for aesthetic appreciation which is not art, for example many children's toys. Also, much that is widely considered art, for example religious art, is not made primarily for aesthetic consideration. Nor can we simply say that everyday aesthetic objects are never primarily made for aesthetic contemplation. Everyday aesthetic phenomena have many intentions and uses and some of these actually are primarily aesthetic, for example flower-arranging. We call something an aesthetic phenomenon when it is perceived aesthetically, and all non-art phenomena can be perceived aesthetically under some circumstances: one needs simply look at it in the right way, or provide it with a suitable framing or background story. Even a clod of dirt can be appreciated aesthetically if framed in the right way.

Since the aesthetics of everyday life is defined in part by negation, i.e., it is

---

8   Glenn Kuehn discusses the issue in "How Can Food Be Art?" in *The Aesthetics of Everyday Life*, 194-212.

applied to objects that are not art or nature, then the actual boundaries of the concept are going to be determined in part by debates over the definition of art. I have discussed this issue generally but I think it would also be worthwhile to take one current definition of art and see how it would mark off the division between art and non-art, and particularly between art and that which is not art but still aesthetically interesting. Robert Stecker has recently defined art in this way: "an item is an artwork at time t, where t is not earlier than the time at which the item is made, if and only if (a) it is in one of the central art forms at t and is made with the intention of fulfilling a function art has at t, or (b) it is an artifact that achieves excellence in fulfilling such a function."[9] This definition gives two paths for achieving art status. The first clearly separates art from non-art by way of the list of "central art forms." During the twenty-first century, these would probably include painting, sculpture, film, dance, and photography, among others. The second path however does allow some artifacts to be included as art which are not normally listed, as long as they achieve excellence in fulfilling a function art has at that particular time. Let's say that providing aesthetic experience is such a function. In this case, any item outside of the normal realm of art would be considered to be art as long as it was excellent in providing aesthetic experience, but not if it was mediocre in doing so. If clean sheets on a line are excellent in providing aesthetic experience then they are art (that is, assuming that they count as an artifact). They are not art if they provide only a minor aesthetic experience and also fail to be excellent in fulfilling any *other* function of art at that time. This is quite an expansion of the concept of art and would include much of what I have called everyday aesthetic phenomena. However it would not eliminate the domain *everyday aesthetics* which could still include every item that, although providing aesthetic interest, failed both to fall into the class of central art forms and to be excellent in fulfilling one of the functions of art at that time. Whether or not Stecker's definition is the correct definition of art is not my concern here. My point is simply that whatever the definition of art is it will also have bearing on the boundaries between art and everyday aesthetics.

Perhaps the most interesting question that can be asked about the limits of everyday aesthetics is whether aesthetic appreciation is the same kind of thing when directed to everyday phenomena as when directed to works of art. The short answer is, "of course not." This should not be surprising since it is

---

9 Stecker, *Aesthetics*, 114.

also true elsewhere in aesthetics. For example, aesthetic appreciation is not the same sort of thing when directed to nature as when directed to art. Artist's intentions and intended meanings play a role in the aesthetics of art that they cannot play in the aesthetics of nature, unless we think of animals as artists, and even so, this would only cover a small part of the aesthetics of nature. In the case of everyday aesthetics, although we may think of a creator's intentions or meaning, for example we may think of an amateur decorator's intentions and the meaning she or he finds in the displays created, we do not think of these creators literally as artists and we do not write monographs about their work, although we might call them artists in an honorific way.

However, although there are important differences between art aesthetics and everyday aesthetics there are also many similarities. As mentioned above, certain key terms are used across the domains. "Beauty" may mean something different when applied to a mechanical repair, a baby, a tree or a Rembrandt, but there is also something similar between all of the experiences of these things when they are called beautiful. That is why there is a general field of aesthetics of which everyday aesthetics is one part.

The nature and limits of everyday aesthetics can also be understood in terms of the history of the field. Such a history has never been written, but we can at least sketch something out in a few paragraphs.

BRIEF HISTORY OF EVERYDAY AESTHETICS

Although there is not a large tradition of work on everyday aesthetics there have always been aspects of philosophical work that can be related to the field.[10] In attempting to sketch out the history of these efforts it is, as usual, a good idea to begin with the ancient Greeks.

Plato in his *Symposium* has the student philosopher begin his love of beauty with the bodies of young men, although the philosopher quickly leaves everyday beauties behind as he ascends the ladder of love. However, Plato would not normally be seen as enthusiastic about everyday aesthetics. His attitude towards fashion, cooking, and cosmetics is as negative as his attitude towards the imitative arts. In *Gorgias*, for example, he speaks

---

10 Sherri Irvin details the lack of articles in the field in "The Pervasiveness of the Aesthetic in Ordinary Experience," *British Journal of Aesthetics* 48, no. 1 (2008): 29-44. Roger Scruton refers to the aesthetics of everyday life as a much neglected topic in "In Search of the Aesthetic," *British Journal of Aesthetics* 47, no. 3 (2007): 232-50.

of cookery as a "mischievous, deceitful, mean, and ignoble activity, which cheats us by shapes and colors"[11] In *Greater Hippias*, Socrates is critical of Hippias's defence of the aesthetic appreciation of the everyday.[12] Socrates himself, however, could be said to be endorsing consideration of the aesthetics of everyday life when he argues in the same dialogue that "whatever is useful we call beautiful, and beautiful in that respect in which it is useful."[13] A functionalist approach to everyday aesthetics is suggested here, functionalism being defined as the claim that something is beautiful to the extent that it is useful, or as Sven Ove Hansson puts it, "the aesthetic properties of an object depend on its functionality."[14]

One would think that Epicurus and the Epicureans would have something to say about everyday aesthetics. In fact, although pleasure is the goal of the Epicurean life, this is chiefly associated with absence of pain; thus disconnected from aesthetics. Still, Epicurus does have one thing to say about the topic. Whereas Plato is critical in his *Republic* of the lovers of sights and sounds, Epicurus believes that a wise person will enjoy such things, for example the spectacle of the theatre.[15] It is not until the end of the nineteenth century that writers influenced by Epicurus, for example Walter Pater, came to focus on the everyday.

Stoic philosophers took a similar approach to that of Plato in rejecting the sensual pleasures of the body. Marcus Aurelius for example writes that "Man's joy is to do man's proper work. And work proper to man is benevolence to his own kind, disdain for the stirrings of the senses, diagnosis of the impressions he can trust, contemplation of universal nature and all things thereby entailed."[16] There is no room for everyday aesthetics, or for any aesthetic values, in his disdain for the senses. One could say that he promotes a negative aesthetics insofar as he claims that every part of life and every object in it is disgusting.

---

11 Plato, *Gorgias*, in *The Collected Dialogues of Plato*, ed. Edith Hamilton and Huntington Cairns (New York: Bollingen Foundation, 1961), 465b, 247.
12 Plato, *Greater Hippias* in *Collected Dialogues*, 294a, 1547.
13 Plato, *Hippias* 1549, 295c.
14 Sven Ove Hansson, "Aesthetic Functionalism," *Contemporary Aesthetics* 3 (2005) accessed March 19, 2011, http://www.contempaesthetics.org/newvolume/pages/article.php?articleID=324.
15 Plato, *Republic*, 475d-476b, 714-15. See Elizabeth Amis, "Philosophers and Literary Critics" in "Hellenistic Aesthetics," *Encyclopedia of Aesthetics* 2, 391.
16 Marcus Aurelius, *Meditations*, trans. with notes Martin Hammond, intro. Diskin Clay (New York: Penguin Books, 2006), Book 8, #26, 75.

However, he is not consistent in this. He also writes that "even the incidental effects of the processes of Nature have their own charm and attraction."[17] He then refers to a common everyday experience: "Take the baking of bread. The loaf splits open here and there, and those very cracks, in one way a failure of the baker's profession, somehow catch the eye and give particular stimulus to our appetite." (An interesting feature of this quote is that the aesthetic pleasure here cannot be attributed to the art of baking or to some sort of functionalism.) He even suggests that fruit rotting on a tree can be beautiful since anyone with "a feeling and deeper insight for the workings of the Whole [i.e., the whole universe] will find some pleasure in almost every aspect...."[18] Such a person will even see beauty in an old man or woman. From the perspective of "the Whole" we can see things as beautiful that would be ugly in isolation, although only someone who has genuine affinity for Nature will be able to have such perceptions. This openness to aesthetic qualities of the apparently ugly in nature can also be applied to such things as the charms and attraction of imperfect and non-functional items in everyday life.

Marcus Aurelius's view is similar to that of Yuriko Saito, who encourages us to appreciate a rotting elk carcass in nature, although Saito stresses that the aesthetic value of the scene is based not simply on knowledge of its role in nature but also on the way in which that role is expressed in terms of the senses.[19]

HUME

David Hume in his famous essay on the standard of taste asks us to consider taste first with regard to wine and only later with regard to literary works.[20] And although he designates taste in wine as bodily and not mental, his theory of bodily taste provides grounds for his theory of taste in literature. So, one might say that everyday aesthetics operates as a jumping-off point for Hume insofar as he is concerned with the aesthetic appreciation of wine. He tells a story taken from *Don Quixote* that suggests a theory of judgment in everyday

---

17 Marcus Aurelius, Book 3, #2, 16.
18 Marcus Aurelius, Book 3, #2, 17.
19 Yuriko Saito, "The Aesthetics of Unscenic Nature," *The Journal of Aesthetics and Art Criticism* 56, no. 2, Special Issue: Environmental Aesthetics (1998): 101-11, 104.
20 David Hume, "Of the Standard of Taste," in *Aesthetics: A Critical Anthology*, ed. George Dickie and R.J. Sclafani (New York: St. Martin's Press, 1977), 596-97, orig. in *Four Dissertations* (1757).

aesthetics based on "delicacy of sentiment," the capacity to distinguish and aesthetically evaluate the different elements of the object. One of the cousins of Sancho could determine that the wine was good but for a slight taste of leather, and the other that it was good but for a slight taste of metal. When the hogshead is emptied, a key with a leather thong attached is found, thus partially vindicating each cousin as having delicacy of sentiment.

In his earlier book, *A Treatise of Human Nature*, Hume claims that we esteem the rich and the powerful because of their "houses, gardens, equipages,"[21] observing that these things, being agreeable in themselves, give everyone pleasure (unlike Kant, he does not clearly distinguish "the agreeable" from "the beautiful"). He further argues that gardens, and other possessions of the rich, are not only agreeable in themselves but we appreciate them because of a vicarious sympathy with the appreciation felt by their owners.

Hume reveals himself to be a functionalist with respect to the aesthetics of everyday life when he says that "the conveniency of a house, the fertility of a field, the strength of a horse, the capacity, security, and swift-sailing of a vessel, form the principal beauty of these several objects."[22] Here, each type of thing has a functionally related predicate appropriate to it: conveniency, fertility, etc. He adds that an object may be considered beautiful because it tends to produce pleasure or advantage in some other person, reinforcing the idea that such aesthetic pleasures are at least sometimes vicarious.

He also observes that "[a] man, who shews us any house or building, takes particular care among other things to point out the convenience of the apartments, the advantages of their situation, and the little room lost in the stairs, antichambers and passages." It is these things that make up the beauty of the building. From this, he concludes that "[t]he observation of convenience gives pleasure, since convenience is a beauty." This remark on the aesthetics of architecture is related to everyday aesthetics in that it stresses the idea that convenience is, or at least can be, an aesthetic property. Although Hume may be using "convenience" here in a way close to the original Latin idea of "coming together in harmony," it also suggests the element of comfort we associate with it today.

Hume's functionalism is also exhibited when he says that the beauty of

---

21 Hume, *Treatise*, Book II, Part II, Section V, "Of Our Esteem for the Rich and Powerful." All of the quotes, save one, are from this section. I owe this reference to Glenn Parsons and Allen Carlson, *Functional Beauty* (Oxford: Clarendon Press, 2008).
22 Hume, *Treatise*, Book III, Part III, Section I, "The Origins of Natural Virtues and Vices," 577.

"tables, chairs, scritoires, chimneys, coaches, sadles, ploughs, and indeed ... every work of art" is mainly derived from its utility or fitness for achieving its purpose. (The phrase "work of art" here refers to *craft* objects of the sort just mentioned, and not to what we would mean by it.) Finally, consistent with his functionalism, he argues that fields are more likely made agreeable by fertility than by "ornament or situation," and personal beauty is mainly based on health and vigour.

Hume's thoughts on everyday aesthetics are sketchy at best. The notion of bodily taste developed in the Sancho's cousins case has merit, but confuses evaluation with subtle discrimination of elements. The notion of functionalism has more plausibility, and a pedigree going back at least to Plato, but leaves out many other dimensions of aesthetic experience, as we shall see later. Nonetheless, he makes an advance by expanding the field of aesthetic properties to include the everyday term "convenience."

KANT

It is seldom mentioned that Kant distinguishes *two* kinds of aesthetic experience: the agreeable and the beautiful (or *three* kinds if one includes the sublime). Kant pays far more attention to the beautiful and the sublime than to the agreeable, and most writers in aesthetics assume, wrongly, that he merely identified the aesthetic with the beautiful, or with the beautiful and the sublime. It might be thought by some that everyday aesthetics could be correlated with Kant's notion of "the agreeable."[23] In this section I will oppose this idea, while recognizing that what he has to say about the agreeable has some relevance to everyday aesthetics. In fact, Kant addresses the aesthetics of everyday life not only in his sections on the agreeable but also, and perhaps more importantly, in his sections on beauty.

First, let me briefly summarize Kant's view on beauty. For Kant, beauty is the object of a delight that is directed to objects evaluated by taste "apart from any interest." He believes the pleasure we take in beauty is "disinterested," i.e., distinct from any practical, moral or intellectual interest. (I think he would allow that you could still find a beautiful thing "interesting" but not in a way that would entail concern for its existence.) Beauty also pleases universally in the

---

23 Christopher Dowling does this in his critique of the very idea of everyday aesthetics in "The Aesthetics of Daily Life," *British Journal of Aesthetics* 50, no. 3 (2010): 226-42.

sense that everyone who looks at the object of taste disinterestedly will appreciate it. This is what he means when he says that when I see something as beautiful I "demand" that others see it as beautiful too, although it would probably have been better if he had said that I *expect* others to see it as beautiful if they perceive it disinterestedly. This leads us to Kant's third point, that the object of beauty has the look of purpose (i.e., it looks designed), even though we perceive it without consideration of its actual purpose. For example, when we appreciate a flower we are supposed not to think of the purpose of its reproductive organs. Even a botanist, when appreciating a flower, needs to set aside his knowledge of botany. Since, in focusing on the look of purpose the emphasis is on the formal qualities of the object Kant is often called a formalist. "Free beauty" presupposes no concept of the object. However, Kant also has a category of "dependent beauty" which allows consideration of purpose, presupposing a concept of the object's perfection. Fourth, the object of beauty is an object of necessary delight in the sense that it causes pleasure through the free play of two fundamental cognitive faculties: the imagination and the understanding. These are in "free play" in the sense that they are not being applied here to scientific knowledge. As Kant explains, when the imagination is simply used for cognition it is constrained by the understanding, but when it is free from cognitive work it provides the understanding with a "wealth of undeveloped material" not included under the standard concepts. This material can be used to enliven the mental powers generally.[24] Since all humans have this ability (what Kant calls "common sense") beauty is not only subjective but universal.

Kant says: "That is agreeable which the senses find pleasing in sensation."[25] Unlike beauty, the agreeable does not merely please, but "gratifies." When we judge an object as agreeable we are expressing an interest in it, i.e., are concerned for its real existence. This is shown by the fact that it provokes a desire for similar objects. Although the agreeable may be experienced by irrational animals, Kant believes *beauty* is only available to humans.

Kant argues that the agreeable is relative to inclination. Hence, the hungry person will find something agreeable that others may not. Taste, in the sense of "discrimination," does not enter into the agreeable. The judgment of the agreeable rests, rather, on private feeling. As opposed to the beautiful, when we talk of the agreeable there is no disputing about tastes.

---

24 Immanuel Kant, *The Critique of Judgment*, trans. James Meredith (Oxford: The Clarendon Press, 1928), #49, 179-80.
25 Kant, *Judgment* #44.

Kant's examples of the agreeable include Canary wine, violet colour, and the smell of a rose. (Unlike Hume, he thought there is no discrimination involved in tasting wine, at least Canary wine!) Kant speaks of "the taste of the tongue, the palate, and the throat," in relation to the agreeable, but also of that which is agreeable to the eye and the ear. When he discusses violet colour, he notes that it may be soft and lovely to one person, and dull and faded to another. He also refers to the tones of wind and string instruments as examples of the agreeable. However, he insists that *pure* tones are objects of beauty, perhaps because our appreciation of them is a function of reflection on their purity. At one point, he associates the agreeable with entertainment of guests, and at another, with "the charming," which he attaches to the use of colour in visual works (for Kant, it is design that makes paintings beautiful, not colour).

Can the concept of the agreeable be used to define everyday aesthetics? Much of everyday aesthetics could be included under the agreeable as Kant defines it; for example, the entertainment of guests. There are, however, various problems with such an approach.

(1) Recent aestheticians have rightly questioned the ideas that aesthetic appreciation can be completely disinterested, and that aesthetic objects can be completely formal. This has undercut Kant's distinction between the agreeable and the beautiful.

(2) The concept of beauty should not be excluded from everyday aesthetics. Kant defines beauty in terms of the play of the imagination and the understanding when responding to objects that have the appearance of purposefulness. It may be true that everyday aesthetic objects do not typically generate such play, even when they produce pleasure. Yet, why should judgments of beauty *require* such play?

(3) Even if we stuck to Kant's use of the term "beauty," it would still be wrong to exclude it from everyday aesthetics. Kant ties "beauty" with the aesthetic pleasure we get from appreciation of good design and pleasing form. This kind of pleasure is surely not absent from the dinner party, the garden, or the use of tiles in the bathroom. Kant himself includes such things as costumes and wallpaper under the category of beauty rather than under that of the agreeable. Since we would generally want to include such things in the field of every-

day aesthetics, his distinction between the beautiful and the agreeable may not be useful in defining it.

(4) It is arguable that the items Kant calls "agreeable" are not exclusively matters of sense, and that there is an imaginative or even a cognitive element in their experience. For example, the entertainment of guests is not entirely a matter of providing sensory delights. Also, Kant sees sexual desire as a matter of appetite, and so it would follow that its satisfaction would fall under the agreeable, and yet it would be wrong to ignore the role that imagination, a cognitive faculty, typically plays in that realm.[26]

Whereas Kant associates the agreeable with purely sensory experience, and the beautiful with experience arising from a play of cognitive faculties, it is arguable that *all* aesthetic experience has sensory, imaginative, and cognitive aspects, although one of these may be dominant in any one experience. Wine connoisseurs would insist that wine appreciation requires not only sense but also cognition (being able to tell the year, for example) and imagination (being able to taste the flavour as "nutty," for example).

There are admittedly some possible counterexamples to the claim that there is a sensory, imaginative, and cognitive aspect to all aesthetic experience. Whether the pleasures of mathematics have a sensory side is controversial, although one could argue that the mental images and drawings mathematicians use may play an important role in the mathematical aesthetics. Great mathematical and scientific discoveries often have a strong imaginative dimension. It might also be argued that some aesthetic pleasures are exclusively sensory. Yet, although the pleasures of massage may appear at first to be completely sensory with no imaginative component, reflection shows that they require elements of imaginative anticipation and association, as well as elements of cognition in coming to know the different dimensions and possibilities of one's own body. Whether or not the pleasures of massage can be aesthetic, however, is a matter of contention.

Later in his book Kant discusses what he calls the "agreeable arts," the object of which is mere enjoyment.[27] Here the representations we apprehend

---

26 Immanuel Kant, *Lectures on Ethics*, trans. Louis Infield (New York: Harper and Row, 1963), 163.
27 Kant, *Judgment* #44, 165-66.

are considered "as mere sensations," whereas in fine art they are considered as "modes of cognition." Under the agreeable arts are included "the charms that can gratify a dinner party." These include the arts of telling entertaining stories, of getting a good conversation going, and of "inducing a certain air of gaiety." Kant observes that what is said and done here is "for the entertainment of the moment" and is not "a lasting matter" subject to reflection. Also included are the arts of table-setting and of providing agreeable background music to foster conversation, and of all sorts of play to make time pass, by which he probably means party games. By contrast, he believes that fine art advances the mental powers "in the interest of social communication."

The distinction between the agreeable arts and the fine arts parallels, but is distinct from, that between the agreeable and the beautiful. Unlike the agreeable *per se*, the main interest in the agreeable *arts* is social. Also, the agreeable arts have a somewhat more complex aesthetic field than "the agreeable." For example, Kant's discussion of "the agreeable" in music focuses on individual tones, whereas his discussion of "the agreeable arts" turns to entire musical pieces. The objections raised above against a strict separation of the agreeable from the beautiful may, however, also be applied to that between the agreeable and the fine arts.

Despite the many problems with his distinction between the agreeable and the beautiful Kant's work is still helpful in creation of an aesthetics of everyday life. Although the aesthetics of everyday life should not be *identified* with the agreeable, this does not mean we should abandon some sort of distinction between the agreeable and the beautiful. It still makes sense to distinguish the agreeable as *primarily* a matter of sense experience from the beautiful as *primarily* a matter of play of imagination and understanding. Yet, as I suggested earlier, the items Kant classified under "the agreeable" usually contain some play of imagination and understanding too, and the items classified under "the beautiful" usually contain some sensory element. Kant's exclusion of the sensory from the beautiful is perhaps the greatest weakness of his overall aesthetic theory. How could the beauty of a Rembrandt seriously be separated from its sensory qualities?

Kant's contribution to everyday aesthetics is not, however, limited to his views on the agreeable and the agreeable arts. Indeed, when he talks about beauty, both free and dependent, he often refers to things of everyday life. That is, his discussion is not limited either to nature or to fine art. For example, when discussing free beauty he mentions "free patterns, lines aimlessly intertwining—technically termed foliage" as things that please. He must be referring here to wallpaper and perhaps to frames on paintings or decorative elements on buildings.[28] He also mentions "designs à la grecque" as an example of free beauty. This appears to be a reference to the fashion in his day of imitating Greek clothing (particularly the ornamental ribbon called the "meander" above the hem).[29] He also makes remarks on ornamental gardens, decoration of rooms, and furniture that shows good taste.[30] Dependent (or "appendant") beauty would include any beauty that "presupposes a concept of the end that defines what the thing has to be," which includes, on Kant's account, not only the beauty of such artistic matters as architecture, but also the beauty of humans and horses.

To reiterate: everyday aesthetics should not be limited to the agreeable, for many everyday objects may also be beautiful and may owe the pleasures they give in part to a play between imagination and understanding. Even many items Kant lists under the agreeable require play of imagination and understanding for their appreciation. Kant does not have a category of everyday aesthetics. Yet he did have many interesting things to say about aesthetic phenomena that neither fell within the realm of the aesthetics of art or the aesthetics of nature. What remains in the category of the agreeable is that which gives pleasure that is purely sensory with no mixture of the imagination or any cognitive element.

HEGEL

Hegel, unlike Kant, explicitly limited aesthetics to art, and so he would not normally be thought of as a source for valuable ideas about the aesthetics of everyday life. However, some of the things he says about art are relevant to our topic. In his *Aesthetics: Lectures on Fine Art*,[31] Hegel speaks of Dutch painters as being able to produce works that display a "pure shining and appearing of objects as something produced by the spirit [a term Hegel uses to mean the underlying spiritual aspect of things, associated ultimately with what he

---

28 Kant, *Judgment* #4, 46.
29 Winfried Menninghaus, "Hummingbirds, Shells, Picture-Frames: Kant's 'Free Beauties' and the Romantic Arabesque," in *Rereading Romanticism*, ed. Martha B. Helfer (Amsterdam: Rodopi, 2000), 32.
30 Kant, *Judgment*, "General Remark on the First Edition of the Analytic," 88.
31 Quotes are taken from the G.W.F. Hegel selection titled "Art, Nature, Freedom," in *Aesthetics: Lectures on Fine Art*, trans. T.M. Knox (1975) in *Aesthetics*, ed. Susan Feagin and Patrick Maynard (New York: Oxford University Press, 1997), orig. 1835.

calls "The Absolute"] which transforms in its inmost being the external and sensuous side of" things. These objects include "velvet, metallic luster, light, horses, servants, old women, peasants blowing smoke from cutty pipes, the glitter of wine in a transparent glass, chaps in dirty jackets playing with old cards."[32] I take him to mean that the external sensuous side of these objects becomes transformed by spirit through the artist's activity when represented in the work of art. In these comments I will take very seriously his idea that art changes the aspect of everyday things that we experience with our senses. In the list given above, the first three items have a shining quality, as can also be said for the glitter of wine. Even the representation of pipe smoke has such a quality, as it is typically luminous. Hegel is not here commending us to aesthetic experience of everyday objects themselves. Rather he is referencing their representation in works of art. However, he is also directing our attention to a transformed experience of the represented objects. So the relationship between the art work and the subject matter is dialectical, the artwork drawing from the subject, enhancing it, and then projecting back, through our experience of it, to our experience of the subject matter.

Still, on the surface at least, Hegel is no fan of everyday aesthetics. He contrasts prosaic reality with the "pure appearance produced by the spirit [i.e., of the artist or the age]" in a painting.[33] He even thinks that the artist's representation "*mocks*" external nature. In support of this he observes that it is really hard to produce a beautiful effect in a physical substance (such as metal), whereas imagination, which is the material of art, is quite easy to work with as, here, one simply draws from one's inner being.

Along these lines, he observes that "precious stones, gold, plants, animals, etc., have in themselves only this bounded existence,"[34] i.e., an existence which requires hard work to bring out what he calls "the pure shining of appearance." He believes that the artist *steals* material from nature, and then "freely disgorges" this accumulated treasure in his works.[35] The imagination collects that which sparkles and shines, treasure-like, but is able to do *more* with it. A paradox ensues: art "furnishes us with the things themselves," but it does so "out of the inner life of mind." (I believe this paradox is resolved once we read

---

32 Hegel, 194. See my "Sparkle and Shine," *British Journal of Aesthetics* 37, no. 3 (1997): 259-73 for further discussion of these neglected qualities.
33 Hegel, 194.
34 Hegel, 195.
35 Hegel, 195.

Hegel's insight as a matter of recognizing the dialectical nature of the relationship between everyday life aesthetics and the aesthetics of art.) Hegel further insists that art confines our interest to ideal appearances of these objects suitable for contemplation. In doing this, "art exalts these otherwise worthless objects."[36] This would seem entirely negative about the things of everyday life. However, it also says that art draws our attention to things or aspects of things we would otherwise not notice. Hegel recognizes this when he observes that art manages to fix such temporary aspects of everyday life as "a quickly vanishing smile, a sudden roguish expression in the mouth, a glance, a fleeting ray of light...."[37] Why value such things unless we have an aesthetic interest in everyday life itself?

Hegel speaks of the fixing activity of the artist as art conquering nature. He wants to keep the luminous subject-matter in *second place* to art, and so he says that "it is not the subject-matter which principally makes a claim on us but the satisfaction which comes from what the spirit has produced."[38] The spirit of the artist has produced (in all its freedom) a certain satisfaction based on this rather lowly subject-matter, the fleeting nature of which it has captured and *conquered*. Hegel even goes so far as to see artistic making as the "extinction" of the sensuous external material. Yet everything he has said indicates that it is more a matter of bringing that sensuous material to life, or manifesting its inner nature. This is even more evident when he turns to discussion of specific painting traditions.

Hegel remarks, for example, that the Dutch painters actualize their own world "once more through art."[39] When we understand their art, he believes, we must understand it in terms of their history, their will to freedom, their careful, clean and neat well-being, and especially their joy in having achieved this.[40] It is this joy which Hegel takes to be the content of their pictures. So, the sparkle and shine of Dutch painting is not just the work of the free-floating imagination of the artist, but something situated historically in the life of a people—a point which, after all, we should expect of Hegel. Rembrandt's *Night Watch*, he thinks, is "fired" by this "sense of vigorous nationality." That is, the luminosity of the painting exists *because* the Dutch spirit is infused into it. Similarly, he believes that a feeling of "freedom and gaiety," which he also con-

---

36 Hegel, 195.
37 Hegel, 195.
38 Hegel, 195.
39 Hegel, 195.
40 Hegel, 196.

siders a "spiritual cheerfulness in a justified pleasure," animates Dutch genre scenes. So, the Dutch spirit, as manifested in everyday Dutch life, is brought back into the painting through the spirit of the artist. Instead of annihilating the everyday, Dutch painting foregrounds and enhances it. In short, Hegel's analysis of Dutch painting shows an awareness of, and approval of, the Dutch painters' appreciation of the aesthetics of everyday life.

All of this moves to another level of analysis when Hegel turns to seventeenth-century Spanish painter Bartolomé Esteban Murillo's paintings of beggar boys. He indicates that there shines forth, in these paintings, a complete absence of care and concern comparable to that of a Muslim Dervish. He finds the representation of these boys to exhibit "the full feeling of their well being and delight in life."[41] This is similar to his approach to Dutch paintings. However he pushes this further to the level of sublime experience when he says that the boys are like Olympian gods since, although they do nothing, anything may come of them.[42] One could argue that this makes them really more like Taoist sages than like Olympian gods (Hegel had recently encountered Taoism for the first time when he wrote these notes). The reference to Muslim ascetics also points in the direction of sublime experience. This all relates to the aesthetics of everyday life insofar as Hegel is not simply referring to the beauty of the art but also to that of the boys themselves.

In sum, although not an advocate of everyday aesthetics, Hegel may contribute to this new field by pointing out ways in which art can pick our features in our everyday lives that deserve aesthetic attention. Also, it is the everyday lives of the Dutch and the Spanish which is manifested in the paintings he admires. Although Hegel disparages everyday life he undercuts this by drawing attention to styles of art most concerned with the everyday. I see the relationship Hegel finds between art and life as dialectical. That is, the art responds to everyday life which in turn is seen in terms of the art. This notion of the importance of the dialectical relation between art and everyday aesthetics will be a central theme of this book. Finally, Hegel's emphasis on luminosity and the shining qualities of objects inspires my own emphasis on the qualities of sparkle and shine as particularly important aspects of everyday aesthetic experience and the theory of aesthetic experience as experience of objects with "aura" which I will develop in Part II.

---

41 Hegel, 196.
42 Hegel, 197.

LATER NINETEENTH-CENTURY AESTHETICS

In the United States, Ralph Waldo Emerson could also be seen as contributing to everyday aesthetics, although his main interest was in the aesthetics of nature. He praised the avant-garde poetry of his time for exploring common things. He thought it "a great stride" that "the feelings of the child, the philosophy of the street, the meaning of household life, are the topics of the time,"[43] and he called on his readers to see the meaning of "[t]he meal in the firkin [a small wooden barrel]; the milk in the pan; the ballad in the street; the news of the boat; the glance of the eye; the form and the gait of the body."[44] That is, one should find aesthetic value in ordinary things.

In Germany and England, Karl Marx's *1844 Manuscripts*, with his concepts of alienated and non-alienated labour, could be seen as at least implying a theory of everyday aesthetics with a special focus on the negative aesthetic experiences of the working class especially during the hours of work. Marx famously states that man "forms things in accordance with the laws of beauty."[45] It is this activity that proves man is what he calls a "species-being," and it is in such material production that man has his active "species-life." By "species-being" Marx means a being that is conscious of its own nature as a member of a species, and of its free and conscious material production. As Marx says, "Man is a species-being, not only because in practice and in theory he adopts the species ... as his object, but ... because he treats himself as ... a *universal* and therefore a free being." By "species-life" Marx means production according to the laws of beauty. He writes that, through this production, nature appears as man's work and as his reality, and that therefore "[t]he object of labor is ... the *objectification of man's species-life*." For example, the shoe he is making embodies his essential human nature. For man, in his productive activity, "duplicates himself not only, as in consciousness, intellectually, but also actively, in reality" and this results in his seeing himself in a self-created world. It follows that, "in tearing away from man the object of his production [which happens in capitalist

---

43 Ralph Waldo Emerson, "The American Scholar," orig. 1837, in *Pragmatism and Classical American Philosophy*, ed. John Stuhr (New York: Oxford University Press, 2000), 25-26.
44 Ralph Waldo Emerson, "Nature," orig. 1836, in *The Essential Writings of Ralph Waldo Emerson*, ed. Brooks Atkinson (New York: Modern Library, 2000), 6.
45 All quotes are from Karl Marx, *Economic and Philosophical Manuscripts of 1844*, "Estranged Labour," (Moscow: Progress Publishers, 1959) tr. Martin Mulligan, accessed April 7, 2011, http://www.marxists.org/archive/marx/works/1844/manuscripts/labour.htm.

production] ... estranged labor tears from him his *species-life*." This is what Marx means by "alienation." Alienated labour degrades human spontaneous, free activity to a means that merely satisfies the needs of capitalism, and man's species-life to a mere means to his physical existence.

In sum, Marx argues that the loss of production according to the laws of beauty under conditions of capitalism gives rise to alienation, i.e., an unnatural separation from one's species-being and species-life. Thus, the everyday activity of production should, ideally for Marx, be aesthetic. Marx also holds that the emancipation of man through overcoming the concept of private property entailed in the capitalist system implies an emancipation of human sensibility.[46] This too, if true, would have implications for everyday aesthetics. What Marx teaches is that everyday aesthetics has a normative dimension. Alienation is an aesthetic loss. Marxist aestheticians and their twenty-first-century intellectual descendents additionally stress the ways in which our everyday lives are filled with commodities and advertisements that are designed to lure us into a false consciousness, a failure to recognize our exploitation and alienation.

It could be argued that the writings of John Ruskin, William Morris, and the various members of the nineteenth-century Arts and Crafts movement are also important forerunners of everyday aesthetics insofar as their aesthetic concerns were not limited to the arts but extended to life generally. In a recent article, Jeffrey Petts correctly chastises everyday aestheticians for mentioning Dewey in this regard, but leaving these English writers out.[47] Petts emphasizes Morris's idea that we (human beings) should both do good work and fill our world with the products of such work. Morris believed that if workers engage in good, non-alienating work, then all of our lives will be better. Moreover, he saw this as a condition for the development and appreciation of the arts in general.

Just as many writers today seek to dissolve the distinction between popular and fine art, so too Morris and the other "Arts and Crafts" writers sought to dissolve the distinction between art and craft. As Petts observes, for Morris, life properly lived is artful.[48] Morris held, for example, that "the true secret of happiness lies in the taking a genuine interest in all the details of daily life, in elevating them by art instead of handing the performance of them over to

---

46 Leonard P. Wessell, Jr., "The Aesthetics of Living Form in Schiller and Marx," *The Journal of Aesthetics and Art Criticism* 37, no. 2 (1978): 189-201.
47 Jeffery Petts, "Good Work and Aesthetic Education: William Morris, the Arts and Crafts Movement, and Beyond," *Journal of Aesthetic Education* 42, no. 1 (2008): 30-45.
48 Petts, 44.

unregarded drudges."[49] The point is two-sided: first that we should take an aesthetic interest in the details of daily life and second that we should elevate such details by way of art. For Morris, if art is not connected with everyday life it is poisoned. Like Marx, he saw the everyday life of his own times as made ugly because of the private ownership of the means of production and the dominance of the capitalist class.

Somewhat earlier, and under the influence of Epicureanism, Walter Pater (1868) encouraged his readers to maximize experiences of aesthetic pleasure. Although he had a special interest in pleasure gained from art, his aestheticism was expressed in a more general way that related to everyday phenomena as when he asks us to observe the exquisite moment "of delicious recoil" when experiencing a spray of water in summer heat. Pater believed that success in life is always to "burn with [a] hard, gemlike flame," which is to say to experience life with ecstasy. This "burning," he writes, may be caused by "any exquisite passion, or any contribution to knowledge that seems ... to set the spirit free for a moment" or, and this is where everyday aesthetics comes in, by "any stirring of the senses, strange dyes, strange colours, and curious odours."[50] The curious and the strange are among the things in everyday life that can "set the spirit free."

Pater encourages us to have a "sense of splendour of our experience." Because life is short, we should pull together everything we are "into one desperate effort to see and touch." Our one chance to have a good life lies in inserting as many "pulsations"—aesthetically powerful moments—as possible into life.[51] This will give us a "quickened sense of life." Although he believes that a life devoted to appreciating art does this best, what really is most important is "the highest quality to your moments as they pass, and simply for those moments' sake." Pater's approach to everyday aesthetics is much more individual-centred than that of Marx and Morris. Nonetheless, as we shall see, the two views are not totally incompatible, and are arguably synthesized in the later aesthetics of John Dewey.

Pater also recognizes that beauty, even in everyday life, can have a tragic dimension. Along these lines, he observes that we may aesthetically appreciate

---

49 William Morris, "The Aims of Art," in *The Collected Works of William Morris* (London: Longmans, Green, 1915), originally 1887, Chapter 23, 94. I owe this reference to Hans Ulrich Gumbrecht, "Aesthetic Experience in Everyday Worlds: Reclaiming an Unredeemed Utopian Motif," *New Literary History* 37 (2006): 299-318.
50 Walter Pater, *The Renaissance: Studies in Art and Poetry* (Oxford: Oxford University Press, 1998), 152.
51 Pater, 153.

character in other humans. He writes: "Not to discriminate every moment some passionate attitude in those about us, and in the very brilliancy of their gifts some tragic dividing of forces on their ways, is ... to sleep before evening." To be aesthetically aware one must be able to appreciate human passions including the tragic dimension of those passions.

In France, Charles Baudelaire drew attention to the ways that the daily life of the city can be appreciated from the standpoint of a special kind of aesthetic observer, which he called the "flâneur." This word is often translated as "stroller" or "lounger," but also carries the implication of savouring the delights of the city.[52] The flâneur can be narrowly conceived as a bohemian type who flourished in the Parisian arcades in the middle of the nineteenth century.[53] However, often, the notion is extended much more broadly. The basic idea is of someone who strolls through the passing scene in an urban world, pleasurably observing it. Certainly the flâneur is interested in such everyday phenomena as fashion, craft, architecture, and manners. Baudelaire's flâneur was a kind of connoisseur of daily life.

In his *The Painter of Modern Life* (1863) Baudelaire describes the painter Constantin Guys as a kind of aesthetic ideal, seeing him as like a figure in a story by Edgar Allen Poe who, having recently escaped a deathly illness, finds himself "pleasantly absorbed in gazing at the crowd ... rapturously breathing in all the odours and essences of life."[54] Baudelaire sees the experiences of the convalescent as like those of a child who "sees everything in a state of newness" and who absorbs form and colour with delight. Baudelaire's interest in everyday life translated over into the arts insofar as he promoted the new artists of his time who were portraying the lives of the streets, even though the beauties there are transitory. His concepts applied particularly well to the Impressionists.

Yet Baudelaire's focusing on the detached intellectual floating through the crowd is limited as an ideal for contemporary aesthetics. First, many of *our* urban spaces are not quite right for the kind of strolling Baudelaire describes. Second, insofar as the life of the nineteenth-century flâneur would have been impossible for a woman or a working class person of that time, it is unclear how it could be applied as an ideal to our own.[55] Third, the flâneur only appreciates

---

52 Charles Baudelaire, *The Painter of Modern Life and Other Essays* (London: Phaidon Press, 1995), Chapter 1, "The Painter of Modern Life."
53 See Keith Tester, ed., *The Flâneur* (London: Routledge, 1994).
54 Baudelaire, 7.
55 Janet Wolff, "The artist and the flâneur: Rodin, Rilke and Gwen John in Paris," in *Flâneur*, 111-37.

public spaces, not the space of home-life: it would not include a housewife's aesthetic appreciation of hanging laundry, which Pauliina Rautio has convincingly argued is an important part of everyday aesthetics.[56] Finally, treating the flâneur as an ideal fails to recognize his problematic social position within a capitalist system (although the flâneur may be critical of capitalist society, who supports him financially, and at what cost?).

An interest amongst Parisian intellectuals in everyday aesthetics has continued up to our own times. In the 1920s and 1930s Walter Benjamin, a Marxist literary and culture critic, picked up on the idea of the flâneur as someone who stood in the margins of the bourgeois class and who, although alienated, "bestowed a conciliatory gleam" over the city.[57] I take this to mean that the city gained for him a gleaming beauty which was a consolation for the alienation he experienced as a member of a capitalist-dominated class society. As Benjamin put it, to the flâneur "a shiny enameled shop sign is at least as good a wall ornament as an oil painting is to a bourgeois in his living room."[58] Benjamin placed particular emphasis on the flâneur's experience in the Parisian arcades, the shopping-malls of the day. He saw the flâneur as intoxicated by the commodities put on display.[59] In this respect, although he was sometimes sympathetic to the flâneur, he was also critical of him for living under an illusion, for not seeing beneath the surface appearances of things. The lesson for everyday aesthetics is that the ideal of the flâneur also holds its dangers.

In the 1960s, Guy-Ernest Debord outlined the concept of the "dérive"—literally a "drift"—which he saw as a rapid walk through various urban environments that refused to recognize conventional divisions and categories, and allowed one to "succumb to the enticements of the terrain."[60] The Situationists were artists who, following Debord, sought to overcome the dominance of everyday life by capitalist consumerism, in which things take on a life of their

---

56 Pauliina Rautio, "On Hanging Laundry: The Place of Beauty in Managing Everyday Life," *Contemporary Aesthetics* 7 (2009), http://www.contempaesthetics.org/new volume/pages/article.php?articleID=535.
57 David Frisby, "The flâneur in social theory," in *Flâneur*, 81-110.
58 Walter Benjamin, *The Writer of Modern Life: Essays on Charles Baudelaire*, ed. Michael Jennings (Cambridge, MA: Harvard University Press, 2006), 68.
59 Benjamin, *The Writer*, 85.
60 Vincent Kaufmann, "The Poetics of the Dérive," in *The Everyday*, ed. Stephen Johnstone, in the series *Documents of Contemporary Art* (London: Whitechapel Ventures, 2008), 95-101.

own and life is reduced to "Spectacle."[61] They concentrated on how images influence or mediate our experience of the world. They tried to achieve their goals through developing art or art-like events that disrupted everyday life. In this way they could be seen as creating a new form of flâneur not susceptible to the illusions of the commodity-intoxicated flâneur described by Benjamin.

Theorists of the nineteenth and early twentieth centuries who were primarily interested in the arts often argued that the artist him- or herself has an enhanced appreciation of aesthetic features of everyday life. Arthur Schopenhauer thought that the genius artist was able to access the world through pure perception in which the artist loses awareness of himself, perceiving a hat, for example, in such a way that the Platonic Form of the hat shines through.[62] Although this process (recommended by Schopenhauer) allows the perceiver to perceive the extraordinary in the ordinary, it fails to capture the particular nature of the object because of its obsession with universals. It also fails to capture the ways in which non-genius observers can appreciate everyday aesthetic phenomena.

Leo Tolstoy, in his book *What is Art?* (1896), although mainly interested in defining art, was also concerned, somewhat like John Dewey later, to address the continuity between fine art and the things of everyday life. He wrote that "[a]ll human life is filled with works of art of every kind—from cradlesong, jest, mimicry, the ornamentation of houses, dress, and utensils, up to church services, buildings, monuments, and triumphal processions. It is all artistic activity."[63] For Tolstoy, the very category of art is so broad as to include much of what we would call the aesthetics of everyday life.

Clive Bell, the British formalist art critic famous for advocating the art of Cézanne, insisted in his *Art* (1914) that we bring nothing from life to our appreciation of a work of art, and that the world of human business and passion is not the world of aesthetic contemplation. This would seem to make him an enemy of everyday aesthetics. However, he also thought that the artist is able to see what he called "Significant Form" in the ordinary objects around us.[64] As he put it "Occasionally, when an artist—a real artist—looks at objects

---

61 Thanks to my student Esuebio Lozano for getting me to think more about the relationship between Situationism and everyday aesthetics.
62 Arthur Schopenhauer, *The World as Will and Representation* (New York: Dover, 1966).
63 Leo Tolstoy, *What is Art?* (New York: The Library of Liberal Arts, 1960), 53.
64 Clive Bell, *Art* (New York: Capricorn Books, 1958), Chapter III "The Metaphysical Hypothesis."

(the contents of a room, for instance) he perceives them as pure forms in certain relations to each other, and feels emotion for them as such. These are his moments of inspiration: follows the desire to express what has been felt."[65] As with Schopenhauer, when Bell's "real artist" looks at a chair he ignores many of the chair's features, for example its association with the intimate life of the family. As he puts it, for the artist an object such as a chair is sometimes able to provoke aesthetic emotion. Unfortunately, also like Schopenhauer, he neglects the particular chair and he excludes non-artists from aesthetic perception of the everyday.

NON-WESTERN

There are also non-Western sources for interest in everyday aesthetics. The Navajo concept of beauty extends far beyond the spheres of art and nature. As anthropologist Gary Witherspoon has put it, the Navajo word for beauty, *hózhó*, "refers to the positive or ideal environment." Witherspoon describes *hózhó* as "beauty, harmony, good, happiness, and everything that is positive" and he observes that it refers to an all-inclusive environment. The goal of the Navajo is to live in the condition of *hózhó* to maturity.[66]

The Japanese are particularly concerned to emphasize everyday aesthetic experience.[67] Japanese aesthetics provides a constant source of reflection on the way in which something extraordinary can be found in the ordinary and the everyday. Drawing on Japanese examples, Barbara Sandrisser has criticized the contemporary notion of "the commonplace" as something ordinary and mediocre.[68] She notes that the term "commonplace" originally comes from the Greek *koinos topos* which she takes to mean place where people met to exchange ideas. (This etymology may be incorrect since the O.E.D. gives the earlier meaning of *koinos topos* as "general theme.") She then refers us to an older Japanese craft-oriented view of the everyday. Following the Japanese, Sandrisser encourages us to accept the vernacular, artistic, and even agricul-

---

65 Bell, *Art*, 44.
66 Gary Witherspoon, *Language and Art in the Navajo Universe* (Ann Arbor: The University of Michigan Press, 1977), 24-25.
67 See especially Yuriko Saito on this in her *Everyday Aesthetics* (Oxford: Oxford University Press, 2007).
68 Barbara Sandrisser, "Cultivating Commonplaces: Sophisticated Vernacularism in Japan," *The Journal of Aesthetics and Art Criticism* 56, no. 2 (1998): 201-10.

tural roots of contemporary sophisticated culture. On her view, an admirable culture is one in which people gain emotional delight from their everyday environments.

Sandrisser admits that the traditional shaping of the environment carried out, for example, by Japanese carpenters has mythical and spiritual dimensions that are difficult to accept or appreciate today. For example, in the tradition of Japanese woodworking, the wood is seen to have a soul, a benevolent *kami*, which needs to be respected. The master carpenter in ancient temple grounds is expected to respect each log within the context of its destiny within a sacred space.[69] Although this approach to the aesthetics of wood-working may seem overly romantic or superstitious, Sandrisser notes that it helped to create the vernacular elegance so admired today in Japanese aesthetics.

Here again, we have reached a point where the commonplace is transcended, exceeding the mundane and the banal. This happens especially through what I have previously referred to as art's dialectical relationship with everyday experience. As Sandrisser observes, Japanese architecture at its best (for example, in the contemporary work of Tadao Ando) gathers together the delights of everyday aesthetics, in the gentle perfume of wood, in the feel of textures, and in our appreciation of weather, foliage, and other natural phenomena.

Sei Shōnagon, who served a Japanese empress during the Heian period, around 1000 AD, wrote the *Pillow Book* in which she gives a well-known list of elegant things: "1. A white coat worn over a violet waistcoat. 2. Duck eggs. 3. Shaved ice mixed with liana syrup and put in a new silver bowl. 4. A rosary of rock crystal. 5. Wisteria blossoms. Plum blossoms covered with snow. 6. A pretty child eating strawberries."[70] The aristocratic community in which she lived was highly aesthetic. The orientation of this list was not to works of fine art but to both ordinary and unusual objects of everyday life.

Sei Shōnagon represents a certain type of aesthetic ideal: the aesthete. Although we often think of aesthetes as mainly interested in the arts, they may also focus on the everyday. For example, the aesthete has been described by Chinese-American geographer Yi-Fu Tuan as taking a child-like delight "in a balloon, the striped awning of a café, a towering construction crane, the fragrance of burning leaves, a military parade, or a sunset without any attempt to see how they might constitute a larger whole and without examining the

---

69 Sandrisser, "Cultivating," 204.
70 Barbara Sandrisser, "On Elegance in Japan," in *Aesthetics in Perspective*, ed. K. Higgins (Fort Worth: Harcourt Brace, 1996), 628.

consequences they may have on human life, society, and nature."⁷¹ Unlike the French flâneur who focuses mainly on the visual, Tuan's aesthete is aware of all aspects of the environment available to all the senses.

JOHN DEWEY

A classic source of inspiration for the aesthetics of everyday life has been John Dewey. One could even say that Dewey is the grandfather of everyday aesthetics.⁷² Although his main interest was in the aesthetics of art, he stressed what he called the "sources of esthetic experience" in "animal life below the human scale."⁷³ He also traced the aesthetics of art to the aesthetic phenomena of prehistoric humans, evidence of which he found in contemporary tribal societies. Like Marx and Morris, Dewey fit his view of everyday aesthetics into an overall philosophy of social improvement. In Dewey's case this involved paying attention to primitive aesthetic experience. As he put it, "[we] do not have to travel to the ends of the earth nor return many millennia in time to find peoples for whom everything that intensifies the sense of immediate living is an object of intense admiration."⁷⁴ Aesthetic phenomena that show this include bodily scarification, waving feathers, gaudy robes, and shining ornaments of gold and silver. However, instead of placing these things within a non-art category called "everyday aesthetics," Dewey expanded the notion of art to include them, saying that they "formed the contents of esthetic arts" for these people. He notes that the domestic utensils of such people were constructed with such care that today they are honoured in art museums. Yet he also observes that in their time "such things were enhancements of the processes of everyday life."⁷⁵

Related to these concerns was Dewey's larger goal to restore continuity between art and the everyday, or as he put it, "between the refined and intensified forms of experiences that are works of art and the everyday events, doings,

---

71 Yi-Fu Tuan, *Passing Strange and Wonderful: Aesthetics, Nature, and Culture* (New York: Kodansha International, 1995), 19.
72 John Dewey, *The Later Works, 1925-1953 Volume 10: 1934*, ed. Jo Ann Boydston and Harriet Furst Simon (Carbondale: Southern Illinois University Press, 1989) [originally *Art as Experience* (New York: G.P. Putnams, 1934)]. Sherri Irvin, refers to this work as "the most general and well-developed existing account of the possibility of aesthetic experience in everyday life" ("Pervasiveness," 30).
73 Dewey, 24.
74 Dewey, 12.
75 Dewey, 12.

and sufferings that are universally recognized to constitute experience."[76] Anyone who has read some of Dewey's aesthetics will recall his discussion of the aesthetic experience of such things as a crackling fire in the hearth, the solving of a problem in a car-mechanic's garage, and the pleasure we may get from eating in a fine restaurant. What Dewey calls "*an* experience" can happen not only with art but in everyday life. I shall return to Dewey at the end of this chapter.

LATE TWENTIETH CENTURY

After Dewey, and with the rise of analytic aesthetics in the English-speaking world, interest in everyday aesthetics declined radically. It was not revived until the work of Joseph H. Kupfer, Roger Scruton, and David Novitz.[77] Kupfer could be said to have written the first monograph on everyday aesthetics in English. Like Dewey, Kupfer argued "that aesthetic values permeate everyday life and ought not to be thought of as the exclusive province of museums and concert halls."[78] Rather than pointing out how objects of everyday life can be artful, Kupfer stressed how our personal and social development is pervaded by aesthetic relations and qualities.[79] He sought to provide "an aesthetic investigation of the human interests and activities which comprise daily living."[80] Kupfer found aesthetic deprivation underlying "overall dissatisfaction" in American society.[81] In this respect he was like Morris and Ruskin. However, although Kupfer had much of value to say on the aesthetics of violence, sexuality, sport, decision-making, and death, his book failed to connect his issues with the larger domain of philosophical aesthetics.

David Novitz, as the title of his book, *The Boundaries of Art*, indicates, was more concerned with boundaries between fine and popular art and between art and non-art than with the notion of everyday aesthetics. Nonetheless, he did have interesting things to say about the aesthetics of grooming, friendship,

---

76 Dewey, 9.
77 Joseph H. Kupfer, *Experience as Art: Aesthetics in Everyday Life* (Albany: State University of New York Press, 1983). Roger Scruton, *The Aesthetics of Architecture* (Princeton: Princeton University Press, 1980), 2nd ed., 2000. David Novitz, *The Boundaries of Art* (Philadelphia: Temple University Press, 1992).
78 Kupfer, 1.
79 Kupfer, 2.
80 Kupfer, 2.
81 Kupfer, 2.

and character, all topics that would fall under the everyday. In his effort to dissolve the boundaries between art and everyday life, he also drew attention to such things as landscape gardening, tree pruning, debating, cooking, and living-room décor. However, his conception of everyday aesthetics was limited to what can be conceived of as skilled arts, thus excluding appreciation of everyday phenomena that are not in any sense crafted, for example the piles of garden clippings placed outside of houses for recycling, the patterns of shadows on a wall, or the abstract layered shapes on weathered billboards.

In his 1980 book on the aesthetics of architecture Roger Scruton described architecture as essentially related to the aesthetics of everyday life.[82] On his view, the aesthetics of building is of a piece with that of decoration, arrangement of rooms, folding napkins and laying places at a table. For Scruton, when architecture has an aesthetic aim it is to try to make something "look right" to the casual observer, rather than to express meaning. Scruton goes too far on this point since expression of meaning is certainly important in architecture, for example the Christian meanings expressed in church architecture. However, the idea that "looks right" is an important aesthetic property is useful in considering not only architecture but also everyday objects. Scruton also defends the view that architecture is not an object of refined taste. This connects with his conviction that *everyone* participates in architecture even if it is only through home decoration. He concludes that proposing an aesthetics of architecture *is* proposing an aesthetics of everyday life. Ironically, his discussion of architectural examples shows the very refined taste he rejects. I would argue, contra Scruton, that advocacy of the aesthetics of everyday life does not require rejection of refinement whether in architecture or elsewhere.

More recently, in a book on the nature of beauty, Scruton speaks of everyday aesthetics in terms of the humanly universal attempt to "match our surroundings to ourselves and ourselves to our surroundings."[83] Handiwork, carpentry, decoration (including laying a table for guests), dress, and tidying one's bedroom, are all incorporated into everyday aesthetics with the dominant ideas still being "looks right" and what "fits." Scruton stresses that the judgment that something looks right is not a mere judgment of utility. For example, a carpenter cannot say that a doorframe looks right simply because it allows the

---

82   Scruton, *Architecture*.
83   Roger Scruton, *Beauty* (New York: Oxford University Press, 2009), Chapter 4 "Everyday Beauty," 82. See also his "Search."

door to open and shut easily and it meets health and safety requirements.[84] He also insists that the aesthetic is socially derived and is motivated "as a guide to our shared environment."[85]

Another important contributor to the field has been Richard Shusterman. He has written several books related to the topic, starting with *Pragmatist Aesthetics: Living Beauty, Rethinking Art*.[86] He has, for example, proposed a new discipline of "somaesthetics" which, as he puts it, is "devoted to the critical, ameliorative study of one's experience and use of one's body as a locus of sensory-aesthetic appreciation ... and creative self-fashioning."[87] Somaesthetics includes not only an analytic dimension which provides theories about the body in its relation to aesthetics, but also a practical dimension which involves specific recommendations for body improvement. Thus somaesthetics looks at everyday aesthetics from the perspective of how one can creatively transform one's own body through such techniques as Yoga and the Feldenkrais method. As I see it, somaesthetics is an important sub-discipline of everyday aesthetics. Yet it would not function well as an overall aesthetics of everyday life since there are many aesthetic phenomena that are not strictly speaking "of the body." For example, although we use a body part, the eye, to appreciate someone's garden visually, we are not attending to the eye when we do so.

Philosophers may be surprised to find that the terms "everyday aesthetics" and "the aesthetics of everyday life" often crop up outside of their field. Visual culture theorists and folklorists have sometimes used these terms to define their own fields.[88] Fascination with the notion of "everyday life" among social critics goes back to the 1960s. These writers tend to see everyday aesthetic phenomena in terms of what is called "expressive culture." Their interest is in the ways that expressive culture reveals matters of social concern, e.g., with regard to race, class and gender. Although they share with philosophers of everyday aestheticians a conviction that activities of everyday life may be

---

84 Scruton, *Beauty*, 82.
85 Scruton, *Beauty*, 90.
86 Richard Shusterman, *Pragmatist Aesthetics: Living Beauty, Rethinking Art* (New York: Rowman & Littlefield, 2000), orig. 1992.
87 Richard Shusterman, *Performing Live* (Ithaca: Cornell University Press, 2000), 138. This is in Chapter 7: "Somaesthetics and the body/media issue."
88 Barbara Kirshenblatt-Gimblett, "The Future of Folklore Studies in America: The Urban Frontier," *Folklore Forum* 16 (1983): 175-234. Harris M. Berger and Giovanna P. Del Negro, *Identity and Everyday Life: Essays in the Study of Folklore, Music, and Popular Culture* (Middletown, CT: Wesleyan University Press, 2004).

richly aesthetic, they focus on "expressive significance" more than on aesthetic experience or aesthetic properties as such. The main value of this work for philosophers may be in the wide range of examples they offer, as well as some of the problems raised and explored. For example, some cultural theorists are interested in the relation between ordinary everyday activities and certain heightened events such as festivals and rituals, the aesthetic qualities of which have not been much discussed by philosophers.

This completes the rough overview of the history of everyday aesthetics up until the 1990s. The more recent history will be discussed in coming chapters. However, first we should consider whether the field is appropriately named. Ossi Naukkarinen rejects "everyday aesthetics" as the appropriate name. He thinks that everydayness implies something "ordinary, boring, usual, habitual, well-known and safe."[89] And this, for him, makes it less attractive as a term for what we are studying than "non-art aesthetics." I disagree. "Non-art aesthetics" covers too much insofar as it would include such fields as the aesthetics of nature and the aesthetics of mathematics. Also, although the everyday includes things usually considered ordinary and boring, they are no longer quite so ordinary, and are certainly not boring, when experienced aesthetically. However, I agree if he means that the aesthetics of everyday life should include that which is non-ordinary in life despite the usual association of the everyday and the ordinary. Naukkarinen is also right that as soon as one attends to the aesthetic dimension of things one has left the realm of the ordinary. That is, the ordinary becomes somewhat less ordinary when it is experienced in aesthetically positive ways.

THE IMPORTANCE OF EVERYDAY AESTHETICS

Some recent writers have gone quite far in their estimation of the importance of everyday aesthetics. For example, Paul Duncum has argued that because of social, economic and technological changes, everyday aesthetics has become pre-eminent, overshadowing fine art.[90] Taking a post-structuralist, semiotic approach, Duncum claims that we live in a world in which culture itself has taken a visual turn. He asks us to consider the ubiquity of television: its power

---

89 Ossi Naukkarinen, *Aesthetics of the Unavoidable—Aesthetic Variations in Human Appearance* (Lahti: International Institute of Applied Aesthetics, 1998), Vol. 3, 65.
90 Paul Duncum, "A Case for an Art Education of Everyday Aesthetic Experiences," *Studies in Art Education* 40, no. 4 (1999): 295-311.

is based on its having been integrated into every aspect of our lives. This point would, of course, be better made today by remarking on the ubiquity of the electronic screen image, of which the TV image is just one example.

Duncum thinks that interest in everyday aesthetics has come about because society has turned to the cultural, and the cultural has turned towards the visual.[91] I am not sure what the "turn to the cultural" means (from what? as opposed to what?). Nor is it clear that contemporary culture is more interested in the visual than in the aural, if youth's continued interest in music is any indication. Also, within contemporary philosophy interest in everyday aesthetics is certainly not limited to the visual.

Like other philosophers interested in the topic, Duncum provides a list of what would make up everyday aesthetics, in this case a list of "sites" rather than a list of items, types of things, or types of experience. He writes that "[c]haracteristic sites of everyday aesthetics include environments such as theme parks, shopping malls, city streetscapes, and tourist attractions, as well as mass media images especially on television and now on computer screens."[92] This list is interesting not only for what it includes but also for what it excludes. Computer screens and virtual worlds are novel and appropriate inclusions. Duncum, however, excludes anything that is refined or exotic. Yet, one can have refined appreciation of various non-art, non-nature sites and phenomena. For example one can have refined appreciation of the various kinds of beauty derived from the application of cosmetics. Also, the exotic is a fairly typical interest in the everyday lives of tourists. Duncum also excludes natural environments from everyday aesthetics, perhaps because of a postmodernist conviction that there are no such things. I too have excluded natural environments from my definition of everyday aesthetics, but only because a field of natural aesthetics already exists and because there are distinctive differences between the ways we approach natural phenomena and the ways we approach the non-natural artefacts, events, and phenomena of our everyday lives.

Duncum takes the importance of everyday aesthetics to be based on the fact that we learn about ourselves and the world mainly unconsciously through everyday processes. He then argues for incorporating everyday sites into art education since, for most children, these sites are more powerful in shaping their identity and world-perception than the fine arts. He thinks that the fine

---

91 Duncum, 295.
92 Duncum, 295.

arts should no longer be the central concern of art education. Instead, art education would be about the ways in which visual culture shapes our values and beliefs. He goes on to predict that everyday aesthetics will continue to grow in importance, for example as electronic media come to pervade our lives and, as Marx correctly predicted, more and more aspects of our lives under capitalism become subject to the market (think about the fact that internet search engines now target advertisements to individual interests). Further, Duncum argues, as the world of virtual reality becomes the world in which many young people live, the world itself will be transformed into signs and images.

Although Duncum's "cultural studies" approach to everyday aesthetics is valuable, it is limited insofar as he takes the theme park, the shopping mall and virtual reality as paradigms. Other, more subtle but equally pervasive sites, for example the backyard vegetable garden and the musty used bookstore, do not to fit in with his typology.[93] Everyday aesthetics should not neglect the sites he describes, but also should not neglect other sites, objects and phenomena. Moreover, the many qualities I will discuss in coming chapters as central to everyday aesthetics are neglected in this approach. Also, the radical separation Duncum posits between an elite aesthetics of fine art and the everyday aesthetics of consumerism neglects the many ways in which fine art aesthetics and everyday aesthetics may fruitfully interact, as for example in the ways that contemporary artists draw our attention to everyday life. Finally, even those young people who may find the visual sites Duncum describes entertaining may not accept the idea that study of them should replace fine arts education, which may still provide the richest and most enduring aesthetic experiences.[94]

EVERYDAY AESTHETICS IN THE VARIOUS ART TRADITIONS

Much art is based on, or inspired by, everyday aesthetic experience. We have already seen this point in Hegel. We see art, at least in part, in terms of everyday aesthetics, and everyday aesthetics, at least in part, in terms of art. The aesthetics of everyday life did not begin with philosophers. If one defines it as the activity of reflecting on aesthetic qualities in everyday life, this was already done with great skill by poets, novelists, painters, musicians, and choreographers. Moreover, architects and designers constantly think about how to improve

---

93 See Yuriko Saito's criticisms in *Everyday*, 51.
94 Thanks to my student Elizabeth Yanez.

our everyday lives aesthetically. There have been high points in these non-philosophical reflections, for example, in the work of Dutch still-life painters and that of contemporary installation artists. However, this should not hide the fact that art's interest in everyday aesthetics is pervasive.

Most painters explore some aspect of everyday life in at least some of their works. Even abstract painters explore the everyday by focusing our attention on the aesthetic properties of certain shapes and colours we encounter on a daily basis. This could also be said for poetry. Of course there is a historical dimension to this. Interest in the aesthetics of the everyday has been greater at some times than at others. In poetry, there was an increase in the nineteenth century, particularly in Wordsworth and Whitman, in part as a reaction against writers such as Joshua Reynolds who rejected the aesthetic value of the everyday.[95] This turn to the everyday continued through certain aspects of modernism and on into the Beat poetry of the 1950s and 1960s and the Slam poetry which began in the 1980s and continues today.

Everyday life was also a particular concern, during the last couple of centuries, to visual artists such as Courbet, Monet, Renoir, Morisot, Bonnard, Hopper, Burchfield, Marsh, and, in our own time, Katz and Andersson. Picasso and Braque brought the objects of everyday life directly into the studio through collage. Rauschenberg and Cornell took this further through assemblage.

Marcel Duchamp famously took a urinal from a hardware store and turned it into art, calling it *Fountain*. Although he proclaimed a lack of interest in the aesthetic dimension of what he did, that dimension is hard to ignore. Artists influenced by Duchamp came to look at everyday items differently.

Attacks on the institution of art by the Surrealists had the effect of turning attention to aesthetic qualities not traditionally associated with art or nature. Andy Warhol took us directly into the world of everyday life, as did the other Pop artists of the 1960s. The super-realist artists of the 1970s continued this trend. Robert Bechtle, for example, drew attention to the look of parked cars on suburban streets. And in the late 1970s and 1980s feminist artists turned this spotlight on the everyday lives of women. Mary Kelly's *Post-Partum document 1973-1979*, for example, explored the relationship between a child and a working-class mother using the techniques of conceptual art.

---

95 George J. Leonard, *Into the Light of Things: The Art of the Commonplace from Wordsworth to Cage* (Chicago: University of Chicago Press, 1994).

Photography, in particular, opened up new domains of appreciation in everyday life. Many of the first photographs by Niépce and Daguerre were of Paris street-life, place-settings, and still-lives. Later photographers drew our attention to the complex qualities of such ordinary things as the green pepper one might buy in a grocery store (Edward Weston). Paul Strand, Helen Levitt, and many others photographed ordinary people going about their lives. Contemporary photographers have explored such topics as the look of suburban streets at night. Jeff Wall has used his set pieces to highlight dramas in everyday life.

Film also had an important connection to everyday life, as has been argued by Michael Roemer.[96] Roemer writes "Because most good films use the language of the commonplace, they tend to have an unassuming appearance, whereas films that make a large claim ... almost invariably prove to be hollow." This leads him to hold that good films must be concrete. Roemer further writes that "there is a great challenge to making the commonplaces of life, that have so long eluded art, yield up their meaning." In film "we are finally able to use the much despised and ephemeral detail of everyday life, the common physical dross, and work it into the gold of art."

Many directors specialize in exploration of aesthetic matters in everyday life. For example Yasujirō Ozu in his film *Late Spring* (1949) lovingly depicts the quotidian in post-war Japan, drawing our attention to little things, like the way the widowed father sits at his desk. Jean Renoir similarly dwells on the way a maid moves from room to room in a bourgeois house in *Boudu Saved from Drowning* (1932). Some movies also depend on depiction of everyday life for their effect: horror films, for example, seduce us into shock by immersing us first in the everyday.

In architecture, a new interest in everyday life came with the rise of modernism and postmodernism. Le Corbusier drew our attention to the aesthetic riches of airplanes and grain elevators.[97] The Italian Futurists did something similar with automobiles and factories. Postmodern architects, such as Robert Venturi and Denise Scott Brown, turned to vernacular use of signs on the streets of Las Vegas for inspiration.[98]

96　Michael Roemer, "The Surfaces of Reality," *Film Quarterly* 18 (1964): 15-22. I quote from the selection of the same name in Feagin and Maynard, eds., *Aesthetics*, 80 first quote, 86 second and third.

97　See Le Corbusier, *Towards a New Architecture* (Mineola, NY: Dover, 1985), orig. 1923.

98　Robert Venturi, Stephen Izenour, Denise Scott Brown, *Learning from Las Vegas* (Cambridge, MA: The MIT Press, 1977).

Music draws inspiration from, and also influences our perception of, the sounds of everyday life. We often attribute aesthetic qualities to everyday non-music sounds. Sounds that we find aesthetically displeasing are commonly called "noise," although not everything we call "noise" is aesthetically displeasing. John Cage encouraged us to pay attention to ambient sound in his famous composition *4'33"* (1948) in which the pianist opens the piano lid and does not play a note for that period of time.

When philosophers attempt to define music they generally distinguish musical from non-musical sounds. For example, Jerrold Levinson defines music as "sounds temporally organized by a person for the purpose of enriching or intensifying experience through active engagement (e.g., listening, dancing, performing) with the sounds regarded primarily or in significant measure as sounds."[99] He wishes to distinguish between music and that which can be treated as music, and he opposes Cage's idea that all sounds are (or can be) music, although he admits that one can be receptively aware of any sonic environment. It is noteworthy that Levinson's definition of music is designed to exclude "elevator music." Even though this type of background music involves sounds temporally organized by a person, it fails to meet the condition of being made for the purpose of "enriching or intensifying experience through active engagement." If background music fails to be music then it enters the world of everyday aesthetics. Similarly, the ambient sounds Cage sought to include in the domain of music can, even if excluded by Levinson's definition, still exist in that of everyday aesthetics.

Starting in the 1970s, and perhaps influenced by Cage, composer and art educator R. Murray Schafer developed a theory exploring our relations with what he called "soundscapes."[100] Soundscapes include all sounds within an environment, human, natural and mixed. John Fisher, drawing from Schafer, remarks on the aesthetic pleasures and displeasures we can gain from non-musical sounds.[101] Fisher describes a number of ways one can listen to non-musical sounds: formalist, associational, and representational.[102] Although

---

99 Jerrold Levinson, "On the Concept of Music," in *Music, Art, and Metaphysics* (Ithaca: Cornell University Press, 1990), 269-76.
100 Raymond Murray Schafer, *The Soundscape* (Vermont: Destiny Books, 1993) and *The Tuning of the World* (New York: Alfred Knopf, 1977).
101 John Andrew Fisher, "What the Hills are Alive With: In Defense of the Sounds of Nature," *Journal of Aesthetics and Art Criticism* 56, no. 2 (1998): 167-79, 168.
102 Fisher, 168.

Fisher is mainly interested in natural sounds, his ideas are also applicable to the human and mixed sounds typical of everyday life. He rightly opposes the view that whatever is not music is noise and cannot give us aural pleasure.

Postmodern dance drew its audience's attention to the aesthetic qualities of such ordinary activities as carrying a mattress across a room.[103] But the relation of dance to everyday life is not limited to this style. Dance, in general, highlights aspects of everyday life, as can be seen, for example, in Monroe Beardsley's analysis of dance as representing such working actions as snow-shovelling and corn-planting.[104]

CONCLUSION

Discussion of everyday aesthetics allows us to talk about things that do not generally come up in traditional aesthetics. It opens a new domain of inquiry. Yet, as I have suggested, this domain is closely related to more traditional fields of aesthetics. For example, the terms that characterize aesthetic experience are often shared between it and the aesthetics of art and nature. Central to all three fields is the term "beauty." However, a number of other terms are shared as well, for example "harmony" and "grace," and even some terms not often mentioned, for example "neat" and "messy." The three fields also share many problems, for example debates over the nature of aesthetic evaluation. They are also related by way of art directing its attention to the aesthetic qualities of nature and everyday life.

What then is everyday aesthetics? We have rejected the idea of defining it in terms of necessary and sufficient conditions, but not the idea of a less ambitious form of philosophical definition. Nor have we rejected the idea of a general account of the field. In what follows I will consider various attempts to define the field as well as attempts to exclude its very possibility. I will discuss and reject the view that it can be defined exclusively in terms of functionality (a view held by Hume, as we have seen), the view that it is a matter of unified experience (associated with Dewey), and the view that it is understandable in terms of the notion of ritual (Sartwell). My favoured position will be that it should be studied in terms

---

103 Noël Carroll and Sally Banes, "Working and Dancing: A Response to Monroe Beardsley's 'What Is Going on in a Dance?'" *Dance Research Journal* 15, no. 1 (1982): 37-41.

104 Monroe C. Beardsley, "What is Going on in a Dance?" *Dance Research Journal* 15, no. 1 (1982): 31-37.

of aesthetic properties. However, this view will also be found to have problems. I will attempt to resolve these and flesh out my position in Part II when I introduce the concept of "aura." None of the views discussed is completely wrong and each has something to offer. In particular, the position of Dewey will be revisited in more detail and with considerable sympathy.

CHAPTER 2
Aesthetic Experience and Aesthetic Properties

It might be argued that there is no such thing as an everyday aesthetic experience; that the everyday implies the ordinary, but aesthetic experience implies something outside the ordinary. M.J. Zenzen, for example, claims that aesthetic experience is extraordinary perceptual experience.[1] It is involved only when "something familiar and personal becomes strange and transcendent" with an aura of other-worldliness. Similarly, Richard Shusterman speaks of it as something that stands out from the ordinary flow of routine experience.[2]

I prefer a somewhat broader meaning for "aesthetic experience." Although the kind of experience described by Zenzen and Shusterman is important, there are also simpler, low-level, forms that do not involve strangeness, transcendence or otherworldliness. As Yuriko Saito has observed, there are many aesthetic predications that entail experiences that are not extraordinary, for example when we say that sheets hanging in the backyard "look clean."[3] These might be said to indicate low-level aesthetic experience. At the same time, Zenzen and Shusterman are right to the extent that when we *focus* on

---

1 M.J. Zenzen, "Ground for Aesthetic Experience," *The Journal of Aesthetics and Art Criticism* 34, no. 4 (1976): 469-47.
2 Richard Shusterman, "The End of Aesthetic Experience," *The Journal of Aesthetics and Art Criticism* 55, no. 1 (1997): 29-41.
3 Saito, *Everyday*.

these phenomena and experience them *as aesthetic* they leave the realm of the ordinary in the sense of the banal and uninteresting.

The term "aesthetic experience" probably gained its prominence from Dewey. Adapting ordinary language, he speaks of a meal in a French restaurant or an experience of a storm at sea as "an experience."[4] For Dewey, "an experience" must be (1) "so rounded out that its close is a consummation," (2) a whole, (3) something that "carries with it its own individuating quality" that pervades throughout, (4) self-sufficient, (5) something that has "its own plot, its own inception and movement towards its close," (6) something that has "its own particular rhythmic movement," (7) a "memorial" or a "summing up" of all that something of that type can be, (8) such that "every successive part flows freely, without seam and without unfilled blanks, into what ensues" but with no sacrifice of part identity, (9) something that has no holes or dead centres, and (10) that "has a unity that gives it its name."[5] It also has to be (11) aesthetic.

I would not deny that there is such a thing as "an experience" in Dewey's sense, although it may be difficult to find one that has all of the qualities mentioned. Nor is it clear that everything we would call "an experience" in Dewey's sense would *have* all these qualities. For example, we might say that an event that was broken off or incomplete in some way was "an experience." A dinner party cut short by a sudden illness of one of the guests might be "an experience" although, qua dinner party, it would be incomplete.

However, it is another matter whether aesthetics generally, and everyday aesthetics in particular, must be defined in terms of Dewey's "an experience." As Sherri Irvin has argued, we can have aesthetic experiences without having "an experience."[6] We can, for example, experience things as having aesthetic qualities. Experiencing things as having aesthetic qualities is a kind of aesthetic experience, although not necessarily one that has the unity or completeness characteristic of "an experience." We can experience a streetscape as beautiful and yet not need to describe doing so as having "an experience." Some aesthetic experiences happen in the moment with no clear beginning, middle and end, or any of the other time-taking complexities Dewey mentions as required for "an experience."[7]

---

4   Dewey, Chapter 3 "Having an Experience," 43.
5   Dewey, Chapter 3 "Having an Experience," 42-44.
6   Irvin, "Pervasiveness."
7   I owe this thought to my student Muchen Megan Li.

Nonetheless, when Irvin says, "[a]n experience that one has every day, like drinking a cup of coffee, can become quietly exquisite and even strangely foreign when done with full attention to the feel of the cup in one's hands, the rim of the cup touching one's lower lip, and the sensation of the coffee in the mouth and going down the throat";[8] one could argue that this is "an experience"! Also, it may be argued that, although it does not cover every aesthetic experience, what Dewey described as "an experience" is an especially important kind of aesthetic event, perhaps even an ideal.

Monroe Beardsley is less friendly to everyday aesthetics than Dewey.[9] Although he thought that we could have aesthetic experience of technological things, he mainly thought of aesthetic experience as related to the arts. He saw it as what the arts uniquely have in common and what distinguishes art experiences from other sorts of experience. Thus, he held that "the experience of listening to a song has more in common with the experience of looking at a piece of sculpture than it does, say, with that of walking in a picket line or that of driving down the Schuylkill Expressway."[10] However, although many experiences of walking a picket line and driving are non-aesthetic, some can be aesthetic, and the aesthetic ones may have much in common with looking at a piece of sculpture or with listening to a song.

For Beardsley, a person is having an aesthetic experience "if and only if the greater part of his mental activity during that [stretch of] time is united and made pleasurable by being tied to the form and qualities of a sensuously presented or imaginatively intended object on which his primary attention is concentrated."[11] This definition, by itself, would not exclude aesthetic experiences based on everyday phenomena, unless the phrase "sensuously presented" implies an artist presenter. For example, one could have a united pleasurable experience based on the sensuously presented qualities of a decorated Christmas tree. However, as in the case of Dewey's "an experience," Beardsley's concept of "aesthetic experience" could not cover all matters of everyday aesthetics, for there are some instances in which aesthetic predicates may be applied without primary attention being given to the phenomenon or the greater part

---

8   Irvin, "Scratching an Itch," *Journal of Aesthetics and Art Criticism* 66, no. 1 (2008): 25-35, 31.
9   Monroe C. Beardsley, "Aesthetic Experience Regained," *The Journal of Aesthetics and Art Criticism* 28, no. 1 (1969): 3-11.
10 Beardsley, "Experience," 4.
11 Beardsley, "Experience," 5.

of mental activity being united. We can see something as having the aesthetic quality of being pretty, for example, while still focusing on other things.

Marshall Cohen argued, contra Beardsley, that the experience of riding in a crowded subway can also have unity, thus (in his eyes) refuting the notion that unity is a sufficient condition for an experience to be aesthetic. Beardsley replied that such an experience is just a "mass of jarringly diverse and confused impressions, without dramatic structure...." That is, he simply denied that riding in a crowded subway *could* have unity and thus could be aesthetic. This is another attack on everyday aesthetics. Yet someone could experience a subway in a unified way by constructing the experience *as unified*. Humans generally construct their experiences by focusing on certain aspects of the phenomenon at hand. This in itself gives experiences a certain unity. And this unity can also be intensified. For example, one could construct one's experience of a subway so that it is quite a distinct unity with dramatic structure. Artists and poets do this, for instance, when observing their subject-matter. One could even argue that making a work of art based on such an experience is itself a way of experiencing that subject-matter as unified. Consider Red Grooms' "Subway" from *Ruckus Manhattan* (1976). Creation of such a work requires construction of experience by the artist both during the preliminary stages of the creative process and as that process continues. This is construction not only of the work of art as an experience for the artist and the audience but of the experience of a subway itself, or of subways in general, *by way of* constructing a work of art. Art that takes everyday life as its subject-matter is evidence that everyday-life experiences can be aesthetic, thus refuting both Cohen and Beardsley.

Although Beardsley is right that "our experiences of good works of art, are in fact generally of a high order of unity—of coherence and completeness—compared with most daily experiences,"[12] he fails to see that *some* daily experiences, for example some experiences upon which artists may draw in coming up with their creations, are nearly as coherent and complete as some works of art. Moreover, and more importantly, he neglects the fact that *in the very act of perceiving* such everyday phenomena, artists, aesthetes, and even ordinary folk, often compose the experience to have unity and dramatic structure.

The preceding point is inspired by a comment by Allen Carlson on the aesthetics of nature. He speaks of the nature appreciator as composing the natural landscape which, in the raw, is "promiscuous and indeterminate." I

---

12 Beardsley, "Experience," 9.

apply this idea here to any non-art experience outside of nature. Carlson was in turn inspired by Santayana who, in *The Sense of Beauty*, said that the natural landscape allows "great liberty in selecting, emphasizing, and grouping its elements" and that a landscape has to be composed to be seen. Carlson, however, like Beardsley and Dewey, requires that the experience be consummatory, determinate, harmonious, and meaningful. As I have argued above, this is not required for everyday aesthetic experience, although it might be an ideal.[13]

More recently, Ronald Moore, consistent with Beardsley, has argued that if you say that some foliage is gorgeous while speeding on the highway, you are not really describing an aesthetic experience, for aesthetic experience requires protracted attention. However, he admits that one can judge a field of flowers as beautiful in a short time-span.[14] Why then does he think seeing gorgeous foliage from a speeding car cannot be aesthetic? Perhaps his point is simply that it is not "an experience" in Dewey's sense, which may be conceded. Yet many everyday aesthetic phenomena are only available for a moment, for example one can aesthetically appreciate the momentary effect of a car's headlights against one's living-room wall.[15]

Yi-Fu Tuan helps us here by distinguishing between two extremes of aesthetic experience: the physical and the intellectual. At one extreme the aesthetic can be a "shudder of delight that is predominantly physical in character" and at the other, a "mediated response, cool yet intense, of intellectual appreciation."[16] From Tuan's perspective Moore would be focusing on the second and neglecting the first. Someone might think that Tuan's "predominantly physical" category eliminates the distinction between aesthetic and non-aesthetic pleasures. However, Tuan allows that some pleasures have not yet reached the threshold of the aesthetic. As he puts it, "[p]leasures may well exist that are direct and naïve: for instance, the taste of cool water when thirsty...." He goes on to argue that "pleasure deemed aesthetic suggests greater distancing,

---

13   Allen Carlson, "Aesthetic Appreciation of the Natural Environment," in *Aesthetics: A Reader in Philosophy of the Arts*, David Goldblatt and Lee B. Brown, eds. (Upper Saddle River, NJ: Pearson Prentice Hall, 2005), 526-33. The Santayana quote appears on p. 526. The harmonious quote is on p. 531. George Santayana, *The Sense of Beauty: Being the Outline of Aesthetic Theory* (New York: Charles Scribner's Sons, 1896).
14   Ronald Moore, *Natural Beauty: A Theory of Aesthetics Beyond the Arts* (Peterborough, ON: Broadview Press, 2007), 142.
15   Thanks to my students Carolyn Robbins and Jeannie Kim for comments on this.
16   Yi-Fu Tuan, "Surface Phenomena and Aesthetic Experience," *Annals of the Association of American Geographers* 79, no. 2 (1989): 233-41.

the effect of a more circuitous psychological path," a path that can be extended by "association, memory and knowledge."[17] He follows this comment with a description of an experience which is heightened by further reflection through the medium of poetry. Thus, on his view, although a pleasure may not be immediately aesthetic, it may be enhanced through the mediation of art so as to cross the threshold. This is a very significant point that further supports my general claims about the importance of the interaction between the experience of art and everyday aesthetic experience.

Tuan's analysis does not so much oppose Moore's as show how an aesthetic experience can evolve out of the non-aesthetic through the mediation of art. The initial experience of a gorgeous fall landscape, which we might have briefly through a car window, is not non-aesthetic, just rudimentary. It can gain the temporal dimension Moore requires through the mediation of something that brings association and complexity, for example poetry or music.

Moore also forgets that, as Tuan puts it, most aesthetic experience requires apprenticeship in the sense of preliminary training that leads up to the experience. We may not be aware of this apprenticeship since the knowledge gained in it need not be conscious. Although knowledge of the past may influence our aesthetic appreciation, we are not normally actively thinking about the past in the moment of appreciation. One can quickly judge a garden as aesthetically delightful while driving past rapidly.

EVERYDAY AESTHETIC PROPERTIES

Perhaps we can better talk about everyday aesthetics in terms of the notion of everyday aesthetic properties. Perhaps we will know how to separate everyday aesthetics from art aesthetics and from nature aesthetics when we know which properties are appropriate to everyday aesthetics. Talk about properties does not, however, imply turning away from experience since to know that something has a certain property requires that one experience it as having that property, at least in aesthetics.

J.L. Austin, who otherwise said little about aesthetics, famously remarked that we should "forget for a while about the beautiful and get down instead to the dainty and the dumpy."[18] This was in line with Ludwig Wittgenstein's

---

17 Tuan, "Surface," 234.
18 J.L. Austin, "A Plea for Excuses," in *Philosophical Papers* (Oxford: Clarendon, 1961), 131.

influential injunction that philosophers should broaden their diet of examples. Arthur Danto gives Austin's quote as support for his claim that art critic Clement Greenberg, and, before him, Kant, failed to recognize a set of aesthetic qualities that is nearly boundless.[19] In the remainder of this book I will be following Austin's and Danto's advice in recognizing and discussing a much broader set of aesthetic properties, although I do not favour Austin's recommendation to forget about beauty.

What then are aesthetic properties? For some philosophers, aesthetic properties are mainly, or exclusively, properties of artworks. However, there is another tradition that sees them simply as characteristics of objects and events that give us pleasure in apprehension of them. James Joyce famously quotes Aquinas as saying, "Pulcra sunt quae visa placent," which he translates as "that is beautiful the apprehension of which pleases."[20] Here, I take beauty to be the paradigmatic aesthetic property. Perhaps aesthetic properties are ones that please in their apprehension. Aquinas's view as expressed in this quotation is, from the standpoint of everyday aesthetics, headed in the right direction since it is quite inclusive. It does not, for example, limit aesthetics to the fine arts. (His actual aesthetic theory is, of course, more complex than would be indicated by this quote alone, but we need not go into that here.[21])

However, this formulation does have some problems (which may not be problems for Aquinas himself, as indicated in the last footnote). First, it is too general: there are many pleasures based on "apprehension" in some senses of that word which are not aesthetic. One sense of "apprehension" is "intuitive understanding" and, although a politician may well get pleasure in his or her intuitive understanding of a political situation, this may not be aesthetic since it has no sensuous dimension. A sensuous dimension is required, given that the term "aesthetic" was invented originally to refer to sensuous, as opposed to

---

19 Arthur Danto, "Embodied Meanings, Isotypes, and Aesthetical Ideas," *The Journal of Aesthetics and Art Criticism* 65, no. 1 (2007): 121-29, 125.
20 James Joyce, *A Portrait of the Artist as a Young Man* (New York: B.W. Huebsch, 1922), 243. Joyce misquotes Aquinas, who actually wrote "Pulchra enim dicunter quae visa placent"—"we call a thing beautiful when it pleases the eye of the beholder" (*Summa Theologica* 1a.5,4). I owe this point to Robert Martin. The translation using "apprehension of which" is, however, common and has interest independent of its accuracy.
21 For a nice overview, see Joseph Margolis, "Aquinas" in "Medieval Aesthetics," *The Routledge Companion to Aesthetics*, ed. Berys Gaut and Dominic McIver Lopes (New York: Routledge, 2001), 31-35.

cognitive, experience. Second, if "apprehension" means "direct or immediate perception" this can give pleasure which is not aesthetic, as for example the taste of cool water when thirsty (mentioned earlier by Tuan). Of course this is not to say that a taste of cool water could never be aesthetic, for example when the experience is complex and carries a feeling of significance. What we need is a distinction between non-aesthetic and aesthetic pleasure. Perhaps to get beyond being mere pleasure aesthetic experience needs to be connected with a sense of heightened significance. I will discuss this in Part II when I develop my idea of aesthetic experience as experience of aura. Still, the phrase, "the aesthetic is that which pleases in the apprehension of it" can be taken as basically correct if "apprehension" is defined in such a way as to exclude non-aesthetic pleasures.

We should not, however, forget the other side of aesthetics, the feeling of *displeasure* that arises in connection with the sensuous or imaginative apprehension of certain things. Whereas the first side comes under the concept of "beauty," using that term very broadly, the second comes under the concept of "ugly," also broadly used. As we develop lists of properties relevant to everyday aesthetics, we should not neglect the negative properties: for example "harsh" with respect to sound, and "dull" with respect to colour. At the same time, we should not assume complete symmetry in our handling of positive and negative aesthetic qualities. Aesthetics has more to do with positive than with negative qualities. That is why dictionary definitions of "aesthetic" frequently mention such positive terms as "beautiful," "refined," "good taste," and "appreciation" and seldom mention negative terms. Also, when we say that something is "aesthetic," without qualification, we mean that it is aesthetically *good*, whereas saying that something is aesthetically bad requires spelling out.

Is there a distinct set of everyday aesthetic properties? One can begin to answer this question by asking whether there is a distinct set of everyday aesthetic property terms. The answer to that question is "probably not" since property terms have a variety of different meanings, both aesthetic and non-aesthetic, and it would be odd to call something an aesthetic property term if its main usage is non-aesthetic. There is, of course, a list of canonical aesthetic terms, for example "beautiful," "elegant," "graceful," and "ugly" and these terms can all be applied to everyday aesthetic phenomena. However, there are properties that, although important in aesthetics generally and in the aesthetics of art specifically, have not been much noticed because they have strong associations with everyday life. The terms used to refer to these properties are not necessarily primarily aesthetic in their usage. Two examples of such terms are "neat" and "messy," which I will discuss in detail in Chapter VII. It is arguable that neatness is an everyday aesthetic property. For example, we gain pleasure in the apprehension of a neat room. Although it is also a property that can be relevant to works of art, we do not much talk about neatness with respect to art. There are exceptions: for example, we may complain that some aspect of a work, for example the plot of a novel, is not neat or is messy, and we may praise a painting for its neat lines. Still, neatness is more closely associated with clothing, household maintenance, handwriting, arguments and papers. Messiness is generally considered to be a negative property. However, it is not always so. We might say a sandwich is messy and mean that as a compliment. Messiness may be appreciated by some people under some circumstances. This is true with many, or perhaps all generally negative aesthetic properties, even "harsh" and "dull."

Neatness is closely related to the qualities of "ordered," "orderly," "organized," "tidied" and "straightened." We like to have ordered files and straightened rooms (although not always!). This liking often involves some pleasure in the apprehension of these things. As mentioned previously, I am taking "apprehension" to mean something more than mere noticing. It includes an element of contemplative satisfaction. For example, I can work hard on ordering my files and then stand back and observe them with satisfaction. This contemplative element distinguishes such experiences from such mere pleasures as the pleasure of drinking water when thirsty. Therefore, it makes sense to call these everyday aesthetic qualities.

Perhaps even more fundamental than these is the quality of "rightness," as in "sounds right," "looks right," and "feels right." The importance of rightness as an aesthetic quality goes back as far as Plato.[22] We have already mentioned Roger Scruton's use of "looks right" and the way in which he associates this property, as well as "fits," not only with everyday life but also with architecture and with aesthetics in general. Nelson Goodman has drawn attention to rightness and "good fit" with respect to architecture.[23] Albert Hofstadter goes so far as to define the aesthetic impulse itself in terms of rightness and fitness, although this would

---

22 See Edith Watson Schipper, "Mimesis in the Arts in Plato's Laws," *The Journal of Aesthetics and Art Criticism* 22, no. 2 (1963): 199-202.
23 Nelson Goodman, "How Buildings Mean," in *Reconceptions in Philosophy and Other Arts and Sciences* by Nelson Goodman and Catherine Z. Elgin (Indianapolis: Hackett, 1988).

leave out legitimate aesthetic properties with no obvious relation to rightness, for example when we say that something glows with beauty.[24]

Most recently, Glenn Parsons and Allen Carlson have used the concept of "fit" in their theory, reminiscent of Hume's, that everyday aesthetics should be based on function. For them, an everyday object only has aesthetic properties if it looks like it fits its proper function.[25] As a general theory of everyday aesthetics this view is weak since it excludes all beauties that violate this criterion. For example, shadows play no function and yet can be beautiful. The aesthetics of play would also be excluded. When a child uses a broom to represent a horse the broom takes on aesthetic properties unrelated to its proper function. Nonetheless, the theory does make us more aware of such aesthetic qualities as rightness and fit.

We should distinguish between the aesthetic sense of "right" as in "looks right" or "sounds right" and other senses, for example, moral. There is also a purely *practical* sense of "looks right" (where "practical" is used in the everyday and not the moral sense) as when an electrical hook-up looks right. Moral and purely practical senses of rightness make no reference to sensuous and imaginative qualities.

The satisfaction of rightness is sometimes ambiguous between the aesthetic and the practical. If a wooden joint looks right to a carpenter, this may give him or her a sense of aesthetic satisfaction. This would be especially true for an expert in Japanese or some other crafts tradition of joinery. However, we often take the *look* of rightness as a mere indicator of nonaesthetic practical rightness. Such rightness is a matter of fitting some explicit standard, and not of aesthetic judgment. Above, I mentioned an electrical hook-up as an example. Although an electrician might gain some small aesthetic satisfaction from noticing that all of the wires look like they are hooked up right, this will be of little value if they are not *actually* hooked up right. It should also be noted that sometimes the expression "looks right" is intended to mean that something *appears* to be right (in the nonaesthetic sense), but may not be. Recognition of nonaesthetic practical rightness may give satisfaction, but not in a sensuous/imaginative display being perceived. This is why I oppose the Parsons/Carlson theory that aesthetic properties are only correctly attributable based on functional fit.

I do not intend however to imply that such qualities as "proportional," "balanced," "integrated," "harmonious," and "beautiful" which have been much more discussed in the history of aesthetics should be excluded from everyday

---

24 Albert Hofstadter, "The Aesthetic Impulse," *The Journal of Aesthetics and Art Criticism* 32, no. 2 (1973): 171-81.
25 Parsons and Carlson.

aesthetics. The home decorator may be as interested in harmony and balance as in organization and neatness. Babies are often referred to as beautiful, as are table-settings for banquets. A list of everyday aesthetic qualities may even end up being very similar to a list of aesthetic qualities in the arts. However, meaning changes with circumstances: the terms may be the same and yet the qualities different in different contexts.

One advantage of focusing on aesthetic quality terms as they are applied in everyday life is that this may shed light on aesthetics generally. For example, attending to "looks right" and "fun" in everyday aesthetics makes us newly aware of how such terms play a role in evaluation of the arts. Some qualities will be more prominent in everyday aesthetics than in other aesthetic domains, some less so. And of course there may be some terms that are applicable in one domain and not in the other, although if so they are hard to find, especially given the possibility of metaphorical application. Again, "fun" might refer to a different quality in everyday aesthetics than in art aesthetics.[26]

Another item to add to the list of qualities that are relevant both to everyday aesthetics and to the aesthetics of art is "clean," as in "looks clean." However, whereas the phrase "looks clean" might be applied to the style or look of a painting, such phrases as "smells clean" and "feels clean" are limited to everyday aesthetics. Consider the medieval Japanese writer Sei Shōnagon's list of "Things That Give a Clean Feeling." The list goes as follows: "An earthen cup. A new metal bowl. A rush mat. The play of the light on water as one pours it into a vessel. A new wooden chest."[27] Shōnagon is not only listing things: she is listing aesthetic experiences in everyday life.

Cleanliness may not be next to godliness, but many admire it aesthetically. Even if its main interest had to do with hygiene, our fascination with it goes beyond germ elimination.[28] Something can *be* clean without looking clean: a floor with a design that makes it look dirty, for example. Something can look clean without *being* clean, for example, a floor that hides microscopic germs. Although we might be disgusted or upset to find that a clean-looking object is not really clean, it is doubtful that this is an aesthetic matter. I will discuss the quality of cleanliness in more detail in Chapter VII.

---

26 Thanks to my student Jeanie Kim for comments on this.
27 Sei Shōnagon, "The Pillow Book," Higgins, *Aesthetics*, 619.
28 See Kevin Melchionne, "Living in Glass Houses: Domesticity, Interior Decoration, and Environmental Aesthetics," *The Journal of Aesthetics and Art Criticism* 56, no. 2 (1998): 191-200, for further discussion.

Allowing such two-word combinations as "looks clean" into our list expands aesthetics. For example, although the term "good" is not by itself aesthetic, the situation is quite different with "looks good," "sounds good," "tastes good," "smells good," and "feels good." The same can be said for similar terms, such as "great." There are also qualities involving the term "well," as in "well-planned," and "well-thought-out." Additionally, there are qualities indicated by the term "too" when applied in a specific aesthetic situation, as in "too high," "too red," and by the term "not enough," as in "not enough red here."

SMELL, TASTE, AND TOUCH

To "smells clean" should be added such related qualities as "smells nice," "smells good," "smells delicious," and their opposites. These have a great importance to everyday aesthetics, in the home, the restaurant, the street, and in our erotic lives.[29] This is one area in which the aesthetics of everyday life departs from the aesthetics of fine art. Discussions of the aesthetics of smell are rare in writings about the fine arts, although it is conceivable that smells could be refined and organized to the point where they are a medium for an art form.[30]

Richard L. Anderson has noted that in the United Arab Emirates there is an informal ritualized gathering of women called the *fualah* during which the hostess brings out a glass-lidded box that holds various bottles with perfumes and incenses.[31] Similarly, there is interest in the West in various kinds of aesthetic experience related to smell. For example, Emily Brady mentions a work in a contemporary art museum in Helsinki, titled *Babylon* by Christian Skeel and Morten Skriver, that features ceramic pots on a long table each containing a different scent.[32] I have also spent considerable time

---

29 See Frank Sibley, "Tastes, Smells, and Aesthetics," in *Approach to Aesthetics: Collected Papers on Philosophical Aesthetics* (Oxford: Clarendon Press, 2001), 207-55.
30 See Larry Shiner and Yulia Kriskovets, "The Aesthetics of Smelly Art," *The Journal of Aesthetics and Art Criticism* 65, no. 3 (2007): 273-86.
31 Richard L. Anderson, *Calliope's Sisters: A Comparative Study of Philosophies of Art* (Englewood Cliffs: Prentice Hall, 1990), 273-74.
32 Emily Brady, "Sniffing and Savoring: The Aesthetics of Smells and Tastes," in *Aesthetics of Everyday Life*. See also Mădălina Diaconu, "Reflections on an Aesthetics of Touch, Smell and Taste," *Contemporary Aesthetics* 4 (2006), http://www.contempaesthetics.org/newvolume/pages/article.php?articleID=385, and "The Rebellion of the 'Lower' Senses: A Phenomenological Aesthetics of Touch, Smell, and Taste," conference paper (Nov. 2002) accessed April 21, 2011, http://www.o-p-o.net/essays/DiaconuArticle.pdf.

in a show at the Museum of Modern Art in San Francisco sniffing various kinds of wine.[33]

Perfumery may be considered an art form; it certainly involves creation of experiences with many levels of complexity as well as temporal development. There are professional fragrance consultants who have trained for years and are able to make elaborate distinctions between scents. There are perfume creators, collectors, connoisseurs, and critics. Perfume experts speak of various levels of smell experience and are able to make subtle distinctions. The Osmothèque in Versailles has preserved over 1700 perfumes recreated from formulae for posterity. (Marie-Antoinette's perfume was recreated in 2007!) The point is not without controversy: some philosophers have held that perfumery is a minor art at best.[34] More recently, Shiner and Kriskovets have argued that perfume can be art if it makes a statement in an artworld context and calls attention to its embodiment. Otherwise, they insist, it is a commercial product that may however provide aesthetic pleasure and even be a classic of design.[35] In short, smell analysis and evaluation can be as complicated and sophisticated as that of wines, cheeses, and coffees.

Let me give another example closer to home. I am not a lover of shopping malls. However, through years of accompanying others who are, I have gained some pleasure in working my way through the various smells made available in soap, perfume, and scented-candle shops. Although these smells are not currently organized in a way that could make them a medium of fine art, the experience of them can afford significant aesthetic pleasure.

Smell has a powerful emotional connection too. Rachel Hertz, a specialist in olfaction, observes that the amygdala, the brain's emotion centre, is the limbic structure that interacts the most with the olfactory centre. When we perceive a scent the amygdala is activated. Hertz describes a personal experience as a child that shows not only the emotional impact of smell but also the frequent relation between smell and the feeling of happiness: "I remember squeezing the translucent turquoise shampoo into my hand and lathering it into a bubbly and delicious foam in my hair, but most of all what I remember is the

---

33 San Francisco Museum of Modern Art, "How Wine Became Modern: Design+Wine 1976 to Now," November 20, 2010–April 17, 2011.
34 Charles Lalo, "A Structural Classification of the Fine Arts," *The Journal of Aesthetics and Art Criticism* 11, no. 4, Special Issue on the Interrelations of the Arts (1953): 307-23, 321.
35 Lalo, 281-82.

exquisite scent that arose from the bubbles. I had never smelled anything like it before—sweet, piney, watery, and mysterious—and it seemed to me to be the most sublime aroma on Earth.... I became intensely happy for the first time in a long time."[36] Note the use of the aesthetic term "sublime" in this description: as I shall argue later, everyday aesthetic experience can also be sublime.

There is a long history of opposition to treating these senses as capable of giving aesthetic experience. In the *Greater Hippias* Socrates asks whether the beautiful is "whatever we enjoy—I do not mean to include all pleasures, but only what we enjoy through our senses of hearing and sight...."[37] He explicitly excludes the senses concerned with food and sex from beauty. Socrates goes on to refer to the common belief that "everyone would laugh at us if we said that it is not pleasant to eat, but beautiful, or that a pleasant smell is not pleasant, but beautiful, and as to sexual intercourse, everyone would contend against us that it is most pleasant, while admitting that it ought to be enjoyed only where there is none to see because it is a disgraceful and repulsive sight."[38] Aristotle, Aquinas, Kant, Hegel and Santayana all also objected to associating the "lower" senses with beauty.[39]

It might be argued that this field of everyday experience is *not* aesthetic because it is not amenable to judgments based on appreciation of complex fields of ordered elements. David W. Prall argued that smells, tastes, and "vital feelings," are not materials of beauty in the sense that colours, sounds, and even textures are.[40] This is because, as he put it, "they are obviously not contents of typical aesthetic judgments."[41] Prall, however, undercut this position by admitting that such qualities may be perceived with sensuous delight, that attention may be focused on them as specific qualities directly apprehended in sense perception, that they can be contemplated aesthetically, and that they can have specific and interesting character. He just thought they are not

---

36 Rachel Hertz, *The Scent of Desire: Discovering our Enigmatic Sense of Smell* (New York: HarperCollins, 2007), 31. Another good discussion by a non-philosopher of the aesthetics of smell is Tuan, *Strange*, 55-69.
37 Plato, *Plato*, 297e, 1551.
38 Plato, *Plato*, 299a, 1552.
39 Shiner and Kriskovets, 275.
40 David W. Prall, "Aesthetic Surface," in *Introductory Readings in Aesthetics*, ed. John Hospers (New York: The Free Press, 1969), 49-60, orig. *Aesthetic Judgment* (Thomas Y. Crowel Co., 1929), 57-75. See Carolyn Korsmeyer, *Making Sense of Taste: Food and Philosophy* (Ithaca: Cornell University Press, 1999) for a further discussion of Prall, 104-08.
41 Prall, 52.

usually considered beautiful. He admitted even that they can be *elements* of aesthetic experience and that they make up much of the beauty of nature. The problem, as he saw it, is that our grasp of them, while aesthetic, is a grasp of something specific and nonstructural unlike the orders of relation found in music harmonies. Yet, as Emily Brady has observed, smells and tastes may exhibit complex structures.[42] And as I mentioned above, fragrance specialists can make incredibly fine distinctions. Moreover, few critics today would agree with Prall that the arts based on sound and sight are necessarily governed by strict structural or critical principles. Prall's point would be more plausible if weakened to say that smells and tastes are somewhat less amenable to be elements in complex art compositions than sights and sounds.

Also, Prall could not have anticipated developments in the contemporary visual and aural arts which give more importance to interesting juxtaposition of elements than to formal relations between lines and colours, tones and rhythms. In recent times, the differences between the visual and aural arts, on the one hand, and the arts of smell and taste, on the other, have become considerably less dramatic. Perhaps this is not the case, yet, for the arts of touch.[43] (The question may be raised whether there even is an art of touch, although massage might count.[44])

Prall further undercuts his original point when he observed that smells and tastes are nevertheless beauties insofar as they are elementary materials of certain limited aesthetic experiences, and that combinations of smells, colours, and sounds can in nature "make up a rare beauty." When he writes, "If there is a beauty of August nights, or beauty in the sameness of a June day, or the fresh loveliness after rain ... such beauty is not all for the eye and ear, and if we do not ourselves know how to blend smells and tastes with sound and form and colour to compose such beauties, we need not foist our limitation upon nature,"[45] nothing is left of his original assertion that smells and tastes cannot really be subjects of judgments of beauty.

---

42 Brady, "Sniffing."
43 An early piece on the aesthetics of touch is Frances W. Herring, "Touch: The Neglected Sense," *The Journal of Aesthetics and Art Criticism* 7, no. 3 (1949): 199-215. A more recent effort that deals with yet another sense modality is Barbara Montero, "Proprioception as an Aesthetic Sense," *The Journal of Aesthetics and Art Criticism* 64, no. 2 (2006): 231-42.
44 Richard Shusterman, "Somaesthetics: A Disciplinary Proposal," *The Journal of Aesthetics and Art Criticism* 57, no. 3 (1999): 299-313.
45 Prall, 55.

Allowing for an aesthetics of smell and taste opens up a space not only for unexplored aspects of natural aesthetics but also for everyday aesthetics, even for profound and complex aesthetic experience in everyday contexts. Moreover, as I suggested earlier, the division between fine art aesthetics and everyday aesthetics becomes less rigid when one considers the work of such central artists of our time as Joseph Beuys and Robert Rauschenberg. These artists did not work with materials that have degrees of qualitative difference worked out in the established orders that Prall expected from art.

More recently the idea that everyday aesthetics extends to what is called the bodily senses (taste, smell, touch) has been attacked by Glen Parsons and Allen Carlson.[46] This is part of a larger critique of what they call Deweyan aesthetics, roughly the kind of aesthetics I am advocating here. Drawing on a tradition that goes back to Socrates, they distinguish between the beautiful and the merely pleasant. Their argument is based partly on ordinary language and partly on an observation about the way we experience things. For them, it is highly awkward to apply the term "aesthetically pleasing" to something like taking a warm bath or having a sexual experience. They think that to call such things aesthetically pleasing would be an unwarranted revision of everyday language. This argument is implausible, however, since the term "aesthetically pleasing" is much more a term of philosophy than of ordinary language. It is not surprising that the Western tradition that began with Socrates, and was mediated by Christianity and Cartesian dualism, would oppose the notion that sexual experience could be aesthetic. However, other traditions, for example of India, go in another direction.[47]

In anticipation of the objection that their view does not work cross-culturally, Parsons and Carlson argue that in the Chinese and Turkish languages there are different words for aesthetic and bodily pleasure, and that in these cultures the word for bodily pleasure is more likely to be used in relation to a warm bath than the word for beauty. This is an odd argument given that the Turkish bath experience is probably highly aesthetic in its many dimensions, and that there was a Chinese aesthetics of food as early as Confucius.[48] Da'an

---

46 Parsons and Carlson, Chapter 7. This chapter is devoted to everyday aesthetics.
47 See Richard Shusterman, "Asian Ars Erotica and the Question of Sexual Aesthetics," *The Journal of Aesthetics and Art Criticism* 65, no. 1 (2007): 55-68.
48 Da'an Pan, "Tasting the Good and the Beautiful: The Aestheticization of Eating and Drinking in Traditional Chinese Culture," *The Cal Poly Pomona Journal of Interdisciplinary Studies*, 16 (Fall 2003), 67-76, accessed December 11, 2011, http://www.csupomona.edu/~jis/2003/contents.html.

Pan observes that in China "[t]he notion of *mei-shi* (lit., beautiful food; i.e., gourmet food) is almost a household word."[49] And even if smells and tastes are seldom called beautiful in the West this is no argument against their being considered aesthetically pleasing.

Parsons and Carlson's central point is that we experience the bodily senses in a radically different way than we experience seeing and hearing. I agree that there are major differences between the senses: for example, seeing is more spatial and less temporal than hearing. However, it is not clear that seeing and hearing form a special privileged group in relation to the other senses. The lynchpin of Parsons and Carlson's argument is that tastes and smells are experienced as localized in the body, unlike sight or hearing,[50] for we can clarify tastes and smells by introspecting on the tongue and nose, whereas introspecting on our eyes and ears distracts us from the qualities of sights and sounds.[51] This is wrong in my experience: the reader can check his or her own experience. The most I can get from introspecting on my tongue and nose is localization of certain sharp stings (i.e., "hot here!" or "salty here!"). And the only way I can get a clearer picture of a taste is to taste the thing again, compare it with other tastes, and distinguish the various elements (for example the spices) used, none of which involves introspecting on my tongue. In conclusion, Parsons and Carlson provide no convincing reason for rejecting the idea that proximal senses can provide us with aesthetic experiences.

EVERYDAY AESTHETICS AND RELIGIOUS RITUAL

We have been exploring various ways to define everyday aesthetics. Recently Crispin Sartwell has argued for understanding ritual as part of everyday aesthetics and, somewhat more controversially, understanding everyday aesthetics in terms of ritual.[52] He bases his thought on the idea that art emerged historically from many non-art activities, including ritual and craft. Although this is true, nothing requires that the aesthetics of the everyday be defined in terms of its

---

49 Pan.
50 Parsons and Carlson, 184. In this, they are opposed to Sibley, "Tastes, Smells."
51 Parsons and Carlson, 185.
52 Crispin Sartwell, "Aesthetics of the Everyday," in *The Oxford Handbook of Aesthetics*, ed. Jerrold Levinson (New York: Oxford University Press, 2003), 761-63. See also his *The Art of Living: Aesthetics of the Ordinary in World Spiritual Traditions* (Albany: State University of New York Press, 1995).

relation to art or its origins. Nor is it the case that art arises *just* from ritual and craft. I will set aside the issue of craft for now and concentrate on ritual. I take "ritual" to refer primarily to religious rites, although it also applies metaphorically to such non-religious practices as ground-breaking ceremonies and to social conventions such as shaking hands. In criticizing Sartwell's emphasis on ritual I do not mean to exclude such things from everyday aesthetics. They have aesthetic properties and may be appreciated aesthetically. However, there are problems with the concept of the sacred as a definer of everyday aesthetics.[53]

The first problem is this. Many, perhaps most, tribal societies, both in ancient times and today, have seen ritual as *set off* from the everyday. Ritual creates a separate sacred space. For example, the Australian Aborigines make a strong distinction between sacred and mundane art.[54] Part of what we mean by "the everyday" is that it is distinct from the sacred and from "ritual" in the religious and quasi-religious senses of that term. Ritual has important aesthetic dimensions, but should not be confused with the everyday. This is true even though in some communities, for instance monasteries, ritual happens literally every day.

A second problem is that the aesthetics of ritual is closer to fine art than to the everyday. As with fine art, ritual is institutional, and its objects of appreciation are institutionally determined. Although much that happens in everyday aesthetics is related in some way to institutions (for example designed objects have a relation to the institutions that produce designers) the institutionality of both fine art and ritual is more direct. A sign of the closeness of art and ritual can be seen in the fact that some art-forms, for example the Japanese tea ceremony, consist largely of rituals or ritual-like activity. Many ritual activities are also evaluated by participants in terms much like those of art,[55] although we should not forget that ritual usually has a different purpose than art (e.g., appeasing gods). Moreover, ritual objects often find a place in art museums because of the skill required in their production, their expressiveness, and their other art-like qualities. Fine art museums, in this respect, are similar to churches. Sartwell himself observes the religious-like veneration we

---

53 See Gumbrecht 299-318, for a discussion of the relation between religious and aesthetic experience.
54 Elizabeth Burns Coleman, "Appreciating 'Traditional' Aboriginal Painting Aesthetically," *The Journal of Aesthetics and Art Criticism* 62, no. 3 (2004): 235-47.
55 Chungmoo Choi, "The Artistry of Ritual Aesthetics of Urban Korean Shamans," *Shamanism: A Reader*, ed. Graham Harvey (London: Routledge, 2002), 170-86.

give to masterpieces of art.[56] Along similar lines, Peter Kivy writes that the performing of music is a ritual, the musical work an "aesthetic distillation of ritual," and the audience a "congregation of co-celebrants."[57] Of course much of music is not like this, for example the performers may just be performing for themselves and mainly focused on the aesthetic pleasures of cooperative work.[58] Nonetheless, there remains a striking similarity between the realms of ritual and art.

We should not, however, be rigid in maintaining a separation of the sacred from the everyday. As already mentioned, many everyday practices are formalized *as if* they were rituals. We even sometimes refer to them as rituals, although this is usually only metaphorical. Harold Osborne has rightly stressed the importance of this in relation to the aesthetics of everyday life. He writes that "esthetic feeling is perhaps most pervasive in what may be called the 'ritualization' of life."[59] He refers here to the rituals of politeness and greeting, as well as to good table manners. He is also thinking of the rituals of courtship, of military pageants and of secret societies. Graduation ceremonies would also fall into this class. And although there is a sacred dimension to most weddings, one can also see the wedding ceremony as coming under everyday aesthetics. Even watching films in public has been referred to as a ritual.

Similar overlaps occur with the sacred. For example, within the home, we often lavish attention on favoured objects as though they were sacred. However, if these practices do not *actually* set aside a sacred space, as when there is a home altar, they are not *literally* sacred. So let us consider these actual, literal, sacred spaces. If the aesthetics of the home is part of everyday aesthetics, and if part of the home becomes a sacred space, then the sacred is, in this case, a part of the everyday. This raises a problem for everyday aesthetics. Is the Mexican home altar a matter of everyday aesthetics or is it a matter of the aesthetics of religion? It is difficult to say. From the perspective of a believer the ritual or sacred aspect of the home altar may take prominence, while from that of a nonbeliever the altar may be seen more as an everyday aesthetic phenomenon.

---

56 Sartwell, "Everyday," 762. He is thinking of a point made by Walter Benjamin in "The Work of Art in the Age of Mechanical Reproduction," in his *Illuminations*, ed. Hannah Arendt (New York: Schocken, 1969).
57 Peter Kivy, "Music and the Liberal Education," *Journal of Aesthetic Education* 25, no. 3, Special Issue: Philosophy of Music and Music Education (1991): 79-93, 90.
58 I owe this comment to Stan Godlovitch, personal communication.
59 Harold Osborne, "Education in an Affluent State," *Journal of Aesthetic Education* 20, no. 4, 20th Anniversary Issue (1986): 103-07.

There are also some societies in which, although there are separations between the sacred and the secular aspects of life, these are more permeable than in our own. When a Navajo man says that he lives and walks in beauty, this may mean that for him everything in his environment is in some sense sacred.[60]

Moreover, just as I have argued that the relation between art and everyday life is dynamic and mutually enriching, this may be equally true for the relationship between the sacred and the secular. When the ordinary becomes extraordinary, when it is transfigured, it begins to enter into a space that is *perceived as* or *as like* a sacred space. Here, I am using the term "transfigured" quite differently from Danto, who makes a strict distinction between the world of what he calls "mere real things" and the world of art.[61] Danto believes that Duchamp and Pop Art showed us how the mere real things of everyday life may be transfigured into the realm of art. My emphasis, however, is on how the things of everyday life become transfigured prior to any such activity, and on how art sometimes contributes to this.

Ellen Dissanayake has convincingly argued that art, play and ritual are all examples of something she calls "making special."[62] Dissanayake, however, *contrasts* "making special" with the everyday.[63] Yet, I would argue, many kinds of "making special," for example aspects of children's play, are important aspects of everyday life. The contrast should not be between the special and the everyday, but between the things of everyday life that are made special through activity or in perception, and those that are not.

Dissanayake does not define art as "making special," but sees it, along with play and ritual, as coming from this root tendency. She speaks of art as "concerned with shaping and embellishing everyday ordinary reality so that it becomes extraordinary."[64] Although I agree that art does this, I do not think this happens only in art. Moreover, only when the everyday leaves the merely ordinary, whether through shaping, embellishing, or (and this is a point Dis-

---

60 For Navajo aesthetics, see Muriel Saville-Troike, "Navajo Art and Education," *Journal of Aesthetic Education* 18, no. 2, Special Issue: Defining Cultural and Educational Relations—An International Perspective (1984): 41-50.
61 Arthur C. Danto, *The Transfiguration of the Commonplace: A Philosophy of Art* (Cambridge, MA: Harvard University Press, 1981).
62 Ellen Dissanayake, "Aesthetic Experience and Human Evolution," *The Journal of Aesthetics and Art Criticism* 41, no. 2 (1982): 145-55, 148.
63 Dissanayake, "Evolution," 148.
64 Dissanayake, "Evolution," 148.

sanayake misses) through being seen as somehow transcending itself, does it become aesthetic.

The transformation I am describing is not merely a matter of noticing or of drawing attention to things one hadn't noticed before. Drawing attention to something is not the same as drawing attention to something aesthetically. I might draw your attention to a money-making opportunity, a mathematical mistake, or an impending rainstorm, and there might be nothing aesthetic involved. As I see it, drawing attention to something aesthetically does involve taking that thing at least to a small extent out of the ordinary. Art does this to its everyday subjects, and when it does, art contributes to our appreciation of the everyday. However, it can be done in other ways as well. The relation of art, ritual and everyday aesthetics is one of dynamic interaction. Much of what would fall under the idea of "making special," for example in decorating a tool, would be in the region of everyday aesthetics. However, it is also on the road to art.

DEWEY, DEFINING ART, AND THE AESTHETICS OF EVERYDAY LIFE

As mentioned previously, Dewey could be said to be one of the originators of the aesthetics of everyday life. If there is anything people will remember from their initial reading in Dewey's aesthetics it is that he wished to start not with the fine arts but with ordinary experiences such as looking at a fire in a fireplace or contemplating the neatness of one's house. His aesthetic theory, unlike many others, begins with, and always refers back to, the live creature interacting with its environment.[65]

In Chapter 3 of *Art as Experience* Dewey makes an important distinction between experience that is confused and incomplete, "inchoate" as he says, and experience that involves development and culmination. The latter, he calls "an experience," of which such things as playing a chess game and solving a problem are examples. (I set forth what Dewey means by "an experience" earlier in this chapter.) This type of activity/experience is aesthetic in that it involves a certain type of satisfaction. For Dewey, inchoate experiences cannot be aesthetic.

A couple paragraphs further, the idea of "an experience" has become something more elevated in his thinking, or at least the examples are more dramatic.

---

[65] Dewey. See my "Dewey's Aesthetics," in *Stanford Encyclopedia of Philosophy*, http://plato.stanford.edu/entries/dewey-aesthetics/ (2011).

It is here associated with such vivid life-events as breaking up with a friend or going through a hurricane, or, somewhat less dramatically, with that meal in Paris that seemed to sum up everything that a meal can be. Almost as an afterthought, Dewey mentions that art too can give us "an experience."[66] There seem then to be two types of "an experience," the ordinary sort and the more dramatic, both of which are relevant to an aesthetics of everyday life.

Dewey's main interest here is in developing continuity between the aesthetic experiences of everyday life and those of fine art. It is not surprising that many of his examples, e.g., watching a fire engine go by, or men working on a skyscraper, are of phenomena that have also been the subjects of the art of his time: for example, photographs of skyscrapers by Edward Steichen. For Dewey, we need to understand the dialectical relationship between fine art and ordinary experience in order to understand aesthetic experience generally. This relationship, and the way that contemporary analytic theories of art fail to capture it, will be the focus of this section.

Many critics have been concerned that Dewey has dissolved the distinction between the artistic and the everyday. For example, Monroe Beardsley, who we already saw as opposed to the idea that we could appreciate a subway ride aesthetically, emphasized *discontinuity* between art and life. He believed that art has an autonomy that Dewey could not accept.[67] Bear in mind that Dewey does distinguish between art and everyday life. Not every example of "an experience" is art on Dewey's account, for art requires manipulation of a medium. Although Dewey softens the boundaries between art and non-art, he does not eliminate them.

In order to see how Dewey's thought about everyday aesthetics can challenge prominent assumptions in contemporary aesthetic theory we would need to understand it in terms of the basic problems of aesthetics. These include the definition of art, the nature of aesthetic experience, expression and the role of emotions in art, the ontology of art, the creative process, the nature of interpretation, the evaluation of art, and the value of art in society. That is, we need to understand this issue in terms of a challenge to standard views in aesthetics that involves questioning boundaries and distinctions throughout the field. This entails, generally, seeing the arts as taking their meaning not simply from an artworld context but from the context of life in general, including everyday life.

---

66 Dewey, 38.
67 Monroe Beardsley, *The Aesthetic Point of View: Selected Essays*, ed. Michael J. Wreen and Donald M. Callen (Ithaca: Cornell University Press, 1982).

It would seem, at first, that everyday aesthetic experience, for example the pleasure one might get in the experience of mowing a lawn, would have nothing to do with the problem of defining art, except perhaps as a possible counter-example to a proposed definition. Most would agree that a good definition of art would *make sure* that mowing a lawn could not be seen as an example of art. Some, however, would allow for incorporating or transforming this act into a work of art. For instance, one could mow a lawn on stage as part of a postmodern dance performance. Or one could mow one's lawn in such a way as to produce an interesting image which, in the manner of "earth art" could then be designated a work of art. However, neither of these acts would give the ordinary act of mowing one's lawn the status of art. Still, postmodern dance and earth art both dramatically drew attention to the aesthetic dimension of ordinary experience, thus creating continuity between art and everyday life. If carrying a mattress on and off stage was an example of dance, as arguably was the case in Yvonne Rainer's *Room Service* (1963), then a dancer mowing a lawn on stage could be the same.[68] And perhaps such a dance would draw attention to unnoticed aesthetic features entailed in the experience of mowing one's own lawn.

There is an immense advantage in seeing art as a kind of experience as opposed to a collection of items. One problem with traditional definitions of art is that they seem designed to help us divide art objects from non-art objects, perhaps in a warehouse. However, it doesn't seem worth much time to work up a definition to assist this kind of activity. It is not even clear that such a definition would be useful for art museum directors when deciding what to collect or exhibit. The issue of understanding the nature of art for Dewey is not one of knowing how to separate art objects from non-art objects. Rather he simply tries to give us the characteristic structure of the experience of art in terms of the relationship between artist, art object, audience, subject-matter, and the surrounding environments of each.

Since art is a form of experience, and since there is continuity between art and life, it is plausible to think that transformation of everyday experience is *itself* part of the nature of art. It is helpful to understand this point in terms of the creative process of the artist.[69] (What follows is not strictly from Dewey, but Deweyan in spirit.) Imagine what it was like for Cézanne to paint a tree.

---

68 Carroll and Banes, 37-41.
69 See my "A Pragmatist Theory of Artistic Creativity," *The Journal of Value Inquiry* 28 (1994): 169-80 for a critique of analytic approaches to creativity.

He sees the tree, even initially, in a way that is radically different from that of non-artists (and also radically different from the more conventional realist artists of his time). He then goes on to transform his experience of it, both during contemplative moments prior to putting paint to canvas, and in reflective looking during the process of painting. The experience of the painting as it emerges in the creative process becomes part of the experience of the tree, and the experience of the tree part of the experience of the painting, the two mixed up in ways that would be hard to disentwine. Art extends beyond the physical object called the artwork, beyond even the intentions of the artist and the response of the audience, to the way that artist and audience experience the subject-matter portrayed. It also involves aesthetic experience of the materials out of which the work is made: this is where the dialectic between art and everyday aesthetics is most evident—in the studio. The aesthetic properties of paint change as it is transferred to canvas and is perceived in relation to other patches of paint and in relation to the subject-matter portrayed.

We can tell a similar story with respect to Duchamp in the hardware store in which he was inspired to create *In Advance of the Broken Arm* (1915). This work is famously a shovel purchased and changed slightly by inscribing on it the words "In Advance of the Broken Arm/(from) Marcel Duchamp 1915" before hanging it from the ceiling in an art space. Once again, my reconstruction is speculative but plausible. When Duchamp looked at the shovel during his initial moment of inspiration, he saw it as, or was beginning to see it as, the work of art it would become. He did not, of course, see it as art in the sense of actually classifying it as art, for if he had he would have thought of it as having been created by another artist and would have looked at it appropriately, for instance, with a view to interpretation. So his experience of the shovel as art-material would not have been the same as our experience of *In Advance of the Broken Arm* in a museum. However, it would have been similar. Some might think that Dewey's concept of art as experience cannot be applied to Duchamp because Dewey emphasized the aesthetic, whereas Duchamp insisted that he had no aesthetic interest in his readymades. However, Duchamp was using the term "aesthetic" in a narrow, formalist sense, and it is arguable that he expected his viewers to have what Dewey would call "an experience."

Dewey does not give an actual definition of art, certainly not one in terms of necessary and sufficient conditions. However, in the neglected eighth chapter of *Art as Experience* he does give a pronouncement that is as close as he gets to a definition. There he asserts, somewhat obscurely, that "[w]hen the structure of the object is such that its force interacts happily (but not easily) with the energies that issue from the experience itself; when their mutual affinities and antagonisms work together to bring about a substance that develops cumulatively and surely (but not too steadily) toward a fulfilling of impulsions, then indeed there is a work of art."[70] First, a work of art is to be distinguished from the art product (e.g., the painting): it is experienced, it is what the art product *does* for the viewer. Second, it has a structure which is a matter of interaction between the art object and the experience of the audience members. Third, it is an experience that evolves towards resolution. This is a theory of art as interaction between artist, developing artwork, and audience. It is not a theory of art simply as expression of internal emotions of the artist, although these may be involved. For Dewey, expression is a function of interaction between the live creature and the surrounding environment, both aspects of this interaction being equally important.

An important aspect of the Deweyan notion of expression is the idea of inspiration. "To be set on fire by a thought or scene is to be inspired."[71] The artist responds with excitement to subject matter in a way that derives from meanings associated with past experience. There are two sides of inspiration: the self and the subject-matter. On the side of the self the elements of inspiration "proceed from the unconscious" and are "fused in the fire of internal commotion."[72] Although at first, the inspiration is not fully formed, the act of expression carries it to completion.

Heightened aesthetic response to something in the environment is seen by Dewey to be at the centre of the artistic process, and consequently as the centre of his approach to defining art. The object of inspiration might be a chair in a room, as was the case for Van Gogh when he painted *Vincent's Chair with his Pipe* (1888). In addition, and this may be going beyond Dewey, inspiration can include things other than what is commonly called "subject-matter." For example, painting can also be about paint. So inspiration can be found in the way that certain pigmented oils perceptually interact with each other during the painting process. If so, inspiration is not limited to representational art.

To put this in context; let us consider Dewey's theory in relation to some well-known analytic theories of art. Perhaps George Dickie's definition of art best exemplifies the way in which contemporary definitions fail to capture the

---

70 Dewey, 38.
71 Dewey, 71.
72 Dewey, 71.

dynamic of art in its interaction with the aesthetics of everyday life.[73] The definition consists of five sub-definitions. (The circular nature of this definition is admitted by Dickie, and even seen as a virtue.)

1. An artist is a person who participates with understanding in the making of a work of art.

2. A work of art is an artifact of a kind created to be presented to an artworld public.

3. A public is a set of persons the members of which are prepared in some degree to understand an object which is presented to them.

4. The artworld is the totality of all artworld systems.

5. An artworld system is a framework for the presentation of a work of art by an artist to an artworld public.[74]

Although this definition does place our understanding of art in broader terms than we find, for example, in Clive Bell's definition of art as "significant form," it entails a closed relationship between artists, artworld public, artworld systems, and works of art.[75] It never mentions things in the world outside of art, such as in nature or in everyday life. It is forgotten that artists respond to such things, and that the world of the artist is not just the artworld. It also misses Hegel's insight that art is just one manifestation of the spirit at a particular stage in history and that this spiritual whole within a culture includes such human phenomena as philosophy, religion, and science, all interacting. To be fair, Dickie would reply that his definition was intended to simply capture the meaning of art in the classificatory sense and that the issues I raise relate more to the evaluation of art. I would reply that, although much less clear, Dewey's theory has the advantage of situating art within a larger context than the artworld.

Noël Carroll's approach is similar to Dickie's. Although Carroll does not give us a definition of art he does give us a procedure for identifying art. He says that such a procedure gives a narrative that explains how a work came to

---

73 George Dickie, *The Art Circle: A Theory of Art* (New York: Haven Publications, 1984).
74 Dickie, *Circle*, 80-82.
75 Bell, *Art*.

be, giving an "acknowledged artmaking context."⁷⁶ Carroll's art-identifying narratives take place within an artworld which, like Dickie's, is relatively isolated from other cultural contexts. For example, Carroll and co-writer Sally Banes argue in one article that a postmodern dance move that involves carrying a mattress in and out of a room (to return to that example for a different purpose) is art because we can tell a story about how it is connected to other avant-garde art practices of the time and to the history of dance.⁷⁷ By contrast, on Dewey's view, what makes art art is its intensification of ordinary experience. He would have held that postmodern dance movement sought to draw our attention to the aesthetics of everyday life by stressing the aesthetic qualities of such everyday movements as walking and carrying. Although it is true that the stories that connected this work to previous artworks helped legitimize it as art, its dissolution of the boundaries between art and life indicates that those stories do not tell the whole story.

I suspect Dewey would have agreed when analytic aestheticians such as Dickie and Carroll rejected narrow formalism (i.e., the view exemplified by Clive Bell's theory that "art is significant form" and that the viewer should focus on formal rather than content properties of a work) in favour of recognition of the importance of the artworld in defining or identifying art. However, this broadening of context did not go far enough. The artworld context needs to be recognized, but another level, what one might call the culture-world context, needs also to be recognized. One could even argue that there are yet other dimensions to our experience of art at an even more general level that need recognition, for example at the level of species. This is accomplished to some extent by Ellen Dissanayake when she speaks about art from an ethnographic perspective, defining it as a form of "making special,"⁷⁸ and more recently by Denis Dutton when he speaks of an art instinct.⁷⁹

In Arthur Danto's approach, the dualism of artworld vs. real world is quite pronounced. For Danto, Andy Warhol transfigured Brillo boxes into the artworld when he placed them (i.e., his painted plywood constructions that looked

---

76 Noël Carroll, "Identifying Art," in his *Beyond Aesthetics: Philosophical Essays* (New York: Cambridge University Press, 2001), 89.
77 Carroll and Banes, 37-41.
78 Ellen Dissanayake, *Homo Aestheticus: Where Art Comes from and Why* (Madison: University of Wisconsin Press, 1995).
79 Denis Dutton, *The Art Instinct: Beauty, Pleasure, and Human Evolution* (New York: Bloomsbury Press, 2009).

just like boxes one might find in a warehouse) within an art-historical context (i.e., within an art gallery) and gave them an interpretation, thus creating the work called *Brillo Boxes* (1970). Transfiguring involves giving the object new intentional properties relevant to its new home in the artworld. It now has an interpretation given to it by the artist, and it no longer has the interpretation given to it by the original designer.

Yet Warhol was surely inspired in part at least by the everyday aesthetic impact of actual Brillo boxes when he created his famous work, and there is no word of this in Danto. Danto treats this work as if Warhol was isolated within the artworld from the rest of the world. One is struck, however, on reviewing Warhol's life (for example in the recent PBS documentary[80]), by how much he was of the world of his time and how much he influenced the way we saw everyday phenomena during those times.

For Danto, artists take things in the real world and transfigure them into the world of art. From a Deweyan perspective, this idea contributes to the idea that the world of art is somehow radically different from the world of everyday life. Yes transfiguration happens, but it happens to the ordinary *itself* through art. Warhol used his medium to transfigure our perception of the ordinary things about us. The original Brillo box and all advertising-laden packages like it were themselves transformed, at least in some aspect of our experience.

Why is Dewey's thesis concerning the continuity between art aesthetics and everyday aesthetics not more widely accepted today? There is a historical reason having to do with the rise of analytic aesthetics in English-speaking countries in the 1950s. Analytic aesthetics developed partly as a reaction against Dewey. Analytic philosophers were particularly opposed to his attacks on various widely accepted distinctions. After all, analysis is pretty much defined by the making of distinctions. This is often phrased in terms of a style of philosophy based on clarity. To those for whom the distinctions attacked are important, Dewey's thinking appears muddy. This is the blind spot I referred to in the Introduction.

Also, there is the charge of Hegelianism which was raised by his early critic Stephen Pepper.[81] It has two parts. The first was to see Dewey as somehow committed, at this stage of his life, to idealist notions of the Absolute. There is no evidence that Dewey became an idealist during this period, much less one

---

80 *Andy Warhol: A Documentary Film*, American Masters (PBS, 2006).
81 Stephen Pepper, "Some Questions on Dewey's Aesthetics," in *The Philosophy of John Dewey*, ed. P. Schilpp (Evanston: Northwestern University, 1939), 369-90.

who accepted Hegel's Absolute. However, this charge is understandable as a reaction to his concept of an infinite experiential background, an issue I will address later. The second part is more subtle and is also relevant to our attempt to construct an aesthetics of everyday life. Dewey famously held views that were not readily acceptable to analytic philosophy. In particular he believed that works of art were organic wholes characterized by what he called a "pervasive quality," an immediately perceived "emotionally intuited" quality that binds the elements of a work of art together.[82] This quality is not something that is either exclusively in the mind or in the physical world: rather, it is in what he called "the situation." He illustrates this by referring to the way we often speak of a situation as being, in itself, irritating. That is, "the situation is irritating" is different from "I am irritated by this" in that it implies something not entirely subjective.

Dewey sees the pervasive quality not statically but in terms of the dynamic of the creative process. It is present in the inspiration moment (what he calls, rather oddly, the "total seizure"[83]) at the very beginning of the act of making a work of art. What is apprehended at this stage is an unarticulated inclusive qualitative whole. This whole is not something exclusively situated in a private world. In poetry, for example, it is present in the matter of a poem *as it is felt poetically*. It continues as the organization principle throughout the creative process which itself ends in consummation, i.e., in a sense of completion for the artist.

Dewey holds that one apprehends the pervasive quality in a work of art through direct intuition. This point might be objected to by anyone skeptical of direct intuitions. However, we should bear in mind that for Dewey such intuitions are not incorrigible, nor are they intellectual intuitions. The pervasive quality may only be emotionally intuited. Dewey speaks of it as the "spirit" of the work of art. It characterizes art as opposed to mere physical objects. This might seem at first to separate art from ordinary life. However, although Dewey wishes to exclude the pervasive quality from physical objects insofar as they are mechanically related to each other, he still finds it in any example of what he calls "an experience." He says "An experience has a unity that gives it its name, that meal [for example] ... The existence of this unity is constituted by a single quality that pervades the entire experience in spite of the variation

---

82 Dewey, 196.
83 Dewey, 195.

of the constituent parts."[84] Again, art, for Dewey, arises out of ordinary life and is therefore continuous with it.

The pervasive quality is to be found in the experience of the creative process as a whole, and not simply in the emerging work of art. It emerges in the significance and value dimensions of the entire experience including the initiating experience of the subject-matter perceived and the continuing experience of the materials of the medium used in the creative process. It should also be noted that for Dewey the creative process and the pervasive quality continue on into the experience of the audience. They do not simply stop with the completion of a work by the artist.

Dewey identifies the pervasive quality with what he calls the "more than spatial" background of organic wholes, of which the experience of art is one example. It is, as he puts it, the indefinite whole that stretches out indefinitely.[85] Experience, unlike ordinary objects such as rocks and chairs, has this indefinite setting. If the sense of this setting, this "unlimited envelope," becomes intense, the experience, Dewey believes, is "mystical." This term might disturb those who read Dewey with a strong affinity for his naturalism. However, the two aspects of his thought are not inconsistent. For Dewey, we always experience ordinary objects as parts of larger wholes, and these larger wholes ultimately within the context of the universe as a whole. Dewey believes that this experience of inclusion is intensified in art. However, I wish to emphasize here that it is present to a lesser degree in the aesthetic experiences of everyday life, especially as mediated by art.

As art intensifies experience, so too, the original (the subject-matter) is transformed. In the case of the painter, the object perceived becomes part of a virtual or imagined world in which relations and expressive properties are intensified. For the audience, one is not only presented with a created world in which materials are transformed, but one's own world is transformed, although indirectly. For example, one sees trees differently after attending a show of Monet's paintings. Or one experiences one's own pity and fear more meaningfully after experiencing pity and fear for the hero of a tragedy.

Some theorists have confused Dewey's thinking here with belief in some sort of transcendent realm. Dewey had no such belief. Although he is not here promoting a religious perspective, at least not one that posits a transcendent

---

84 Dewey, 44.
85 Dewey, 197.

deity, he *does* think his account has the advantage of explaining the religious feeling that accompanies intense aesthetic experience. When he speaks of being "introduced to a world beyond this world," instead of referring to transcendent realm, he believes that this world is the "deeper reality" of our world of ordinary experience.[86] This experience of the work of art is felt not only as a deepening of the sense of an "enveloping undefined whole," but as an expansion of ourselves to find ourselves. Egotism is erased in the process, this marking another parallel to religious experience in many traditions. *This*, for Dewey, is the common substance of the arts, this subject-matter, ultimately the "aura" of everyday objects (as I will term it in the next chapter)—their capacity to be transformed in this way. This sense of unity is not something to be ignored even though it is not a form of guaranteed knowledge or intellectual intuition of some higher reality.

The dynamic interaction of art and perception may be looked at from the perspective of the art appreciator. However, it is perhaps best understood from the standpoint of the artist in the act of creation. Take a painter who is working with paints. As she manipulates the paints, they take on meaning. The meaning is inexplicable in literal discourse. It is not something that may be handled by the methods of science. It brings in the past and projects into the future. The work becomes alive. She revises the work in order to enhance and elaborate the pervasive quality. As the work becomes alive the artist herself becomes more alive. Expression then occurs. Thus for Dewey aesthetics and art both have to do with animation of everyday experience. As the paint *and* the artist are animated in experience so too is the subject matter, whether it be present in the artist's field of vision, or in imagination or memory.

Drawing from Dewey, Beardsley proposed that we should see an aesthetic experience as a special kind of experience mainly associated with the arts. However, this once again cuts the arts off from everyday life. I don't think that Dewey even had a notion of a distinctive thing called "aesthetic experience" as opposed to "an experience." For Dewey, experience gets aesthetic when it is complete, integral, and developmental. Experience is not divided into parts: scientific, philosophical, business, aesthetic, and so forth. Science, philosophy and business can also be aesthetic, and are aesthetic in their highest instances.

To Beardsley's insistence that the experience of song has more in common with the experience of sculpture than with the experience of driving Dewey

---

86 Dewey, 199.

would reply that an experience of listening to a song can have a lot more in common with the experience of driving than with looking at a sculpture in some instances. Unlike Beardsley, when Dewey speaks of a work of art as an organic whole he does not mean that it is thereby isolated: to be an organic whole means to be in relation to other organic wholes in a nested series of backgrounds. The very intensity of the pervasive quality is impossible without the presence of these backgrounds. That is, we experience the pervasive quality in relation to a complex background (for example, cultural, historical, and biological) which adds to the intensity of the quality itself.

Neither does Dewey separate his aesthetic theory from his ethical, political and social concerns. The good life is the end of political ameliorative action, and the good life is characterized in part by strong aesthetic experience. The main source of unhappiness in our society, Dewey argued, is the current economic arrangement: "The psychological conditions resulting from private control of the labor of other men for the sake of private gain ... are the forces that suppress and limit esthetic quality in the experience that accompanies processes of production."[87] Although opposed to the Marxist idea of the dictatorship of the proletariat, Dewey clearly believed in two essentials of Marxist thought, that labour is oppressed and that alienation characterizes capitalist society. So too, Dewey looked for a solution to societal problems in a transformation of everyday life, including work life. In his case the revolution would come slowly and only within the context of a basic commitment to democracy.

Today, the situation has not much changed. The lives of working-class people are still largely alienated. Things are even worse when one goes to developing countries. The excesses of capitalism during the industrial revolution are being repeated at this moment in China and in numerous other places in the world. In our time, relatively privileged academics tend to isolate themselves from the troubles of this world through a process of separating art from everyday life using strategies like that of the artworld style of defining art.

SOME SUMMATIVE THOUGHTS

Although it has many forerunners, everyday aesthetics is essentially a new discipline. As a sub-discipline of philosophical aesthetics it takes on the typical problems of philosophy as applied to its domain. Aesthetics of art can be

---

87 Dewey, 346.

described as what happens when philosophers approach the arts. Theory of knowledge (can art gives us knowledge?), metaphysics (what kinds of things are works of art?), ethics (can art be immoral?), theory of interpretation (what is the meaning of art?), and theory of evaluation (is there such a thing as taste?), all play a role in the aesthetics of art, as does the fundamental "what is?" question (what is art? what is aesthetics?). Something similar happens when philosophers approach the aesthetics of everyday life. An expansion of the field of aesthetics began when philosophers turned to the aesthetics of the natural environment in the 1970s. One could even say that the aesthetics of everyday life is a continuation of this expansion. The aesthetics of everyday life may have gotten off to a slow start because it was thought that the domain is already covered by the philosophy of art and the aesthetics of nature. However, the aesthetics of art and nature do not include the aesthetics of such things as home decoration or the appreciation of flickering patches of light on a wall. Another inhibitor may have been the thought that there are no issues or philosophical problems in the aesthetics of everyday life that are not already covered in the aesthetics of art and nature. In this chapter we have begun to see that there actually are many such issues. As we shall see in coming chapters, although issues are shared between the different domains of aesthetics, they take on a different character and different importance in each.

One of the first things needed in constructing a new field is to attempt to delimit its boundaries. And yet when we consider the realm of everyday aesthetics we enter into pre-existing battlegrounds. That is, if the everyday is defined in terms of what is not art, not nature, not math, not science then we must consider that there are many debates surrounding what counts as art, nature, math and science. The debates surrounding the nature of art are of special significance in relation to the nature of everyday aesthetics. Is quilt-making part of the aesthetics of everyday life or of the aesthetics of art? What about food preparation? The answer depends on how one defines art. Perhaps ultimately these border disputes do not much matter. Quilts, for example, are regularly shown today both in craft and art museums: it is not a live issue whether quilts are art. One thing, however, that might sometimes be forgotten is that often quilts are made for the home and only appreciated there. Quilts may have been ignored qua everyday objects, in the effort to categorize them as art. Similarly, aestheticians of nature are interested in the question of whether their domain includes human-made environments as well as pristine and relatively pristine nature. So, the issue of what falls within everyday aesthetics depends in part on the outcome of the debate over what falls within the domain of nature.

Various theories have been presented about the aesthetics of everyday life that would categorize it in various ways. Some philosophers, most notably Scruton, understand everyday aesthetics as subsumed under the decorative arts. This makes the field too narrow, as is the case also when Sartwell attempts to understand it in terms of ritual. Hume, and more recently Carlson and Parsons, understand it solely in terms of functionality. This approach is also too narrow in that it excludes appreciation of items contrary to their intended function or of items that have no particular function, for example shadows.[88] Kant, as I suggested in the first chapter, might have categorized everyday aesthetics under the agreeable, and yet he often includes items that are both non-art and non-nature in the category of pure beauty, and many of the items he categorizes under the agreeable do more than just give sensual pleasure. Zenzen and Shusterman insist that only extraordinary experiences should be included, but this has been effectively countered by Saito and Irvin with their emphasis on application of aesthetic predicates in ordinary life situations. I went on to suggest that everyday aesthetics may be defined by determining a special set of properties. But this approach is problematic since it is difficult to find properties that are exclusively applied to any of the particular fields of aesthetics, whether everyday, art or nature. Still, an exploration of the application of property terms in everyday aesthetics furthers our understanding of the field, and an expansion of the number of properties considered aesthetic makes the very existence of the field possible. Although Dewey's concept of "an experience" is too narrow to delimit the field of everyday aesthetics, his advocacy of continuity between everyday aesthetics and aesthetics of art provides the most telling background for the theory of everyday aesthetics we have seen yet. As we shall see in Part II, his concept of "pervasive quality" along with his controversial notion of "background" is suggestive of my own theory of aesthetic experience as experience of objects as with "aura" which itself makes possible an authentic aesthetics of everyday life. Dewey's concept of "background" in particular allows for development of the notion of applicability of the concept of the "sublime" to everyday aesthetics.

---

88 Jun'ichiro Tanizaki, *In Praise of Shadows*, trans. Thomas J. Harper and Edward G. Seidensticker (New Haven: Leete's Island Books, 1977), orig. 1933.

The field of everyday aesthetics is vast. No one person could speak with expertise about the aesthetics of sports, of facial beauty, of costume, of political eloquence, of food, and of every other sub-field of interest. What most readers will be looking for is some sort of glue that holds the field together. However, I doubt that such a glue is forthcoming. Morris Weitz famously argued that a definition of art in terms of necessary and sufficient conditions will never come about, and this is mainly because, as he argues, "art" is an open concept. He believed that a definition of art would foreclose on the conditions of creativity in art.[89] There is a different reason for why we cannot expect a formal definition of the aesthetics of everyday life. Even if there is no final definition of art, art is still an essentially contested concept.[90] That is, like other abstract notions, such as science, democracy, and social justice, there are many uses of the term and great disagreement over its meaning. People find it not only enjoyable but often necessary to try to define art. Defining art, or at least trying to give some characterization of what is essential to art, is part of the overall process of determining what it is to be a human being. Defining everyday aesthetics has no such compelling interest, except perhaps for the handful of academics most immediately concerned with the issue. Nor is the openness of the concept of "everyday aesthetics" necessary for creativity in the way it might be for the concept of "art." And yet the *domain* of the everyday in its aesthetic dimension is intensely interesting both philosophically and in other ways. The interest does not lie in debates over defining "everyday aesthetics" but over issues within the fields that overlap with other aesthetic domains.

As I have observed, the domain of the everyday has been most notably of interest to artists: to novelists, poets, dancers, film-makers, video artists, musicians, and so on. These individuals are continuously inspired by events and objects in their everyday lives. Inspiration is an essential part of the creative process, and it is always a surprise that philosophers of art usually have so little to say about this. John Dewey, however, leads the way in making us aware that the very categories that are of interest in the fine arts have their origins in everyday life. The very concepts of aesthetic valuation (beauty, grace, elegance, etc.) may be found within everyday aesthetic domains as much as in the arts.

---

89 Weitz.
90 The idea of "essentially contested concepts" was first developed by W.B. Gallie in "Art as an Essentially Contested Concept," *Proceedings of the Aristotelian Society* Supplement 56 (1955-56): 169-98. See also his "The Function of Philosophical Aesthetics," in *Aesthetics and Language* (Oxford: Basil Blackwell, 1967), 13-35.

CHAPTER 3
Everyday Aesthetics and the Environment

Of special importance is the relationship between everyday aesthetics and environmental aesthetics. There is considerable overlap. Environmental aesthetics points the way to appreciation of everyday aesthetics by focusing on the entire lived experience of, for example, a walk in the woods. Moreover, environmental aesthetics is not limited to the aesthetics of nature; it also, increasingly in recent writings, includes the aesthetics of human environments. But is everyday aesthetics just a part of environmental aesthetics? In this chapter, I will argue that it is not, although the relationship between the two is very close. Given that environmental aesthetics is closely tied to environmentalism, a related question is whether environmentalism should be the primary focus of everyday aesthetics. Again, I will argue that it should not be.

Several contemporary philosophers have looked into these and related questions. In this chapter I will discuss four: Arnold Berleant, Allen Carlson/Glenn Parsons (the two can be taken as holding the same position), Arto Haapala, and Yuriko Saito.[1] The first two explicitly approach aesthetics from

---

1   Arnold Berleant, *Living in the Landscape: Towards an Aesthetics of Environment* (Lawrence, KS: University of Kansas Press, 1997). Saito, *Everyday*, and her "Everyday Aesthetics," *Philosophy and Literature* 25, no. 1 (2001): 87-95. Allen Carlson, "Environmental Aesthetics," in *A Companion to Aesthetics*, ed. David Cooper (Cambridge: Blackwell, 1995), 142-44, and "Environmental Aesthetics," in *Stanford Encyclopedia of Philosophy*, http://plato.stanford.edu/entries/environmental-aesthetics/ 2010.

the perspective of environmental aesthetics. Haapala takes a more existential approach but can also be seen as basing appreciation of the everyday on awareness of one's environment. Although Saito does not explicitly present an environmental aesthetics her approach is strongly influenced by this tradition. Like some of the earlier philosophers discussed in the last chapter all four are concerned with delimiting the field of everyday aesthetics. My intention here is not to discuss the entire range of their views on environmental aesthetics but the relation between their central views and everyday aesthetics.

ARNOLD BERLEANT

One of the main assumptions of environmental aesthetics which is explicitly found in Berleant's version is that an environment should be appreciated holistically. This assumption is due to the above-mentioned close connection between environmental aesthetics and environmentalism. Environmentalism is closely associated with the idea that natural environments are ecological wholes. Holism, for Berleant, also requires that, in aesthetic appreciation, all the senses be involved. A holistic approach can be valuable, but is it necessary?

Consider my daily walk to work. I may appreciate the nature of the day (sunny and fresh), the seasonal variations of the plant life (spring has arrived!), the flowery smells of plant-clippings (brought out by a recent rain), the cultural richness of my ethnically diverse community (notice the statue of the Virgin on that front porch), the architectural niceties of ordinary buildings (the California bungalow that looks a bit like a Frank Lloyd Wright creation), the sounds of song-birds in the spring, and the fashion statements of students as I enter the campus. This *could* be seen in terms of Berleant's environmental aesthetics. All of the senses are involved, and the environment experienced could be seen as simply that part of my city that I cover in my walk. However, these various items would probably not be seen by any biologist to form an ecological whole since many of the experiences I describe consist of human artifacts, and most of the plants along my walk are not native species, or are not arranged in a natural way. Unless ecology is taken to include the human species and all that it does, the usual ecological approach to environmental aesthetics does not really fit the everyday experience of a walk in an urban neighbourhood.

Moreover, the aesthetic delights of my walk may be relatively isolated from each other, and my overall experience less holistic, than Berleant requires. I am an amateur photographer, and I often look at scenery of everyday life as potential shots through an imagined frame. When I look in this way it is not the case that all my senses are involved. And yet this is one valid way to appreciate the environment. If environmental aesthetics *requires* holistic and engaged experience in which all the senses are concurrently involved, it may be a problem to see everyday aesthetics in these terms.[2]

Berleant's strategy for dealing with everyday aesthetics is to incorporate urban aesthetics under environmental aesthetics.[3] He recognizes that environmental aesthetics was originally focused on the natural environment, but believes it can now include the aesthetics of everyday life. Thus, for him, environmental aesthetics will deal with how we should approach the "landscapes of home, work, local travel and recreation."[4] He observes that "we engage the landscape aesthetically as we drive to work or school, go shopping, walk the dog, or picnic in a park."[5] Thus, for Berleant, everyday aesthetics is a matter of landscape appreciation. But what does he mean by "landscape"? One dictionary definition of "landscape" is that it is an extensive section of rural scenery which can be seen from a single viewpoint.[6] Often this is seen on the model of the perception of a landscape painter. Berleant insists, however, that landscapes need not be seen from this perspective. Also, as we have seen, he does not limit landscape to rural scenery. He even speaks of workspaces as landscapes. Although the domain is broad, it still seems that for Berleant everyday aesthetics is limited to appreciation of expanses of land and similar spaces. That is, since landscape aesthetics is the paradigm, everyday aesthetics under the rubric of aesthetics of the environment becomes urban landscape aesthetics.

There are problems with taking the aesthetics of the natural environment as paradigmatic of a larger aesthetic that includes both itself and everyday aesthetics. The current ideal of nature appreciation based on environmentalism excludes appreciation of many kinds of landscapes influenced by human activities, especially ones that are environmentally unsustainable. Yet contemporary photography, assemblage, and 3D art have taught us to appreciate

---

2 See my "A Defense of Arts-Based Appreciation of Nature," *Environmental Ethics* 27, no. 3 (2005): 299-315, for elaboration of a similar point, but focused on appreciation of nature.
3 Arnold Berleant, *The Aesthetics of Environment* (Philadelphia: Temple University Press, 1992), 11.
4 Berleant, *Landscape*, 16.
5 Berleant, *Landscape*, 20.
6 "landscape," *Dictionary.com Unabridged* 1, no. 1 (Random House, July 2009), http://dictionary.reference.com/browse/landscape.

many landscapes that would be repulsive to most environmentalists. Some of my own strongest aesthetic experiences have come from viewing junkyards and storage areas along the train route from San Jose to San Francisco.[7] My taste in this respect has been influenced by trends in late twentieth-century art. Berleant implies, however, that such things as telephone poles, power lines, commercial strips, trailer parks, suburban malls, and parking lots should not be appreciated since they express negative aesthetic values.[8] Yet these phenomena are often the subjects of contemporary painting and photography, which provide a way for us to experience them in aesthetically positive terms.

Moreover, an exclusive focus on the total environment would draw our attention away from appreciation of relatively isolated objects, things for example that do not really appear to exist in a landscape. Consider a key scene in the 2001 movie, *American Beauty*. The boy-next-door is a drug pusher and a voyeur, and yet he shows his new girlfriend a video he made of a plastic bag shuffling back and forth against a building wall in a gentle swirl of local wind—an image of extraordinary beauty. From the landscape perspective this experience is too isolated and too mediated (by art) to be of any value. It shows lack of concern for the total environment, for there is no landscape present, and only one of the senses is engaged. (Some videos would also engage the sense of hearing through a sound-track, but the point would be similar.) Yet, this video-within-a-movie makes us aware of possibilities of powerful aesthetic experience of individual objects. Although it may be argued that this object is experienced in relation to an environmental element, e.g., wind, there is no visible ecology. Also, from the point of view that sees aesthetic experience as subordinate to the moral demands of environmentalism, the video simply records the existence of a plastic bag not properly recycled. This perspective would ignore the beauty of the image.

Berleant's environmental aesthetics is tied to an attack on traditional aesthetic theories of distance, disinterestedness and contemplation. He partly does this to emphasize senses other than sight. For example, in the context of the aesthetics of urban landscapes, he calls on us to be sensitive to the feel of the surface texture of a road we are walking and the distinctive smells of a neighbourhood.[9] This is a valuable recommendation. However, it is not necessary

---

7   See my "The Aesthetics of Junk and Roadside Clutter," *Contemporary Aesthetics*, http://www.contempaesthetics.org/newvolume/pages/journal.php 6 (May 17, 2008).
8   Berleant, *Landscape*, 20.
9   Berleant, *Environment*, 72.

to reject the ideas of distance, disinterestedness and contemplation in order to stress these phenomena. One can appreciate the surface texture of a road in a distanced, contemplative or disinterested fashion. Moreover, it is arguable that aesthetic awareness of such things *requires* some detachment from purely practical considerations, if only for a moment. Being intensely engaged in an experience of the road is distinct from being engaged in some activity that requires using the road for some purpose.

Berleant's attack on disinterestedness and distance would discourage the visual contemplation exemplified in the plastic bag example. More generally, it would disallow appreciation of raw urban scenes. It would also exclude appreciation of anything associated with practices which themselves are unethical. Yet, as Kant famously argued, one can aesthetically appreciate a palace even though one knows that it was built on the blood and sweat of the oppressed.[10] Also, although engagement of all of the senses can contribute to a powerful aesthetic experience, this should not preclude the possibility, and value, of aesthetic experience that focuses on one sense, and is relatively disengaged, as for example in appreciating a landscape through a train window.

INTERLUDE: EVERYDAY AESTHETICS AND THE AESTHETICS OF NATURE

Although in the time of Wordsworth and Thoreau an appreciation of everyday life meant appreciation of something close to pristine nature, today the matter is almost reversed: that is, appreciation of nature becomes (usually) part of appreciation of everyday life. Most of us live in urbanized spaces where experience of nature is highly mediated. The plants and trees I appreciate on my daily walk have mainly been planted and maintained by humans. They do not play roles in traditional ecologies. The animals I see are either domesticated or ones that have adapted to living in a human-controlled environment. (This was even true to some extent of the landscapes appreciated by Wordsworth and Thoreau!) In addition, I appreciate my environment, including both natural and artificial aspects, via the mediation of cultural meaning.[11] Although most everyday aesthetic experience includes a natural component my appreciation of that component is more a matter of everyday aesthetics than of nature aesthetics.

---

10 Kant, *Judgment*, #2, 43.
11 Scruton, *Beauty*, 67.

During my daily walk I go over a bridge that spans a creek (Coyote Creek). To my good fortune, this creek has not been cemented in, and so the view of it is quite verdant. Such views give me an aesthetic pleasure that is part of my everyday experience. I know that three hundred years ago, when it was more pristine, the creek would not have presented the same vista. For example, more erratic water flows would have assured fewer large trees. However, this thought does not lessen my appreciation of the creek as I see it today. I have been told that local water district plans for flood control would take out most of the trees. This would make an aesthetician of nature happy, but not me since it would be detrimental to my everyday aesthetic experience.

My appreciation of the life of the streets and my appreciation of Coyote Creek cannot be sharply distinguished: the two are continuous, as is my appreciation of the streets and my appreciation of the day, the weather, and the cloud formations above. The aesthetics of everyday life is not in isolation from the aesthetics of nature. However, it has priority for me. By contrast, the aesthetics of nature would play a more prominent role for someone who lives in the wilds of Alaska. I do feel nostalgia for times in which the aesthetics of pristine nature was more prominent, a nostalgia that actually contributes to my appreciation of Coyote Creek as it is today. Sometimes, when I look at it from a bridge, it looks as if set in a primeval jungle. However, this is a matter of appreciation mediated by imagination, not by knowledge of the primeval state of the river itself. Also, appreciation of the creek is mediated by cultural construction of the concept of "nature" itself, for instance as it is influenced by poets like Wordsworth. As I look at the creek I have a certain concept of what nature should look like, and this concept has been influenced by poems I have read, movies I have seen, and art I have observed.

In sum, (1) an element of the aesthetics of the everyday is the aesthetics of those aspects of nature ordinarily available and continuous with other aspects of everyday experience, (2) one can legitimately see the aesthetics of nature as just an aspect of everyday experience when that experience is essentially of a human environment, and (3) whenever we do appreciate nature it is in terms of our culture and its concepts, including our culturally-determined concept "nature" itself.

ALLEN CARLSON

Allen Carlson, whom we have already discussed in relation to the notion of functional beauty, has important things to say about environmental aesthetics. This is mostly in relation to the aesthetics of nature, but also has relevance to the aesthetics of man-made environments. Carlson insists that experiencing nature as a static two-dimensional object, for example through landscape painting or photography, distorts our appreciation of it. He believes that the only proper way to appreciate natural objects is in terms of correct scientific knowledge.[12] He also shares with Berleant (and me) a desire to expand the traditional conception of aesthetics beyond the narrow domain of the philosophy of art, not only to the aesthetics of nature but also to the aesthetics of everyday life. Setting aside the question of whether his is the best approach to appreciation of nature, the issue here is whether we must similarly approach the aesthetics of everyday life in terms of this primacy of scientific cognition. Are we, for example, required to experience the aesthetics of the home in terms of sociological studies of home-life? Is there really an appropriate science background for correct appreciation of a streetscape?

The science-based approach to appreciation is, I believe, less relevant here than in relation to nature. As Eric C. Mulis, in a review of Carlson's *Nature and Landscape*, argues, Carlson's view works much better for larger than small spaces, the later being infused with personal meaning not amenable to a science-based approach. As Mullis puts it, "home décor, landscaping, and rows of vegetables tend to be much more aesthetically significant to individuals than are the terrain and territory within which homes are situated [since they are] sites of activity, cultivation, and care." Such small places are "primarily informed by subjective value and personal history." He concludes that "the natural environmental model [Carlson's view] works well in settings that lend themselves to a cognitive, fact-based approach, but [has] little to say about the personal aesthetic experiences of the places in which we live and call home."[13]

Moreover, the aesthetics of everyday life is already well-covered by something other than science, namely by the arts. In a sense, as I suggested previously, artists (poets, choreographers, novelists, film-makers, etc.) are often the true experts in the aesthetics of everyday life, even if their views have not been philosophically elaborated. They help us to "compose" and frame experiences and, in doing so, to appreciate the everyday. Perceiving their works, and not only realist ones, allows us to see how elements of everyday life may be perceived aesthetically. Although sociological knowledge would add some

---

12 Allen Carlson, "Appreciation and the Natural Environment," *The Journal of Aesthetics and Art Criticism* 37, no. 3 (1979): 267-75.
13 Eric C. Mullis, review of *Nature and Landscape* by Allen Carlson, *The Journal of Aesthetics and Art Criticism* 69, no. 2 (2011): 238-40, quotes from 239.

dimension to the aesthetics of the home, for example by showing how power relations affect choice of decoration, it is not required for that experience to be either appropriate or intense. It is also probably less useful aesthetically than knowledge of the arts (for example the paintings of Bonnard) that treat the same subject-matter.

Carlson says that his theory about the aesthetics of the natural environment has implications for aesthetics in general and that his model for appreciation of nature implies that in appreciating *anything* the appreciation should be centred on the thing itself.[14] This view seems plausible at first. However, it implies that we can and ought to appreciate the object as it is independent of us, i.e., independent of any imaginative associations or hypothetical projections we might have about it. Is this advisable, or even possible?

As we saw earlier, Carlson and Parsons, have recently expanded Carlson's theory to cover not only natural and landscape aesthetics but also the aesthetics of everyday life (and even the aesthetics of art).[15] They argue for the primacy of the concept of functional beauty. When they turn to everyday aesthetics their view is that appropriate framing of everyday phenomena does not have to be in terms of science but can also be in terms of function. They believe that an artifact is aesthetically good if it looks fit for its function, and that this is what is needed for an everyday aesthetics. As we saw in the first chapter, this idea can be traced back to Hume, and earlier to Plato.

Functional beauty is important in everyday aesthetics. However, to speak of the environment of everyday life as "highly utilitarian,"[16] as Carlson and Parsons do, is to overemphasize function. Some of the environment of everyday life is utilitarian, but some is not utilitarian at all. Anyone who reads *Functional Beauty* should also read *The Substance of Style* by Virginia Postrel as a kind of corrective. Postrel exhaustively documents the increasing importance of surface (and non-utilitarian) aesthetic qualities in our everyday lives.[17] Take for example the prominent attention now given to men's bodies in physique magazines, contests, and so forth.[18] So, although I agree with Carlson and Parsons that "looks like it

---

14 Allen Carlson, *Nature and Landscape* (New York: Columbia University Press, 2009), 36.
15 Parsons and Carlson, Chapter VII, "Artifacts and Everyday Aesthetics," is particularly relevant.
16 Parsons and Carlson, 12.
17 Virginia Postrel, *The Substance of Style: How the Rise of Aesthetic Value is Remaking Commerce, Culture and Consciousness* (New York: HarperCollins, 2003).
18 Postrel, 29.

fits its function" is an aesthetic quality, I doubt it is the prime quality in everyday aesthetics. In addition to neglecting the non-utilitarian, the theory is oriented primarily towards artifacts and leaves out events and experiences. A paradigm of everyday aesthetics for Parsons and Carlson might be appreciation of a corkscrew. Yet, as we have seen, the domain of everyday aesthetics reaches far beyond useful objects to include such things as urban landscapes, shadows on walls, the look on a child's face, and items collected for display on a mantelpiece.

I would also argue that "looking fit for its function" is only sometimes aesthetically important. I look at a glass on my table and I think that it looks fit for holding water, as would many other glasses. However, this glass looks particularly good aesthetically, and this is not because it looks like it can hold or deliver water better than others, but because it has a certain pleasing solidity and it has fluting that reminds me of a Greek column. Sure, it helps that the fluting makes for a graspable surface: function *does* play a role. However, it does not determine aesthetic value by itself.

Consider another example. Carlson and Parsons say that the function of a watch is to tell time. However, all working watches tell time. Whether a watch tells time well, or looks like it is going to tell time well, does not determine whether it is graceful, delicate, or elegant. Where function comes in has more to do with whether or not we find something *un*attractive: a smashed watch does not look fit for its function and thus fails to look good as a *watch*, although it might still have interesting aesthetic features. Remember that the Venus de Milo is still beautiful even though her arms are missing. "Beautiful broken watch" is not an oxymoron.

One feature that may contribute to making a shovel beautiful is that it works well. However, as with watches, there can be beautiful shovels that are not functional and functional shovels that are not beautiful. Although I might call the snow shovel that shovels snow best the most beautiful, I might not. Even in the case of shovels I might prefer one that combines attractive design and somewhat less shovelling capacity. Moreover, even functional beauty is not understandable just in terms of function. Something only has functional beauty if it works well in a beautiful way.

Dewey clarifies the role of functionality in everyday aesthetics when he considers the theory that the beautiful is the efficient.[19] He observes that the association of shape with function, as in a spoon, helps in identification. As

---

19 Dewey, 119. Chapter VI, "Substance and Form."

with artistic form, shape involves organization of parts in which the meaning of the whole enters into and qualifies the parts. This, he argues, has led theorists like Herbert Spencer to identify beauty with efficient adaptation of parts to the whole. (Note that Spencer's theory, unlike Carlson and Parsons', does not focus on whether something *looks* fit for its function.) Yet, Dewey observes, any such identity will fail as there are things that are graceful independent of their efficient function. As he says, "[t]here is more to grace than just lack of clumsiness, in the sense in which 'clumsy' means inefficiency of adaptation to an end."[20] He distinguishes between shapes as such, in which only functionality is considered, and aesthetic form. He then develops a broader sense of usefulness in which "the useful" is what fulfills all the "structures" or "organs" of the live creature involved in the experience in such a way as to bring that experience (which is a complex of elements) to completion. This conception of the useful goes beyond both Spencer and Carlson/Parsons insofar as it does not see it just in terms of efficiency. An object can be useful to the self *as a whole* even though a "specific efficiency" might be sacrificed. Such an object has "dynamic," as opposed to mere "geometric," shape. For example, I like to wear a Timex watch that, although inexpensive, has an elegant design based on watches from the 1950s. It is useful to me in a much broader sense of "useful" than mere functionality, i.e., insofar as it expresses certain things I value. Although I miss my Cassio's ability to give the date and day of the week, I am willing to sacrifice these features for the grace of the Timex.

Carlson insists that in order to appreciate nature we must compose it: we must, as he puts it, select, emphasize and group. This is why he opposes the view of Yi-Fu Tuan on the aesthetics of nature. Tuan, no doubt influenced by the Chinese philosophy of Daoism, holds that we should approach nature as though we were a child: "An adult must learn to be yielding and careless like a child if he were to enjoy nature polymorphously."[21] Contra Tuan, Carlson thinks this approach would only lead to confusion and that this sense of confusion would be neither satisfying nor worthy of the title "aesthetic." He thinks the experience would not be aesthetic because it would be too unlike the aesthetic appreciation of art. Appreciation of paintings, for example, ends at the frame. From Carlson's perspective, the appropriate frame for the appreciation of nature would exclude certain phenomena, for example, the

---

20 Dewey, 119.
21 Yi-Fu Tuan, *Topophilia: A Study of Environmental Perception, Attitudes, and Values* (New York: Columbia University Press, 1974), 96.

sound of traffic. Tuan's approach, however, may be defended as allowing us to attend to the experience itself in all its complexity: both the natural phenomena (the ant crawling up one's leg) and the human phenomena experienced at the same time (the sound of traffic). Tuan's position, as Carlson recognizes, is similar to Berleant's in its holism. Unlike Carlson, I think that Tuan's form of appreciating nature can be legitimate, as also Berleant's. Carlson is right that we must compose the experience, but the frame need not exclude the sound of traffic.

Carlson and Parsons similarly attack Yuriko Saito when she discusses how to appreciate a baseball game.[22] Saito, like Tuan and Dewey, allows us to compose the aesthetic object to include such things as the smell of hot dogs and the heat of the sun as well as the events in the field. Consistent with Carlson's criticism of Tuan, Carlson and Parsons think that this approach makes evaluation difficult, since it allows different observers to select different aspects of the event to appreciate. For them this position leads to unacceptable relativism. Presumably they would want us to focus on the aesthetic properties of the game itself while ignoring all other aspects of the experience.

The gain is not worth the price. One can, of course, focus on the aesthetic properties of the game itself, and here some measure of objectivity can be achieved, for instance by means of Hume's concept of the good judge. However, that hardly means that there is anything wrong with Saito's framing of the experience. Again, although framing is required, the appropriate frame is not pre-determined, nor does the frame we choose have to keep different categories of things distinct.

Carlson and Parsons wish to gain seriousness for the aesthetics of everyday life by keeping it in line with the aesthetics of art where they think relativism has less hold. Although an extreme relativism should be avoided, there can be no escape from the relevance of non-art contexts in the appreciation of art. Similarly, there can be no escape from relevance of non-baseball-game contexts in the appreciation of baseball. Just as it can be valuable to appreciate the hot dogs and sun as part of the overall baseball experience, part of the aesthetic experience of a painting includes that which surrounds it, not only its frame but also its context. Moreover, the different perspectives under which a painting can be perceived give rise to different experiences, and this is part of the value of the painting itself.

---

22 Parsons and Carlson, 55; Saito, "Everyday Aesthetics," 89.

Although it makes sense to assume that appreciation of something should be "driven" by the object itself, how should this be interpreted? Carlson, following Kendall Walton, holds that appropriate appreciation should be in terms of the object's proper classification.[23] On this view, we should appreciate a work of Mondrian in terms of his own style and genre and not in terms of another style and genre. Assuming that this is true, does it apply to everyday aesthetics? Are we required to appreciate a shopping mall or a table setting in terms of its proper style?

Although it makes sense to say that some appreciations are appropriate and some are not, it does not follow that appropriateness of appreciation is a matter of whether something has been properly categorized. Carlson and Walton assume that the way something is to be categorized has an objectively right or wrong answer. I would argue that the appropriateness of appreciation is largely relative, not in the sense that anything goes, but in the sense that it requires judgment in relation to the specific situation. Moreover, this judgment includes decisions about how something is to be categorized. Aristotle expressed a similar point in relation to ethics when he argued that to achieve excellence is to find the median, and that this requires knowing that what one does is directed to the right person, to the right extent, at the right time and with the right motive.[24] On this view, moral excellence is a matter not of proper categorization but of subtle and complex judgment. If this is true, and I think it is, something similar should be the case for aesthetic appreciation. Walton believes that whether an artwork appears bland or expressive depends on its being perceived in terms of its proper category. Yet appropriateness is context-dependent. Whether one's dress is appropriate depends on whether one is talking about a wedding or the beach, 1920 or 2011. The context too depends on interpretation. For example some might interpret a beach wedding as primarily a beach event and others as primarily a wedding event.

Nor do I think we should put so much faith in the concepts of "appropriate" and "proper." The appropriate decision is not always the best, unless we are willing to allow that some quite improper things are sometimes the most appropriate. Propriety can be trumped by revolutionary aptness. It might be quite improper to see a modernist novel in postmodern terms, and yet doing so may be illuminating.

---

23 Kendall Walton, "Categories of Art," *Philosophical Review* 79 (1970): 334-67.
24 Aristotle, *Nichomachean Ethics*, Book II, trans. Terence Irwin (Indianapolis: Hackett, 1985).

So is propriety the right approach to appreciation of everyday phenomena? Here, once again, it is helpful to look at how *artists* perceive such phenomena. We find that revolutionary artists often look at everyday phenomena in ways that go beyond or violate what is considered their appropriate category. Monet's first impressionist paintings were quite improper for their time insofar as they featured surface aesthetic features and evanescent lighting effects. Yet they were appropriate as solutions to his artistic problems. Seeing roadside garbage as possible elements in an artwork would have been considered inappropriate by most people when Rauschenberg first used them in his "combines." And yet, in the end, he taught us how to see the debris of city streets differently.

Carlson and Parsons hold that an advantage of their position is that it is cognitivist. Correct appreciation of everyday phenomena is based, for them, on scientific or practical knowledge. Yet if the arts can give us a form of cognition not accessible to the sciences or common sense, then appreciation of everyday aesthetics through the arts could be seen as cognitivist too. Thus Carlson and Parsons' theory would not be superior because it is cognitivist. It is also arguable that a deep understanding of a thing does not merely categorize it but brings it alive again by giving it new meaning that relates to one's own experience. Here I am inspired by Hans-Georg Gadamer's idea of "fusion of horizons."[25] On this view, although one can understand a shopping mall in a superficial way by subjecting it to science-like classification, a true understanding requires overcoming the radical distinction between subject and object. It requires recognition that one can, as an understanding agent, never stand outside one's frame of reference, never escape all of one's assumptions. We understand something when we can see what it is by our own lights, within the context of our own life experience, in such a way as to make it deeply meaningful. Although this approach is contrary to the object-centred approach of Carlson and Parsons, this does not mean it is subject-centred. Rather it is an approach that involves a dynamic interaction of subject, object and surrounding contexts.

Finally, there is a problem that arises out of Carlson's opposition to the "object of art model" for appreciating nature.[26] Carlson thinks that removing a natural object from its environment, whether in reality or in imagination, means treating it like a work of art, and this entails not appreciating it as it is in itself. Hence

---

25 Hans-Georg Gadamer, *Truth and Method* (New York: Continuum, 1989).
26 Allen Carlson, "Aesthetic Appreciation of the Natural Environment."

he objects to putting natural objects on mantelpieces, at least as a form of nature appreciation. Presumably he would also oppose placing non-art artifacts on a mantelpiece as well since we would be treating them like art by isolating them from original context. However, this involves some confusion about how we appreciate art. As Paul Ziff has observed, when appreciating a painting, we are at least subliminally aware of the frame and the gallery walls.[27] And, except for the strictest formalists, we confront the work in terms of whatever information we have about the context of its creation. This is why we pay attention to the label on the art museum or gallery wall. Carlson is simply mistaken then when he says that art works are self-contained in the sense that the environments in which they are created or displayed are irrelevant.[28] Even when we know nothing of the context of creation we have a tendency to view the work in terms of how it was probably created. This would imply that the ways we appreciate art, nature and everyday life are closer than Carlson would admit.

I am not denying that natural objects and non-art artifacts (such as, for example, a collection of antique cameras) can take on different qualities when moved from their environment of creation to an environment of display (e.g., a mantelpiece). This is also true for works of art. Whether this is aesthetically inappropriate is another matter. People collect objects and put them on mantelpieces for a variety of reasons. One reason, for example, is that they have a keen scientific interest in the objects. But even if the owner of a mantle covered with different kinds of stones is a geologist, the stones are not generally there as part of science. That is, they are not there as objects in an experiment or as an exercise in classification. Rather, people, even geologists, put objects on mantels because they like the way they look. So how is this aesthetically wrong?

The aesthetics of everyday life embraces the rock placed on the mantelpiece, whereas a science-centred aesthetics of nature treats this form of appreciation as misguided. When the cognitivist aesthetics of nature is extended to such everyday phenomena as the rock on the household mantelpiece it misfires. There is nothing wrong with appreciating rocks on mantelpieces. The rocks here are in a new context and take on new meaning, although they carry some of their meaning from their context of origin. Note also that the rock on the mantelpiece cannot be appreciated in terms of Carlson and Parsons' functionalist model since it serves no non-aesthetic function. Of course clocks and framed photographs of family

---

27 Paul Ziff, "Anything Viewed," in Feagin and Maynard, eds., *Aesthetics*, 27.
28 Carlson, "Aesthetic Appreciation," 451.

members are appropriately displayed on mantelpieces, and Carlson would have no problem with that. But many other things go on mantelpieces just because they look interesting or nice and not because doing so fits their function or displays the way their form fits their function.

ARTO HAAPALA

Arto Haapala shares with the other philosophers discussed in this chapter a conviction that everyday aesthetics has been unduly neglected.[29] He observes correctly that, when we visit a city for the first time, its strangeness makes us sensitive to aesthetic features we might not notice in familiar surroundings. This is part of the reason for tourism. However, rather than stressing strangeness, his main interest is in the ordinary in the everyday—not aesthetic objects that attract attention but the everyday as such.[30] Related to this, he also emphasizes the personal dimension of everyday aesthetic experience insofar as the self is situated in a familiar place.

I agree that the relation between self and place should play a central role in everyday aesthetics. The aesthetic experience of the familiar is associated with such terms as "comfortable," "friendly," and "homey," all of which have aesthetic uses. However, it is problematic to understand the aesthetics of everyday life *generally* in terms of familiarity, for the unfamiliar also plays a role in the aesthetics of everyday life. Strangeness too can be aesthetically positive, and not just the strangeness of tourist sites. Someone once had a life-sized stuffed lion doll in the back of his pick-up truck in our neighbourhood. This was delightful even though, and partly because, it was strange. However, more importantly, ordinary everyday objects, even ones that are quite familiar can become strange in appearance, and this can be aesthetically positive. Artists in particular have long been able to make this happen. This, for example, was a large part of what the Surrealists were about.[31] It also plays an even larger

---

29 Arto Haapala, "On the Aesthetics of the Everyday: Familiarity, Strangeness, and the Meaning of Place," in *Aesthetics of Everyday Life*, 39-55. See also his "Strangeness and Familiarity in the Urban Environment," in Aarto Haapala, ed., *The City as Cultural Metaphor: Studies in Urban Aesthetics* (Lahti: International Institute of Applied Aesthetics, 1998), 108-25.
30 Haapala, "On the Aesthetics," 40.
31 See Michael Sheringham, *Everyday Life: Theories and Practices from Surrealism to the Present* (Oxford: Oxford University Press, 2006), Chapter 2, "Surrealism and the Everyday," 82.

role in art photography. Both in art and in perception, ordinary objects can become transformed in such a way that we can see something extraordinary in them. Ordinary street items can be transformed into something special under the raking light of sunset when covered by a new blanket of snow, or when observed from a different perspective or frame of mind.

By contrast to Haapala, Hans Gumbrecht thinks of the aesthetic experiences happening in everyday life as interruptions of the ordinary.[32] He mentions for example the elegantly folded toilet paper ends we sometimes find in our hotel rooms. Something like this can trigger a form of aesthetic experience that imposes itself as an interruption within the flow of the everyday. Gumbrecht speaks of moments in our everyday lives in which something suddenly appears in a new light via changes in the framework within which we see it.[33] Like me, he sees everyday aesthetics in terms of when the ordinary becomes extraordinary. Gumbrecht recognizes the importance of defamiliarizing experience in everyday aesthetics. For example, he tells us that one day while looking at his ears in a mirror shaving, he was astonished by their suddenly unfamiliar form.[34] He implies that this experience was aesthetically powerful.

By contrast, and drawing from Heidegger's idea that we only notice a hammer when it is broken, Haapala finds everyday aesthetic experience related deeply to functionality, although unlike Carlson and Parsons, his main focus is on the functionality of our surroundings.[35] For him, everyday aesthetic experience comes about in a place we find familiar but hardly notice. He thinks that this makes the aesthetics of everyday life very different from the aesthetics of art, for art (at least in its contemporary form) focuses on surprise, wonder, and shock, and not on the functional and the familiar.

It is true that an object's being broken sometimes helps us to see it aesthetically, especially when we are not focused on fixing it. A broken old car in a field is often a subject for photographers. However, when my computer breaks down I am mainly interested in how it can be fixed, not in its aesthetic properties. Moreover, negative change in an object is not the only reason for experiencing it differently. We often begin to look at familiar things aesthetically when, although they have not changed at all, our own point of view has changed: for

---

32 Gumbrecht, 299-318.
33 Gumbrecht, 302.
34 Gumbrecht, 308.
35 Martin Heidegger, *Being and Time*, trans. John Macquarrie and Edward Robinson (Oxford: Blackwell, 1997).

example, we might look at grain elevators or factories differently after seeing a documentary on the American painter Charles Sheeler.

There is also something problematic with the example of experience of a previously unnoticed but-now-noticed-because-broken hammer as a paradigm of aesthetic experience. During a recent visit to the Fowler Museum of Anthropology at UCLA I was reminded of the great beauty that functional objects can have in tribal societies. Surely these objects were not made so beautiful only to be noticed when they were broken. Artifacts are given aesthetic qualities by their makers so that they will be noticed when the object is still in working condition.

Also, if we look at art overall, as opposed to more disturbing forms of contemporary art, there is no special stress on surprise, wonder and shock. In fact, contemporary art, especially, tends to focus our interest in everyday aesthetics. For example, an avant-garde art film might dwell on such things as street-lights and food preparation. (Think of the films of Andy Warhol.) In addition, art that surprises and shocks, for example "Piss Christ" (1987) by Andres Serrano, a photograph of a plastic crucifix in urine, can give us aesthetic appreciation of ordinary things we never thought could be appreciated, for example the colour of urine. Moreover, it is not clear why surprise and wonder should be excluded from the aesthetics of everyday life. Finally, as we have seen in the critique of Carlson and Parsons, functionality cannot, by itself, define everyday aesthetics.

Haapala writes that he does not normally pay particular attention to the buildings or his surroundings on his daily route through Helsinki. He implies that this is as it should be, observing that "we see the surrounding buildings through their functionality rather than as objects to be visually contemplated."[36] Yet as I walk through my neighbourhood, I do not see the buildings primarily in terms of their function as housing. Normally, I just casually view them, gaining pleasure from their many architectural and garden features. How should we decide between the two approaches to walking through a neighbourhood?

Haapala suggests that for most people the function of buildings in familiar surroundings is just to be there, serving as background, as something we are used to.[37] Yet, no one really conceives of the function of these buildings as providing familiar background. Although sometimes, while walking through my neighbourhood, I am also walking to work thinking about my classes and paying little attention to my surroundings; this just shows that I am not then

---

36 Haapala, "On the Aesthetics," 48.
37 Haapala, "On the Aesthetics," 49.

experiencing my surroundings aesthetically. And if I am aesthetically experiencing them subliminally, I doubt this takes the form of experiencing them as having the function of providing a familiar background. They do provide a familiar background, but that is not a function: it is not part of their use for me. Haapala might argue that their familiar presence is comforting and that "comforting" is an aesthetic quality. Even so, for something to be "comforting" aesthetically I need to dwell on it in some way. For example, I may look around my house and dwell on how comforting it is in its familiarity.

Also, it is not clear that Heidegger would agree with Haapala. When Heidegger, in his famous article on the origin of the work of art, argues that Van Gogh succeeds in revealing the equipmentality of equipment and the thingly quality of a thing by way of his painting of a peasant-woman's shoes, I take it that he is insisting that great art enhances and intensifies our experience of the everyday.[38] His larger lesson would be that we should experience the everyday with wonder. This often requires that we defamiliarize it, making it strange. And this is accomplished quite effectively, as Heidegger suggests, through great works of art.

Most people would see the photographer Henri Cartier-Bresson as a model of someone who maximizes everyday aesthetic experience. Haapala, however, writes that, "in the context of art the everyday loses its everydayness; it becomes something extraordinary" and that, therefore, Cartier-Bresson's photography *contributes* to the neglect of everyday aesthetics. For example, the photographer's "A Bank Executive and His Secretary" (1960) takes ordinary things out of daily context and puts them into an art context, making them objects of wonder.[39]

Did Cartier-Bresson's photography contribute to the neglect of everyday aesthetic experience? Surely the photograph teaches us to notice scenes we might not normally notice. Surely the scene he photographed was aesthetically interesting to him even before he snapped the shot—otherwise he would not have taken it. This is not to say that the wonder or interest he felt in looking at the scene was the same as what he might have felt when looking at the completed photograph. Still, the two are not unrelated. If the business of everyday aesthetics were to encourage us to see everyday scenes as lacking in wonder, then Haapala would be right. However, why should anyone do this?

---

38 Martin Heidegger, "The Origin of the Work of Art," in *Poetry, Language, Thought*, trans. A. Hofstadter (New York: Harper and Row, 1971).
39 Haapala, "On the Aesthetics," 51.

Still, there is a kernel of truth in Haapala's position, namely that there are two kinds of aesthetic experiences in everyday contexts. The first consists of the ordinary low-level experiences that actually serve more as a background to everyday life than as a focus of interest or contemplation. These experiences are often not expressed verbally and, when they are, they are expressed in such terms as "clean," "clear," "well-ordered," "pleasant," "good-looking," "attractive," "pleasant," "pretty," "tasteful," "looks nice," and "comfortable." I will discuss many of these terms in Chapter Five. The second sort of everyday aesthetic experience, which Haapala tries to downgrade, consists of things in the everyday world that we find aesthetically striking. They could be indicated by the very predicates I just mentioned, but with something added to note their heightened character, something that might be expressed by terms such as "very," "quite," "strikingly," "remarkably," and "amazingly." They can also be marked by such terms as "beautiful" and "fine." Thus, a street-scene might seem vaguely pleasant except at sunset when it suddenly becomes quite beautiful. Experiences of the latter sort are much less common. However, these more unusual experiences are often inspiration for art (or even for life!), and often they are only had by non-artists through the mediation of art.

Haapala makes a valuable contribution to everyday aesthetics when he observes that we always place ourselves in a specific environment, for instance the city in which we live, and that we spread a network of experiential connections from that place.[40] Any relatively complete aesthetics of everyday life needs to recognize the role that a sense of place plays in our network of aesthetic experience. As Haapala observes, this is a process of making sense of one's environment through making connections and through making strange aspects of our surroundings familiar. Yet there are other ways of making sense of our environment. For example, when we find it oppressively boring we can make sense of it by making it strange. Ordinarily, and for most people most of the time, everyday objects and environments are uninteresting. There can be blandness to daily life. That is why we have decoration, festival, courtship, drugs, religion, and art. All of these transform the ordinary. They make the ordinary seem extraordinary. Everyday objects and events, when unenhanced, may have low-level aesthetic qualities, but they are also aesthetically uninteresting. Only by enhancing the everyday, whether through active engagement or through contemplation, can we give life the colour it needs to be meaningful.

---

40 Haapala, "On the Aesthetics," 46.

Haapala is right to imply that the aesthetics of the home is central to everyday aesthetics. The underlying experiences of comfort, attachment, and "the homely" (in the positive sense of that term) that attend satisfying aesthetic experiences at home ideally extend into one's neighbourhood and into other places within which one feels comfortable. However, although the homely and the comfortable are important aesthetic qualities, this is no reason to exclude the fascinating and the strange. Moreover, once we attend to the everyday it is transformed. The ordinary qua ordinary is uninteresting or boring and only becomes aesthetic when transformed. There is also a distinction between properties that give a low-level pleasure and displeasure in their apprehension, for example the comfortable and the uncomfortable, and those that generate an intense form of pleasure, for example the fascinating. Art, along with ritual, love, festival, and decoration, enhances our experience of the everyday. It does this indirectly by providing a medium through which the ordinary becomes extraordinary. It transforms our perception to this end. The dialectic between art and the everyday gives meaning to each: hence the aesthetics of everyday life should not distance itself from the aesthetics of art.

YURIKO SAITO

In her recent book, *Everyday Aesthetics*, Yuriko Saito, like Haapala, argues for greater distance between aesthetics of everyday life and the aesthetics of art, and also from the aesthetics of special or extraordinary experiences. She thinks that everyday aesthetics has been neglected because aesthetics up until now has been art-centred. She is opposed to this hierarchy of aesthetic discourse. Instead, she finds many differences between everyday aesthetics and art aesthetics: paradigmatic art has features not always present in everyday aesthetic phenomena, for example framing devices and the privileging of "higher" senses (sight and hearing). She also believes that if we render ordinary experiences strange by re-contextualizing them (in the manner of contemporary artists) we compromise "the very everydayness of the everyday." Here she is arguing against Yi-Fu Tuan's idea that we should appreciate everyday activities such as when a ploughman creates a straight furrow by viewing it "with the pleasure of an artist."[41]

Although aesthetic experiences are not required to be extraordinary or memorable and aesthetic properties may apply without being part of what Dewey called

---

41 Saito, *Everyday*, 50. Tuan, *Strange*, 100.

"an experience," the very experiencing of something as aesthetic does take it *to some degree* out of the ordinary. Thus Tuan's description of everyday aesthetic experience as viewing the world with an artist's pleasure is, on my view, quite appropriate. Similarly, although there are many differences between art aesthetics and everyday aesthetics and, although it is true that the aesthetics of art has too long dominated aesthetics as a whole, we should not neglect the dialectical relationship between the two. This relationship is important to both everyday aesthetics and art aesthetics. For example, art aesthetics is incomplete without understanding its grounding in the everyday. Many artists respond to changes in aesthetic qualities in our everyday lives as much as to changes in the artworld. For example, Andy Warhol artistically responded to the aesthetic pervasiveness of product packaging in our lives. Everyday aesthetic experience responds in turn to changes in the way the world is represented artistically. For example, people who have been in a major disaster frequently refer to the experience as like being in a movie, and clothes fashions often respond to changes in the fine arts. Also, although the everyday has been neglected by aestheticians, it has not been neglected by poets, painters, musicians and other artists. They have explored it in great detail particularly in the last two centuries. Consider, for example, Pierre Bonnard's exploration of everyday interiors or Ed Kienholtz's of the back seat of an old car. Instead of distancing themselves from their investigations philosophers should see such artists as blazing the trail for everyday aesthetics.

Saito emphasizes our *negative* aesthetic responses in everyday aesthetics: in particular how such responses can prompt us to action. For example, we might respond to what we consider an eyesore through attempting to eliminate it. She contrasts what she calls our "usual" reaction to a dilapidated building, which is to repair or tear it down, with the "unusual" reaction of gaining aesthetic pleasure from noticing its different textures, colour variation, and historical richness. On her view the second, "unusual," approach would make everyday aesthetics too much like art aesthetics. Although I applaud her association of an aspect of everyday aesthetics with practical action, I disagree with weakening the close relationship between aesthetics and pleasure. On my view, positive aesthetic experience, and the pleasure that attends it, is primary to aesthetics generally and to everyday aesthetics in particular. To say something is aesthetically good is to say it gives pleasure. Of course, the types of aesthetic pleasure range widely. For example, the pleasure associated with viewing a Greek tragedy is quite different from that associated with an amusement ride. Moreover, emphasis on reactions that lead to cleanup and repair need not pull everyday aesthetics away from the centrality of pleasure. The activity of repairing a building can be pleasurable, as can contemplation of the repair made. It is by way of pleasure that repairing a building enters into aesthetics.

This is not to say that aesthetic pain plays no role in everyday aesthetics. The pain that comes from looking at an eyesore can be part of a larger aesthetic experience that involves elimination of that pain. However, the goal of aesthetic experience is pleasure. The total experience of giving a dinner party may include not only the pleasure of the result but the toil of creation.

Moreover, the "usual" and "unusual" ways of looking at things are not necessarily in conflict. There is no reason why we cannot benefit by switching between such perspectives in much the way Peggy Brand has suggested that we toggle between interested and disinterested perception in viewing political art.[42] Toggling is fine as long as the end goal is richer aesthetic experience and a deeper form of pleasure.

Nor is the second approach clearly more unusual. I grant that things like dilapidated buildings might evoke the "should be repaired" response more often than the artist-like response. However, much of our lives consist in contemplating our surrounding environment in the "unusual" way, for example sitting in a café and observing people, or just taking a walk. As I walk down the street I am constantly scanning the environment for aesthetically interesting phenomena, not for messes that need cleaning.

Appreciating designed objects, such as high-end toasters, is relatively easy since these objects are designed for appreciation. However, it takes an artist's eye (or something like it) to appreciate something quite ordinary, boring or drab. Ed Ruscha did just this in his 1967 book of photographs, *Twentysix Gasoline Stations*. That is, his photographer's eye picked out and recorded these gas stations which we art-viewers could then appreciate indirectly through his art or directly after leaving the gallery. Interestingly, in relation to Haapala's and Saito's emphasis on the ordinary, rather than glamorizing these buildings or making them strange, Ruscha photographed them so as to retain and express their ordinariness. Thus even the everydayness of the everyday can be aesthetically appreciated by way of perceiving through the eyes of an artist. In this case the everydayness of the everyday is itself taken to some extent out of the ordinary.

---

42 Peggy Brand, "Disinterestedness & Political Art," in *Aesthetics: the Big Questions*, Carolyn Korsmeyer, ed. (Oxford: Blackwell, 1998), 155-70. Also found in *N. Paradoxa* 8 and 9 (November, 1998 and February 1999), accessed July 24, 2011, http://www.ktpress.co.uk/nparadoxaissue8and9.pdf.

Of course Saito's advocacy of the everydayness of the everyday does not imply rejection of intense aesthetic experiences of everyday phenomena. She speaks positively, for example, of finding what she calls "aesthetic gems" in everyday life, and says she is not so much interested in *replacing* this kind of experience as in giving equal billing to what she calls the "usual approach," i.e., the impulse to repair or clean. Yet this metaphor of hidden gems assumes that they may be clearly distinguished from things that are not gems, thus disallowing the possibility of perceiving *anything* as an aesthetic gem. It divides the everyday into two domains: one that contains a few special experiences and another that contains a great many ordinary ones, thus neglecting the importance of ordinary experiences *becoming* extraordinary.

I also question whether seeing that something needs repair is always or even usually an aesthetic matter. Usually we just have to get down to fixing the thing, and that is just a chore. Saito could reply that although the "need to repair" response is sometimes non-aesthetic, as when it is purely practical, it *is* aesthetic when it is perceptually focused. For example, seeing that the peeling paint looks so ugly you want to scrape it off and commence re-painting is, for her, an aesthetic experience. To this, I would reply that seeing something peeling as ugly and then wanting to repaint it is not aesthetic (in the sense of contributing to aesthetic experience) unless it is part of an overall experience characterized by a kind of pleasure. Also, one should distinguish between ugliness that simply invites its elimination and ugliness that invites its contemplation: only the latter is aesthetic. Ugliness of the first sort is, of course, an aesthetic property, albeit a negative one.

There is no reason, of course, why different people could not validly respond to dilapidated buildings in different ways. There could even be tolerance for different perspectives here. Troubles arise, however, when these perspectives come into conflict; when one person wants to renovate a building, whereas another wishes to preserve it in its decayed, but visually interesting, state. This is a practical matter that is resolved through the usual social mechanisms and does not invalidate the usefulness of either perspective. Still, imagine the aesthetic disaster if the French Quarter of New Orleans was restored each building to its most pristine state. The combination of elegance and decay that gives this place its distinct character would disappear, replaced by a museum-like quality.

Saito thinks it is important to attend to ordinary objects as ordinarily experienced because such aspects of aesthetic life have what she considers serious practical consequences. Following this, as with Berleant and Carlson, one of the main thrusts of her book concerns the relationship between everyday aesthetics and the ethics of environmentalism. She understands the significance of everyday aesthetics mainly in terms of ethics, and the ethics of environmentalism plays a large role in this. (This is why my discussion of her is placed in this chapter.) She observes that consumer choices that are not "environmentally sustainable" (by which she means ones that do not promote healthy eco-systems) are often governed by aesthetic principles. For example, people may find non-sustainable green lawns to be more pleasant than native plant gardens. Thus she holds that we should be educated to the environmental consequences of our aesthetic preferences.

I agree with this. However, I believe we should situate these concerns within the broader question of the role of everyday aesthetics in human flourishing, of which environmentalist issues form just a part. Adjusting our aesthetic preferences to what is environmentally sustainable or to what is morally proper is just one part of the significance of everyday aesthetics. Another part involves encouraging more aesthetic experiences in the everyday realm, and promoting the conditions that support those experiences. Although Saito affirms this goal, she believes it should be tempered by moral considerations. I worry that aesthetic concerns may be swamped by moral ones. To her credit, Saito avoids this trap insofar as she criticizes what she calls "environmental determinism" (the theory that ecological value of an object determines its aesthetic value), arguing that aesthetic judgment should be based ultimately on what we can directly perceive rather than on ethical considerations.[43]

Saito believes that Japanese aesthetics is in particular to be admired since it contributes to the moral life by cultivating a respectful, caring and considerate attitude towards others (including non-human others) via aesthetic means. She believes that cultivating a respectful attitude to the essences of non-human things will contribute to moral sensitivity.[44] Her paradigm of this is the Japanese craftsman who attends to and exhibits the quintessential character of, for example, a tea cup. This idea is similar to my own, as I will develop it in the next chapter, that aesthetic properties should be distinguished by whether or not the object that has them has "aura." I understand aura in terms of something having the quality of heightened significance in which it seems to extend

---

43 Saito, *Everyday*, 83.
44 Yuriko Saito, "The Moral Dimension of Japanese Aesthetics," *The Journal of Aesthetics and Art Criticism* 65, no. 1 (2007): 85-97, 86. Most of the material in this article was later incorporated into her book. However, the article provides a nice short version of many of her main ideas.

beyond itself. This can happen when something perfectly exemplifies its type in the way Saito describes.

Saito observes that the Japanese stress the essence of the object or material even when it is not considered artistic. The unknown eleventh-century Japanese author of a book on garden-making called *Sakuteiki* believed that creating the scenic quality of landscape can be achieved only when the "request" of the main garden stone is observed in the placing of the other stones.[45] Saito finds a similar concern or "design strategy" not only in the contemporary Japanese arts of flower arrangement, haiku, and packaging but in the European/American "arts and crafts" movement of the nineteenth century with its valuation of "truth to materials."

She also believes that this view requires that things should be appreciated on their own terms and in relation to their own proper kind. Here, she relies on Carlson's idea of appropriate appreciation and Walton's theory that we must perceive a work in its correct category, views I have criticized earlier in this chapter. However, the Japanese aspect of her thought and the aspects she borrows from Carlson and Walton may not be consistent. She writes, with seeming approval, that "Japanese gardeners meticulously shape and maintain trees and shrubs by extensive" manipulation.[46] This would *not* be a case of proper appreciation of nature according to Carlson's natural environmental model of aesthetic appreciation. Carlson would (or should, based on his principles) be horrified by Saito's description of Ikebana as a form of letting the flower express itself through "cutting of branches, leaves, and blossoms so that only the essential parts defining the particular plant can be clearly delineated."[47] He would see the flower as already clearly delineated *before* the cuts. Although Carlson does show appreciation for Japanese gardens in one of his articles, he appreciates them as something between art and nature, and not as nature itself, and he admits that he finds Japanese gardens difficult to appreciate since they are neither pristine nature nor fine art.[48] In short, Saito cannot support her essentialism with Carlson's naturalism. This is not so bad, however, for, as I will show later, something like Saito's essentialism may be supported on other grounds.

---

45 Jiro Takei and Marc P. Keane, trans., *Sakuteiki Visions of the Japanese Garden: A Modern Translation of Japan's Gardening Classic* (North Clarendon, VT: Tuttle, 2001).
46 Saito, *Everyday*, 112.
47 Saito, *Everyday*, 117.
48 Allen Carlson, "On the Aesthetic Appreciation of Japanese Gardens," *British Journal of Aesthetics* 37, no. 1 (1997): 47-56.

The basis for Saito's advocacy of "being true to the materials" is her idea that morality is a matter of not imposing one's own fantasies on others, including non-sentient others. Although imposing fantasies on others is wrong, I suspect that fantasy's relative, imagination, is required for the sympathetic identification that allows us to act morally.[49] It is, I believe, the only basis upon which any sort of moral equilibrium and understanding can be achieved. How does this apply to the idea of being true to materials? One cannot literally sympathize with a garden stone, and a garden stone cannot literally make requests. To make sense of the notion that it *can* make requests, one must be able to speak of this idea as only fictionally true. Nor is there any innate nature of the stone beyond what science can ideally tell us. To act *as though* stones have innate natures in the significance-heightened way Saito is suggesting is, nonetheless, valuable. "Truth to materials" is an important value if we remember that materials are centres of meaning, and meaning is gathered and shaped in historically conditioned experience. This is why what seems an obvious case of "truth to materials" in one culture (for example, honouring the request of a stone) may seem outlandish in another. The essential nature of the materials emerges in our interaction with the materials-as-experienced insofar as we are live creatures in Dewey's sense.

Saito sees the Buddhist notion of "forgetting oneself" as a precondition for this sensitivity to objects, opposing this to the notion that we should impose our own ideas on the material. Yet, the Buddhist view captures only part of the truth. Following the Buddhist path can generate wonderful craft objects. However, it is an illusion to believe that one can fully forget oneself. Sensitivity to objects is mediated by the conditions of one's experience, and, as I have suggested, we can only authentically connect with the object through sympathetic imagination. Artists, including the craftsmen so admired by Saito, are most practiced at this. The rest of us can only hope to see "with the eyes of an artist," as Tuan would put it.

Someone might reply to Saito that listening to the object's "voice" is not really possible since that voice depends on our own selection, interpretation, and construction.[50] Although she concedes the point, she finds it "less interesting" than determining the kind of attitude that gets us closest to transcending ourselves, achieving self-discipline, and creating valuable objects. I agree that

---

49 Cf. Dewey, especially Chapter XIV "Art and Civilization." Thanks to Yuriko Saito for this reference.
50 Saito, *Everyday*, 138.

attitude is important but disagree that the ability to appreciate exists only because there are pre-existent essences waiting to be revealed. The possibility of appreciating anything is a function of the human capacity to perceive with imagination. This capacity draws as much from the human unconscious, and from historical forces, as from the artist's materials and subject-matter. "Listening to the materials" is really being sensitive to ways in which they can be used for imaginative perception and self-expression: it is not determined by a strict objective/subjective distinction.

When Saito stresses the idea of care for materials she contrasts the Zen approach to that of Kant. Kant was skeptical about experiencing a thing-in-itself whereas Zen is optimistic that the being-suchness of the "non-human other" may be experienced directly.[51] I share Kant's skepticism. However, I also share Zen's optimism. How is this possible? Being-suchness is experienced, but it is only *seemingly* experienced directly. It is really experienced as something partially constructed. If we recognize that direct experience of being-suchness is an illusion (although sometimes a useful one) we can avoid the errors that come from taking our intuitive sense of rightness as indicating unchanging truth.

So, although I agree that we perceive essences, the essences we perceive are historically conditioned and are found within human experience: they are not in an external world of things-in-themselves or in a Zennist self-transcendence.[52] When essences are experienced they are as much products of imagination as they are of the thing whose essence we believe ourselves to perceive. Essences are real, but they must be re-interpreted as biologically, culturally and historically emergent.

Buddhists say that if we do not achieve suchness, for example in recognizing that a flower is a flower, we make things into what they are not. I disagree. It is illusion to think that there is a suchness of a flower independent of us. Things come alive in experience only when seen imaginatively and in a way that really works, i.e., when they are seen in an *interesting* or *powerful* way as what they *are not*. This is the reason for the importance of metaphor not only in the arts

---

51 Saito, "Moral," 88.
52 I have developed my ideas on this in: "Metaphor and the Philosophy of Art: Dynamic Organicism," *Theoria et Historia Scientarium, An International Journal for Interdisciplinary Studies*: Special Issue *Metaphor*, ed. Tomasz Komendzinski, 6 (2002/1): 43-64; "Metaphor and Metaphysics," *Metaphor and Symbolic Activity* (Special Issue on Metaphor and Philosophy) 10, no. 3 (1995): 205-22; and "The Socratic Quest in Art and Philosophy," *The Journal of Aesthetics and Art Criticism* 51, no. 3 (1993): 399-410.

but in everyday life. Only through this can the flower come alive as something for us. It is said that, for Buddhists, suchness is best revealed in such mundane things as "noticing the way the wind blows through a field of grass, or watching someone's face light up as they smile."[53] The Buddhist and the everyday aesthetician are allies on this point. For both, it is important to savour the moment. Buddhists say that we know we are experiencing suchness when we say "Yes, that's how it is" and see at the same time that reality is incredibly beautiful. The experience Buddhists are describing here is valuable, but this does not validate the metaphysics. We are still, as Dewey put it, live creatures interacting with our environments.

The craftsperson's materials can speak to the craftsperson, but only in the way that a fictional character in a novel can speak to a novelist. Such imaginative experience of nature and of materials should, however, be distinguished from conscious imposition of a design conceived independently of the material. This is the practice, often associated with the Western technological tradition, which Saito and I both question. The imaginative experience I am describing should also be distinguished from the relatively arbitrary imposition of fantasy images onto phenomena, as when one sees faces in a cloud.[54]

In sum, Saito believes there are two ways to appreciate the everyday, first as a search for the extraordinary in the ordinary and second by an emphasis on the ordinary in the ordinary. Although she sometimes implies that both are important, she associates the first with the much-attacked theories of aesthetic attitude and disinterestedness, and her sympathy is mainly with the second. This can be seen in her efforts to emphasize the moral dimension of everyday aesthetics and in her downplaying of the relationship between the aesthetics of art and the aesthetics of the everyday. By contrast, I think that art, whether it is the Japanese Tea Ceremony or contemporary video art, plays an important role in getting us to notice the everyday. Nor am I convinced that interest in the aesthetic qualities of such ordinary things as neatening a room should lead to downplaying the extraordinary in everyday life. I agree with Saito that we should attend not only to the rewards of aestheticizing such things as transience and decay (as, for example, in the Japanese concept of *wabi-sabi*) but also

---

53 "Tathātā/Dharmatā," *Wikipedia*, accessed April 4, 2010, http://en.wikipedia.org/wiki/Tath%C4%81t%C4%81/Dharmat%C4%81.
54 Cf. Emily Brady, "Imagination and the Aesthetic Appreciation of Nature," *The Journal of Aesthetics and Art Criticism*, Special Issue: Environmental Aesthetics 56, no. 2 (1998): 139-47.

to the more common role that negative reaction to such qualities plays in our lives. Yet I wonder whether it is possible to approach the ordinariness of the ordinary without making it extraordinary, without approaching it, therefore, in an art-like way.

THE ARTIST IN HIS OR HER CREATIVE PRACTICE

Carlson, Saito and others I have discussed in this chapter are right to oppose the dominance of the aesthetics of art in aesthetics as a whole. However, these philosophers underestimate or downplay the dynamic relationship between the aesthetics of art and the aesthetics of everyday life. The reason for this may be neglect of the point of view of the artist in the creative process, especially neglect of the way in which the artist him or herself attends to the aesthetic qualities of everyday life. Nietzsche once said that aestheticians "instead of envisaging the aesthetic problem from the point of view of the artist (the creator), considered art and the beautiful purely from that of the 'spectator,' and unconsciously introduced the 'spectator' into the concept 'beautiful.'"[55] Perhaps these philosophers have not thought sufficiently about how artists respond to their sources of inspiration both in nature and in everyday life, nor about the role imagination plays both in the way artists and others perceive aesthetically.

I have remarked a couple of times on the everyday lives of artists. I have suggested that artists are the true experts in the aesthetics of everyday life. I argue now that it is artists who are best able to see the extraordinary in the ordinary. They regularly take the things of everyday life and transfigure them, first in their perception, and then through their art-making. It is seldom noticed or discussed that the artist's studio is filled largely with non-art objects, including artist materials, photographic sources of inspiration, and unfinished works. All of this belongs to the realm of everyday aesthetics.

The artist's studio and how the artist perceives things in her studio have been neglected in analytic aesthetics because the theory of the creative process developed in that tradition has tended to downplay the importance both of inspiration and of imaginative perception, both of the subject and of the

---

55 Friedrich Nietzsche, *Genealogy of Morals*, Third Essay, Section 6, 539-40, in *Basic Writings of Nietzsche*, trans. Walter Kaufman (New York: Modern Library, 2000). I owe this reference to Yuriko Saito.

materials used in making the artwork.⁵⁶ By contrast, phenomenologist Roman Ingarden talks about the object of perception for the artist in a way that illuminates the experiences of the artist in his or her studio: "The role of this 'object' is to move the artist in a particular way: it forces him out of a natural quotidian attitude and puts him into a completely new disposition. This 'object' may be a particularly eyecatching quality of some thing, as for instance, of a pigment both saturated and 'shining,' or a specific shape. It must however be a quality which draws our attention to itself because it excites in us an emotionally colored experience and an atmosphere of a certain surprise at its particularity and its wonderfully penetrating character."⁵⁷ This quote features not only the idea of appreciating everyday objects by escaping the everyday attitude towards such objects but also references that quality of "shining" in an object which I will describe as "aura."

CONCLUSION

The theories discussed in this chapter all attempt to define an aesthetics of everyday life. They all contribute significantly to the field, but are problematic in various ways. Berleant's theory tries to construct an aesthetics of everyday life simply by extending the aesthetics of nature into this new domain. However, his emphasis on total engagement of the senses with the total environment excludes engagement of individual senses with individual or isolated aspects of the environment. The preference he gives to engagement over contemplation also disallows a richer theory that includes both. His moral critique of negative aesthetic phenomena further disallows their artistic and imaginative perception. Carlson's cognitivist approach to the aesthetics of nature is also applied by extension to the aesthetics of everyday life. Both in its approach to nature and in its approach to everyday life this strategy fails to take into account the importance of imagination in aesthetic experience. It also neglects any perception that goes against scientific or common sense categories, perception that is not "appropriate." Carlson and Parsons' further extension of the cognitivist perspective in their development of functionalism as the central idea in everyday aesthetics suffers from similar problems. "Looks fit for its function" is an aesthetic quality but fails as the primary quality of everyday aesthetics. Haapala, in his effort

---

56 See my "A Pragmatist Theory" to see how Dewey avoids this problem,
57 Roman Ingarden, "Phenomenological Aesthetics: An Attempt at Defining Its Range," *The Journal of Aesthetics and Art Criticism* 33, no. 3 (1975): 257-69, 263.

to focus on the ordinary and to downplay the extraordinary, fails to see how the ordinary becomes extraordinary and how art, for example the art of photography, can enhance everyday experience. Saito, who has produced the most elaborate theory of everyday aesthetics so far, also goes too far in downplaying the dynamic relationship between art and everyday aesthetics. Finally, Saito develops her notion of the "quintessential" which anticipates my own theory of "aura" as it will be developed in the next chapter.

Part II: A Theory of Everyday Aesthetics

CHAPTER 4

Aesthetic Experience as Experience of Objects with Aura

In the first chapter I reviewed the history of attempts to describe and delineate aesthetics of everyday life. In the second chapter I set forth in a preliminary way my own approach which focuses on expanding the field of properties considered aesthetic, and I attempted to show how this approach is consistent with the main thrust of Dewey's aesthetics, recognizing that he may have overemphasized the concept of "an experience." In the third chapter I critically considered four other approaches to everyday aesthetics all inspired by recent work in the aesthetics of nature with a special concern for environmentalist and other moral issues. Earlier, I had suggested a theory of my own that focused on aesthetic properties and aesthetic experience. I found that it had weaknesses but suggested that it is worth pursuing. What we need now is a theory about what is distinctive of an aesthetic property and an aesthetic experience that overcomes those weaknesses.

Aesthetic experiences are of things that have aesthetic properties. When you experience something aesthetically you are experiencing its aesthetic properties. Conversely, when you experience a thing's aesthetic properties you are experiencing it aesthetically. To have a theory of aesthetic properties one needs to go beyond the aesthetics of everyday life to aesthetics in general. A theory of aesthetic properties is needed to talk about the wide variety of properties that apply specifically to everyday aesthetic phenomena. In short, we need to know what makes the properties discussed aesthetic.

Since this inquiry reaches beyond everyday aesthetics it may seem that addressing it from that standpoint puts the cart before the horse. The natural order of inquiry would seem to be determination of the nature of aesthetic experience and of aesthetic properties first, and then application of this knowledge to various domains of aesthetics. Since everyday aesthetics is controversial it might be thought preferable to begin with the aesthetics of art. However, it is precisely because aesthetic experience and properties have been primarily understood from the perspective of the aesthetics of art that everyday aesthetics and its important dialectical relationship with the aesthetics of art have been neglected. At the very least the aesthetics of everyday life lends a fresh perspective to our understanding of the nature of aesthetic experience. More importantly, it covers the very grounding of aesthetic experience in general. As Dewey put it, to understand the relatively rarefied experiences of art one must first try to understand aesthetics "in the raw,"[1] by which he means at a level prior to the refinements of art.

There have been many theories concerning the nature of aesthetic properties. Mine is that an aesthetic property is one in which the aesthetic object takes on "aura" within experience. Although everyone experiences aura in a variety of manifestations, the concept of aura is difficult to define. Like most of the concepts covered in aesthetics, for example "beauty" and "art," it is doubtful that it can be defined in terms of necessary and sufficient conditions.[2] That is, it is doubtful that it can be defined in the way "triangle" or "water" may be defined. Although such a strict definition may never come out I will attempt to give a rougher sort of definition, at least indicating what I mean by "aura" and how this concept may be useful in understanding the nature of aesthetic experience and aesthetic properties.

Aura is a phenomenological characteristic of an object experienced attended with pleasure or with some combination of pain and pleasure (as when we are fascinated with the ugly). Whether the pleasure or pain/pleasure that attends aura can really be distinguished from the aura itself I will leave open. A phenomenological characteristic of an object is not *in* the object as an external thing and is not merely the result of the physical character of the object. Phenomenological characteristics may be described by way of what Edmund Husserl called the phenomenological method.[3] This requires bracketing considerations of the real

---

1 Dewey, 3.
2 For a discussion, see my "Anti-Essentialism," *Encyclopedia of Aesthetics* 2, 125-28.
3 Edmund Husserl, *Ideas Pertaining to a Pure Phenomenology and to a Phenomenological Philosophy—First Book: General Introduction to a Pure Phenomenology*, trans. F. Kersten (The Hague: Nijhoff, 1982).

objective or science-based nature of the object. To describe it phenomenologically we need to focus on the object-as-experienced. Nor is a phenomenological characteristic just something subjective or purely personal. For example, an object as-experienced can be shared by others. For example, two of us may see a particular act as morally wrong, and although the moral wrongness of this act is not something that can be determined by any scientific method, our seeing the act as immoral is not something purely personal or subjective. Thus the distinction between subjective and objective is bracketed (set aside, not thought about) in phenomenological description.

A phenomenological view of aesthetic experience is one that starts with conscious experience and then analyzes the structure of that experience. Central to phenomenology is Husserl's idea that experience has intentional structure, which is to say that each experience has a "noesis" and a "noema," the first being what gives meaning to an intentional act (whether that be the act of thinking, remembering, judging, imagining, or feeling), and the second being the intentional object of that act (whatever is thought about). For example, if one is thinking about a future dinner party the noesis is the thinking and the noema, what you are thinking about, is the party. From the phenomenological perspective, aura is an aspect of the noema or intentional object of any experience characterized as aesthetic. I am not here addressing the issue of objectivity. In a later chapter I will look into whether some things are *improperly* experienced as having an aesthetic property. At this stage I am just interested in characterizing aesthetic experience.

People sometimes use the term "aura" in a way similar to mine. However, I will be adapting it for my own purposes. "Aura" will be associated in the minds of many with Walter Benjamin who spoke of the loss of aura in the age of mechanical reproduction.[4] He thought of aura as having to do with unique existence and authenticity. That is, presence of the original carries with it an aura of authenticity. An original painting has an aura, on this view, that a copy or a photograph of that painting lacks. I will not be using the term in this way, i.e., as referring to the sense of authenticity possessed by an original.

Although people usually interpret Benjamin as someone who is negative about aura (who believes that the loss of aura in our age of mechanical reproduction is not a bad thing) he does give a hint of a theory of aesthetic experience as experience of aura when he refers in his essay to what he calls "natural

---

4 Benjamin, "Work."

aura." He defines this as "the unique phenomenon of a distance, however close it may be."[5] He illustrates this phenomenon in this way: "If, while resting on a summer afternoon, you follow with your eyes a mountain range on the horizon or a branch which casts its shadow over you, you experience the aura of those mountains, of that branch."[6] The definition emphasizes a kind of psychological distance, a bracketing of the object from practical concerns. Although many people associate Benjamin's concept of aura with tradition and authenticity, the illustration indicates that one can experience aura without these. This opens up a wider application for the notion of aura.

What can be meant by the aura of "a branch which casts its shadow"? Benjamin's brief reference leads me to the following thought. (What follows should not be taken as an explication of Benjamin but as an example that contributes to a phenomenological account of aura.) Walking home from work on an April afternoon I look at the shadows of trees cast on the sidewalk. They are really quite beautiful. One thing that explains this beauty is that the tree is doubled in a way quite different from that which happens in a mirror reflection. The doubling is mainly two-dimensional and mainly one-coloured. Although three-dimensionality is suggested by a certain fuzziness in the more distant leaves, the shadows are mostly flat. These two changes make the shadows seem to belong to another world. That is, looking at the shadows as the branches themselves wave in the wind is as though one were looking into an alternate reality. The two-dimensionality and mostly non-representational nature (sure they represent trees, but often they do not look like trees) make these shadows much like contemporary abstract art works, except animated. I suggest that their aura (at least in my own experience of them) is what Benjamin referred to as "a unique phenomenon of distance" or what Edward Bullough earlier referred to simply as "distancing."[7] That they cannot be touched or changed in themselves, but only by way of touching or changing the trees that cast them (or by changing the light source, as in a solar eclipse), lends to this distanced quality. I do not want to say that the shadows of trees are easier to appreciate than trees themselves. However, the distancing that may be carried out through taking an aesthetic attitude in looking at the trees themselves is

---

5   Benjamin, "Work," 222.
6   Benjamin, "Work," 222.
7   Edward Bullough, "'Psychical Distance' as a Factor in Art and an Aesthetic Principle" in *Aesthetics: A Critical Anthology,* ed. George Dickie and R.J. Sclafani (New York: St. Martin's Press, 1977), 758-82 [orig. 1912].

already to some extent carried out when one looks at their shadows. Note also that these shadows on the sidewalk play no role in ecology and do not fall under the aesthetics of nature, at least as currently conceived.

Benjamin's essay is mainly remembered for its central point that original works of art lose aura in the age of mechanical reproduction. He further holds that mechanical reproductions themselves, for example photographs, cannot have aura. He also thinks that the urge to bring things closer, as happened when working-class people collected images of celebrities in the 1920s and 1930s, involved an elimination of aura. I doubt that photographs are less capable of aura than paintings, and it is more likely that people collected images of celebrities precisely because they had aura. Nor does aura, contra Benjamin, depend on the existence of ritual or cult, as he himself recognized when he spoke of natural aura. However, Benjamin did capture something about the nature of aura when he spoke of "the unique phenomenon of distance," as did Bullough when he also referred to psychological distance when describing experiencing a fog at sea and aesthetic experience in general.

The associated ideas of "aesthetic attitude" and "distancing" are not currently popular in aesthetics. This is largely because they are taken to imply a kind of dualism in which the viewer is seen as ideally detached from the world he or she perceives. However, my account of Bullough's notion of "distancing" is quite different from traditional ones. I interpret it in terms of imaginative perception. In the final chapter I will go into this in detail. Here, I will simply say that, as I see it, there *is* such a thing as the aesthetic attitude, a matter of looking or otherwise sensing in a certain way, and that this attitude tends to generate aesthetic experiences when we take it in approaching everyday phenomena. I will not concern myself here with whether an aesthetic attitude is needed for appreciating art objects, although I suspect that the structure of the artwork itself does much of the work of distancing.[8]

Many attacks on the aesthetic attitude are attacks on formalism insofar as those who advocate the aesthetic attitude are taken to encourage us to dwell on such formal qualities of the object of appreciation as harmonious relations of lines and colours. A classic example of formalism was Clive Bell's view that the art should be defined in terms of what he called "Significant Form" and that "Significant Form" in the context of the visual arts is a matter of certain rela-

---

8   See George Dickie, *Art and the Aesthetic* (Ithaca: Cornell University Press, 1974), for the classic attack on the notion of the aesthetic attitude. See my "Practical George and Aesthete Jerome Meet the Aesthetic Object," *The Southern Journal of Philosophy* 28, no. 1 (1990): 37-53 for a reply.

tions of lines and colours that gives a special aesthetic experience.[9] In my view, the aesthetic attitude is not to be understood as necessarily focusing on formal properties. One may also focus on the symbolic or content-oriented aspects of the object perceived insofar as they give an experience of aura. In the language of Husserl, the aesthetic attitude is the noetic aspect of the experience, the noema of which is the object perceived with its attendant aura.[10]

To avoid possible misunderstanding, I am not using "aura" to refer to what Theosophists believe they can see emanating from persons and things. Theosophist Rudolf Steiner wrote: "The color effects which the 'spiritual eye' can perceive raying out round the physical man and enveloping him like a cloud (somewhat egg-shaped) are called the HUMAN aura."[11] Although I do not believe there are "spiritual eyes" or colour effects of this sort, I suspect this belief is based in part on experience of aura as I have defined it. That is, Theosophists are probably mistaking phenomenological aura for the metaphysical aura they think they see. Unlike its theosophical counterpart, phenomenological aura is not inconsistent with any laws or findings of contemporary science.

I will now give a series of characterizations of "aura," each of which has failings, but each of which also may be helpful in determining its nature. My first inclination is to say that when something has aura it is experienced as having heightened significance. When ordinarily perceived, a shadow is meaningless, but when perceived aesthetically it seems to have more meaning, to have an aura of significance. However, this idea may lead to confusion since "significance" can mean not only having meaning but also having importance, and many things seem or are very important to many people without having aura or being aesthetic in any way. A bear about to attack you has great significance and perhaps no aura at all, at least at that moment.

Similarly, one might be tempted to see "aura" as meaning "valence" i.e., "emotional force or significance, specifically the extent to which an individual is attracted or repelled by an object, event, or person."[12] For example, some sheets drying on a line can have valence, which is to say one could become attracted to looking at them as they take on emotional force or significance.

---

9   Bell, *Art*.
10 Husserl, *Ideas*, 1.
11 Rudolph Steiner, *Theosophy*, 1910, at sacred-texts.com, accessed June 9, 2011, http://www.sacred-texts.com/eso/theo/theo17.htm.
12 *The New Shorter Oxford English Dictionary*, ed. Lesley Brown (Oxford: Clarendon Press, 1993). Thanks to Carolyn Korsmeyer for drawing my attention to this possibility.

However, we can speak of something as having emotional force for someone without knowing anything about the way that person is experiencing that thing. One can just observe her behaviour, noticing that she is attracted to or repelled by the object in question. So having valence is not sufficient for aura.

Another way of describing aura is to say that when something has aura it seems to go beyond itself or be greater than itself. A beautiful man may have aura in that he seems to extend beyond himself, to dominate his space phenomenologically. There is a paradox, however, in the very notion of a thing going beyond itself. For, if it is beyond itself then it is no longer itself. The same goes for something being greater than itself. Perhaps this may be resolved by distinguishing between the object ordinarily seen and the object extraordinarily seen. When it is seen as greater than or beyond itself it is seen as greater than itself ordinarily seen.

The word "aura" comes from the Greek for "breath" or "breeze," and therefore one of its meanings is "a subtle emanation or exhalation."[13] It is also described as "a surrounding glow" which can be extended figuratively to the atmosphere around a person, thing or place. This notion of (metaphorical) breath or glow that emanates from, or at least surrounds, something fits the idea of that thing going beyond itself, hence the main reason I choose the term "aura" as defining aesthetic experience.

To be sure, neither my use of "aura," nor Benjamin's, fits everyday use exactly. Through searching on the Web I have found that the term is most often used in combination with other terms connected by "of." There are many "auras of." Most of these have something aesthetic about them, but some do not. Here are some examples: aura of romance, of elegance, of splendour, of luxury, of beauty, of love, of inaccessibility, of sadism, of daring, of success, of legitimacy, of safety, of faith, of history, of terror, of the uncanny, of disapproval, of menace, of invincibility, of mystery, of love, of uniqueness, of transgression, of high tech, of authenticity, of political corruption, of art, of managerial efficiency, of controversy. There are also adjectival forms, as in divine aura, genteel aura, Wall Street aura.[14] In each case the object said to have a certain aura seems to

---

13 *Shorter OED*, 148. This is the second meaning given after "A gentle breeze, a zephyr." The other meanings given in this paragraph are also from this entry.
14 These examples are given in the *OED*: "1876 Emerson Ess. Ser. ii. i. 28 The condition of true naming, on the poet's part, is his resigning himself to the divine aura which breathes through forms. 1921 Glasgow Herald 25 Aug. 5 The genteel aura of the upper circle. 1959 Economist 27 June 1164/2 No such charges were brought against Mr Strauss, though his Wall Street aura rankles with progressive Democrats."

glow with the named property. This is quite different from saying that it possesses that property. For example, something can have an aura of legitimacy and not be legitimate at all.

Another way of describing aura is to say that when something has aura it seems more real, more alive. We naturally see living things as having some inner power of future actualization: there is more there than meets the eye. Prehistoric and animistic peoples claimed that certain objects possessed a soul. Today we are not so literal, secularists among us even rejecting human souls, and yet there is something of this idea in our notion that something has a power or potentiality.

The idea of vividness as central to aesthetic experience has been explored by D.L. Pole. He argued that there are many varieties of aesthetic experience.[15] Some of the varieties he mentioned had more to do with art than with the everyday. However, one of them was heightened consciousness, such as can happen, for example, through drugs. He then described a non-drug-induced experience of this sort. While working alone late at night a scholar rises from his books "with the feeling that all the world of ordinary objects has acquired, as it were, a new edge, a new depth of quality or vividness."[16] We can say that Pole's scholar is experiencing ordinary objects as having aura.

It would seem at first that the possibility that aura experiences could be induced by drugs would *exclude* them from identification as aesthetic. I do not think it should. Perhaps the impulse to deny that drug experiences can be aesthetic is based on confusing having an aesthetic experience with making a correct aesthetic judgment. An object may be experienced aesthetically under drugs and yet not be deemed correctly to have aesthetic merit. Merit would require that it give rise to aesthetic experience when the subject is *not* drugged. It would also require that at least some others be able to have the experience.

The idea of aura is closely associated with the notion of beauty. Beauty remains the paradigmatic aesthetic concept in the aura conception of aesthetic experience. That which is beautiful is said to "shimmer," "sparkle," "shine," "glisten," "illuminate," and "gleam" all of which are examples of the emanation characteristic of aura.[17] Although all instances of applying aesthetic property terms to things are instances of describing an experience of aura, this is most evident for the properties I have just listed. These exemplify a way in which something can

---

15 D.L. Pole, "Varieties of Aesthetic Experience," *Philosophy* 30, no. 114 (1955): 238-48.
16 Pole, 241.
17 For further discussion of this, see my "Sparkle and Shine."

seem to go beyond itself. Things often have aura when they literally sparkle and shine, and even more often when they metaphorically do so.

My concept of aura owes something to the medieval notion of "claritas," generally translated as splendour, radiance, or shining. Aquinas, for example, thought claritas was essential to beauty. "Shiny" may appear to be just an everyday aesthetic quality, but it has a profound relation to the more complex quality of beauty. I have previously discussed Hegel's special use of the term "shining." He even defined beauty as "the sensible shining of the idea." For him, the sensible in the artwork is elevated to pure shining.[18] The idea may also be applied to the everyday as when things are perceived with the eyes of an artist.

Although aura is what aesthetic properties have in common, in that if a thing has an aesthetic property it has aura, aura itself is perhaps not best referred to as a property. (I have no problem calling it a characteristic.) When something has a property, for example a car having the property of redness, it is supposed to be like some person owning property. Thus "property" implies something that can be added to or subtracted from the thing which has it (hair, for example can gain or lose the property of whiteness), unless of course the property is essential. Aura, however, is not some detachable part of the thing-as-experienced. Rather it is an intensification of that thing or its qualities. (Nor does a thing lose its essential nature when it loses aura.)

Since aura is not a property it is also not a property of a property. It is not the case that each aesthetic property has the property of aura. If that were so then there would be a problem of things having multiple aesthetic properties with multiple auras that would conflict or mix. Only when something has aura can it be said to have an aesthetic property. Aura is what aesthetic properties have in common.[19]

COMPETING THEORIES OF AESTHETIC EXPERIENCE

Another approach to the concept of aura as defining aesthetic experience is to show how the idea is similar to and different from earlier theories of the aesthetic. The idea of aura is, for example, somewhat similar to Monroe Beardsley's idea of intensity, which he sees as a kind of concentration of experience.[20] However, something can be intense and concentrated without

---

18 See John Sallis, *Stone* (Bloomington: Indiana University Press, 1994), 3.
19 Thanks to Stephanie Ross for drawing my attention to this problem.
20 Monroe C. Beardsley, *Aesthetics: Problems in the Philosophy of Criticism* (Indianapolis: Hackett, 1981).

being an aesthetic experience or having aura. I can, for example, feel intense pain, or even pleasure, without aura.

Beardsley also said that an aesthetic experience must have unity. Yet unity is neither necessary nor sufficient for aesthetic experience. Something can have a unity that is quite ordinary. Moreover, fragmented, non-unified things, can have aura, for example a fragment of an ancient sculpture. Unity must give aura to the object to be aesthetic. Still, the notion of unity can be helpful in understanding aura, especially when we are speaking of organic unity. The appropriate notion of unity is captured to some extent in the idea that an organic whole is greater than the sum of its parts.[21] That is, aura happens when we see something as greater than the sum of its parts. "Being greater than a sum of its parts" would be an example of a thing going beyond itself. However, gestalt perceptions are greater than the sums of their parts and not all such perceptions have aura (for example, the diagrams in psychology textbooks illustrating gestalt perceptions do not). So "greater than the sums of their parts" is not sufficient for aura.

Thirdly, Beardsley speaks of aesthetic experiences having complexity, which is to say a diversity of distinct and inter-related parts. Complexity can also contribute to something having aura, and the term "complex" can refer to an aesthetic property. However, some forms of complexity are not aesthetic at all, for example complexity that can give no pleasure or complexity that is not perceivable.

For each of these qualities either they are ordinary descriptions of non-aesthetic things or they are taken aesthetically, and hence are descriptions of aura. Some quality, for example, may increase in intensity, and some object may be more unified, without being more aesthetic, unless the intensity is of an aesthetic quality, or the unity is aesthetic. However, in the latter case that would defeat the purpose of explaining the aesthetic in terms of intensity and unity.

Finally, even when intensity, unity, and complexity are taken together they do not necessarily amount to aesthetic experience, and that is because one can conceive of something having such an experience without having an experience of aura. One can, for example, imagine an artificial intelligence machine that could experience all three, say for the purposes of spying, and yet never have the sense of a thing going beyond itself associated with aura.

---

21 I discuss this in some detail in "Moore and Shusterman on Organic Wholes," *The Journal of Aesthetics and Art Criticism* 49, no. 2 (1991): 63-73.

Still, I do not intend the concept of aura to be very far from traditional aesthetic concepts, or in particular from Beardsley's conception of the aesthetic. I see it as a replacement for previously popular concepts in aesthetics, one that does not have their disadvantages.

The concept of aura recognizes that aesthetic experience is not simply equated with pleasure. There are pleasures that do not involve aura, for example the pleasure we take in the taste of ordinary candy (but not necessarily that which we take in a piece of exquisite Belgian chocolate!). Moreover, aura can sometimes attend experiences of disgust: not the sort of disgust that simply repels us, as in putrid odours, but that which attracts or fascinates.[22] As Carolyn Korsmeyer has said, "A good deal of recondite and sophisticated eating actually seems to be built upon (or even to be a variation of) that which disgusts, endangers, or repels."[23]

Although aura is not an affect it is attended by an affect, either that of pleasure or a special mixture of pleasure and displeasure.[24] Two feelings that attend aura are "fascination" and "interest." When we are fascinated with something it is commonly because it has aura. When we see something as having aura it is fascinating. Although not all interesting things have aura (something can be intellectually or financially interesting and not have aura), all sensuously interesting things do.

Many recent attempts to define the aesthetic have focused on the idea of experiencing a thing as intrinsically valuable or as valuable for its own sake. Jerrold Levinson defines aesthetic pleasure in this way: "pleasure in an object is aesthetic when it derives from apprehension of and reflection on the object's individual character and content, both for itself and in relation to the structural base on which it rests."[25] He also says, "to appreciate something aesthetically is to attend to its forms, qualities, and meanings for their own sakes, and to their interrelations, but also to attend to the way in which all such things emerge from the particular set of low-level perceptual

---

22 Carolyn Korsmeyer, "Delightful, Delicious, Disgusting," *The Journal of Aesthetics and Art Criticism* 60, no. 3 (2002): 217- 25.
23 Korsmeyer, 219.
24 Noël Carroll has raised objections against affect-oriented theories of aesthetic experience in "Aesthetic Experience: A Question of Content," in *Contemporary Debates in Aesthetics and the Philosophy of Art*, ed. Matthew Kieran (Malden, MA: Blackwell, 2006).
25 Jerrold Levinson, "What is Aesthetic Pleasure?" *The Pleasures of Aesthetics* (Ithaca: Cornell University Press, 1996), 6.

features that define the object on a non-aesthetic plane."[26] This theory tells us nothing about the pleasure that comes from this activity. Nor does it tell us why we would feel such pleasure. A scientist might reflect on an object's character and get pleasure from that reflection without that pleasure being aesthetic. Moreover, the concept of "for its own sake" is vague despite its common usage. Levinson probably means by it that, in aesthetic experience, we get pleasure from things as they are in themselves independently of personal considerations or human associations, focusing on intrinsic rather than instrumental values. This may be sometimes valuable, but I do not think it is required for aesthetic experience. Nor is it clear that things are ever valued for their own sake. When we value things we value them in relation to many other things. When I appreciate a piece of driftwood on a beach I may be valuing it in relation to what I can say about it to a friend, to my interest in contemporary art, to the driftwood sculptures of Deborah Butterfield, to my feelings about the beach on which it sits, or to my feelings about nature in general. At most, one can say that sometimes in appreciating something we *feel* that we are appreciating it as valuable in itself.[27]

Noël Carroll agrees with Levinson in focusing on form and content, but considers pleasure unnecessary and eliminates the "for its own sake" clause. He defines an aesthetic experience as "one that involves design appreciation and/or the detection of aesthetic and expressive properties...."[28] He therefore describes his theory as content-oriented, and contrasts it both to theories that are affect-oriented and ones that are axiological (value-oriented).[29] Affect-oriented theories stress experiential qualia. An example is Aquinas's account of aesthetic experience in terms of delight in contemplation. Axiological theories focus on the values gained by aesthetic experience. Levinson's theory is an example. Content-oriented approaches focus on the distinct objects of aesthetic experience. In Carroll's case these objects are design qualities and aesthetic properties (including expressive properties). Some theories combine components from each of these categories.

---

26 Levinson, "Aesthetic Pleasure," 6.
27 Carroll offers his own objection against "valuing for its own sake" on evolutionist grounds, "Aesthetic Experience Revisited," *British Journal of Aesthetics* 42, no. 2 (2002): 145-68, 156.
28 Noël Carroll, "Art and the Domain of the Aesthetic," *British Journal of Aesthetics* 40, no. 2 (2000): 191-208.
29 Carroll, "Revisited," 156.

I agree that design appreciation and detection of aesthetic properties are important to aesthetic appreciation, but I do not think they are definitional. As usual, I will test this theory against the phenomena of everyday aesthetics. It is true that some aesthetic experience of everyday objects involves design appreciation. However, if design appreciation is simply a matter of detection of aesthetic and expressive properties of objects (which seems to be Carroll's view) then a computer which is excellent at detecting properties would count as having aesthetic experience, and that would be false. Carroll seems to think of aesthetic experience as a matter of noticing properties and then valuing them—a rather mechanical conjunction. On my view, these two are not separate moments: the very act of noticing aesthetic properties cannot be detached from that of experiencing something as having aura. Carroll is so concerned to provide a theory that grounds aesthetic judgment objectively he neglects the experience itself. This is intentional on his part, as he questions defining aesthetics in terms of some distinctive phenomenology.

My theory does not fit any of Carroll's theory types. It is not axiological since I reject valuing things for their own sakes. It is not affective since it does not see aura as an affect or experiential feeling-tone. Rather, aura is a characteristic of the object-as-experienced. Finally, it is not content-oriented since it does not accept the strict subjective/objective distinction required for such a theory. Instead, it overlaps all three types. However, since it is phenomenological it is closest to what Carroll refers to as an affect-oriented theory.

Carroll's main argument against affect-oriented theories is based on the assumption that any experience of art is an aesthetic experience and hence if an art experience does not entail some special experiential feeling-tone, for example pleasure, then this shows that such feeling-tones are not necessary for aesthetic experience. He observes that Damien Hirst's artworks (for example, his *Away from the Flock*, 1994, which features a lamb cut in half and placed within a glass box) inspire disgust and hence not pleasure. He also argues that noticing the structure of a Cubist painting can be aesthetic but pleasure-neutral.

Carroll's examples, however, show the problem with his theory. Although there is a disgust element to Hirst's works, those who value experiencing them also gain pleasure from them. There is something meditative and eerie about walking past and around these pieces. Carroll must confuse "pleasure" with "pleasant" in the sense of being merely agreeable. Perhaps he assumes that "pleasure" is defined as the aesthetic affect produced by the aesthetic property of being pleasant. But something does not have to be pleasant to produce pleasure: and this is the case with Hirst's work. "Pleasant" is just one of many aesthetic property terms, whereas pleasure is characteristic of all aesthetically positive experiences. As for the Cubist painting, noticing its structure and gaining no pleasure from this is not an aesthetic experience at all.

Carroll just assumes that if a work of art is the object then the experience is aesthetic. Yet there are many non-aesthetic experiences of works of art, as when they are being shipped from place to place. Also, something can be aesthetically neutral or even aesthetically negative and not be experienced aesthetically. Contra Carroll, one is *not* having an aesthetic experience when forced to endure an inept performance of a Wagnerian opera.[30] An aesthetically negative experience is not an aesthetic experience. Similarly, in nature aesthetics, simply noticing that a tree is "droopy" without any attendant pleasure is not (contra Carroll) having an aesthetic experience. You can also notice that rotten fruit is "disgusting" without the experience being aesthetic. As mentioned in the last chapter, if you say that something is aesthetic no one assumes you could mean that it is aesthetically negative.

Carroll argues that we can aesthetically appreciate a realist novel, for example Zola's *Germinal*, and that this is a counter-example to affect-oriented theories. One such theory says that aesthetic experience is characterized by an emotional response of felt release from worldly concerns. Yet, as Carroll argues, realist novels often require an experience in the reader of being trapped and oppressed by social conditions.[31] I agree that the affect-oriented theory described by Carroll fails to capture the aesthetic experience of a realist novel. However, Carroll's own description also fails to capture it since one would not believe it was a good novel unless the feelings of oppression involved were themselves situated within a larger pleasurable whole. One of the nice features of aura theory is that it allows for aura to emerge out of what Carroll calls a plunge "into the practical flow of life" every bit as much as from escaping that flow. This it why aura theory its particularly appropriate for everyday aesthetics. Aura is not a release from the everyday. However, it *is* a release from the mundane or boring aspects of the everyday. What aura theory provides is what Eaton and Moore have

---

30 Carroll, "Revisited," 152.
31 Carroll, "Revisited," 152.

argued Carroll leaves out, i.e., the "filled with a sense of wonder" aspect of aesthetic experience.[32]

Gary Iseminger shares with me an interest in defining the aesthetic in terms of phenomenology.[33] Unlike Husserl, however, Iseminger understands phenomenology as dealing with a subjective state, as talking about a specific aesthetic state of mind. He calls that state of mind "appreciation," and says that "[s]omeone is appreciating a state of affairs just in case she or he is valuing for its own sake the experiencing of that state of affairs."[34] Aside from the problems with "valuing for its own sake" which I have already addressed, this theory, in requiring the valuing of experiencing, is needlessly self-conscious. This requirement might be useful for works of art but not for objects of everyday experience. I do not need to value the *experiencing* of my backyard garden in order to value it aesthetically. Also, although Iseminger rightly attacks Carroll for thinking that the aesthetic state of mind is *just* a matter of tracking properties, his own theory is not that different from Carroll's insofar as, for him, aesthetic experience is the state of mind in which tracking properties is itself found valuable for its own sake. However, what Iseminger finds valuable is a state of mind, i.e., the mental activity of tracking, rather than the properties tracked. Of course one *can* find valuable a state of mind that happens when tracking things (I might for instance value the state of mind I get into when tracking the disintegration of a log burning in my fireplace), but this is only one sort of aesthetic experience, and an unusual one at that. Normally we are not so self-reflective in aesthetic experience. We are mainly interested in the aesthetic quality of the fire itself, and only rarely in the state of mind we get into when we notice that quality. So, although I agree with his move to phenomenology, I think he has lost something valuable in Carroll's account, i.e., the emphasis on aesthetic properties themselves. Husserl's phenomenology does not neglect the noematic aspect of intentionality and in that way is superior to Iseminger's. What makes the state of mind involved in tracking (or, rather, "contemplating," as the term "tracking" really implies a process that is too mechanical) certain aesthetic properties *aesthetic* is that the properties are experienced with aura. That is, aura theory explains and subsumes the experience Iseminger describes.

---

32 Marcia Muelder Eaton and Ronald Moore, "Aesthetic Experience: Its Revival and Its Relevance to Aesthetic Education," *Journal of Aesthetic Education* 36, no. 2 (2002): 9-23, 14.
33 Gary Iseminger, "The Aesthetic State of Mind," *Contemporary Debates*, 98-110.
34 Iseminger, "State of Mind," 99.

ADVANTAGES TO AURA THEORY

In comparison with the other theories of aesthetic experience reviewed above, there are several advantages to the idea of aura as defining aesthetic experience. First, it includes both the noetic and the noematic aspect of experience, both the experiencing of the object and the object-as-experienced, whereas Iseminger and Carroll each emphasize only one side.

Second, aura covers other positive aesthetic qualities than beauty, although beauty remains the central concept of aesthetics. Something that has grace, delicacy, charm, or some other aesthetic quality has aura. And, as I have argued, negative aesthetic qualities can also have aura.

Third, experiences of aura can be situated on a continuum of intensity. We can speak of a low level of aura, as when a room looks brighter when it is cleaned. There are mid-level experiences, for instance when a baseball throw is considered graceful. We can even speak of high levels, as when the starry heavens are experienced as sublime. Sublime experience can also happen with a simple everyday object, a point I will explore in the last chapter.

Fourth, and related to the third point, the concept covers the best aspects of the idea that imagination is central to aesthetic experience. The experience of aura at its most intense level is described by Kant when he says that in fine art the symbol is what he calls "an aesthetic idea" and that aesthetic ideas seem unending in their reverberations. Kant believed that the productive imagination of the genius artist creates another world ("a second nature out of the material supplied to it by actual nature").[35] When something, and not just a work of fine art (contra Kant), has aura in this extremely intense way it seems to point to another world. Proust's madeleine is such an object which I will discuss in the last chapter. However, this also happens in somewhat less intense situations, as in the account I gave at the beginning of this chapter of experiencing tree shadows on pavement when I said that they seem to inhabit another world. Through this Kantian connection, we can see that aura applies not only to beauty but to the sublime. Sublime objects are charged with even greater significance and intensity than we find in more ordinary objects experienced with aura.

A fifth advantage is that, contra Kant this time, it is not required that one be disinterested to experience an aesthetic object as having aura. However, I am not opposed to disinterestedness or distancing as a strategy for achieving aesthetic experience. Perhaps the idea of disinterestedness lives on in the notion

---

35 Kant, *Judgment* #49, 176.

that insofar as one is experiencing aura one is not focused on how the object in question can be used for other non-aesthetic projects.

A sixth advantage, related to the fifth, is that the claim does not imply anything about how the aura comes about, whether through contemplation, the aesthetic attitude, the aesthetic point of view, losing oneself, or by concentrating on certain features in the aesthetic object. Although all of these strategies can be useful, we also have spontaneous aesthetic experiences that are not preceded by any strategy.

A seventh advantage is that there is no necessary connection between aura and formalism. Although Clive Bell may have been right that certain relations of lines and colours give us an experience of aesthetic emotion, there are many other ways to gain aesthetic emotion. Still, when we experience something as having aura it does seem as though we are, to use Bell's phrase, "lifted above the stream of life."[36] Paradoxically this is also an experience of being more alive. Experiencing something, even an ordinary thing, as having aura is experiencing it as being more real, more authentic, and more alive (in the metaphorical sense of that term) because lifted out of mere ordinariness.

Aura is not *in* me but in the object-as-I-experience-it. This is subjective in one sense, but it is not merely personal. Thus it is not unreasonable for me to expect at least some others to experience something as having aura when I do. Nor is it unreasonable for me to expect something that has had aura one time to have it again later. Most things are not experienced with aura most of the time, but just about everything could be experienced with aura. Not every object *is* aesthetic, but every object *could be*. When ordinary things are experienced aesthetically they are experienced as having aura. Anything beautiful has aura. However, there are also low-level examples of aura, i.e., of a clean room. When we experience something as standing apart, as visually or aurally interesting, or when we experience a smell or taste as evocative or rich, then we have an experience of aura in everyday life. I am walking down a street and see a brick pathway leading down through greenery to a house situated between the road and the creek: the scene is visually interesting, magical in a way, worth dwelling on a bit: it has aura.

AGAINST NON-AESTHETIC DEPENDENCE THEORY

There is a deep assumption, common in contemporary analytic aesthetics, which stands in the way of aura theory and its expansion of terms considered

---

36 Bell, 26.

aesthetic. Once this assumption is overcome it will be possible to talk about a much larger range of aesthetic terms. It is commonly said by analytic aestheticians that aesthetic features depend on non-aesthetic features. The technical term for this idea is "supervenience theory." Supervenience has been defined in this way: "A set of properties A supervenes upon another set B just in case no two things can differ with respect to A-properties without also differing with respect to their B-properties."[37] This idea is used in a variety of philosophical subdisciplines. Its main use in aesthetics is to claim that aesthetic properties supervene on the physical properties of the thing considered: the aesthetic properties can't change unless the physical properties change. Some philosophers who advocate supervenience theory argue for a larger supervenience base than physical properties. For example, some people believe that cultural background can be included in the supervenience base, although it is usually thought that this cultural background itself supervenes on a physical base. However, whether the base is narrowly physical or broad enough so as to include personal or cultural factors, the general move of supervenience theorists is to claim that aesthetic properties fully depend on non-aesthetic properties. This claim has usually been made about art, but may also be applied to everyday aesthetics. It is generally thought that this dependence provides some objectivity in aesthetic judgments. I will argue here that this move is both unnecessary and harmful.

Supervenience theory is often seen as an alternative to reductionism. In aesthetics, supervenience theorists often look back to the somewhat similar theories of Frank Sibley. Sibley argued that aesthetic judgments are never supported by reference to non-aesthetic features, that they are not condition-governed.[38] However, Sibley still believed that non-aesthetic qualities within works of art (and presumably within non-art aesthetic objects) *make* them have aesthetic features—that aesthetic qualities *depend on* non-aesthetic qualities. One of the most problematic features of this theory is that it relies on the dubious idea that there is a clear division between aesthetic and non-aesthetic terms.

Analytic aestheticians do not universally accept this division. A few years

---

37 Brian McLaughlin and Karen Bennett, "Supervenience," in *Stanford Encyclopedia of Philosophy* (2005), accessed June 10, 2011, http://plato.stanford.edu/entries/supervenience/.
38 Frank N. Sibley, "Aesthetic Concepts," in *Art and Philosophy: Readings in Aesthetics*, ed. W.E. Kennick (New York: St. Martin's Press, 1979), 542-64. Originally, *Philosophical Review* 68 (1959): 421-50.

ago Marcia Eaton provided an argument against it and against supervenience theory. As she put it, "which properties figure in aesthetic attributions is a culture-bound matter. If loudness or yellowness or cylindricality or design (all candidates for base properties in most supervenient systems) is a property of an object and if it is considered worthy of attention or reflection in a culture and if a viewer shares the traditions of that culture and if the viewer assents to 'That object is loud (or yellow, etc.),' then that viewer appreciates the object aesthetically (to some degree)."[39] She thinks aestheticians have failed to notice simple aesthetic properties because they have focused on complex properties such as "balanced" and "unified." She notes in a later book how physical-sensory properties may be used aesthetically. For example, the term "loud" can be a positive aesthetic quality, as when someone says that a musical work was wonderfully loud.[40] Supervenience of aesthetic on physical properties may be refuted by the fact there are often aesthetic differences between physically identical objects based on differences in history, context, surroundings, title, and interpretation of the viewers. As Eaton says, "even if we could identify the set of base properties [on which aesthetic properties are supposed to supervene], it is possible for two things to be exactly alike with respect to base properties and for it still to be the case that one is F and one is not-F."

Eaton's point also applies to other objects of aesthetic experience, whether they are handled by the aesthetics of natural environments or are objects of everyday aesthetics. Examples of the latter might include persons' faces, household utensils, and shadows on the street. In agreeing with Eaton I do not deny that aesthetic objects can have such physical properties as weight, and that these properties exist independently of their being experienced. Nor do I deny that one can also be aware of or attend to physical properties of the same object that one appreciates aesthetically, for example paying attention to the chemical composition of a paint-brush stroke for the purpose of determining age. Nor do I deny that aesthetic properties would be changed if physical properties are changed. What I deny is that there are some aspects of aesthetic objects, *as experienced*, upon which aesthetic properties depend.

---

39 Marcia Muelder Eaton, "The Intrinsic, Non-Supervenient Nature of Aesthetic Properties," *The Journal of Aesthetics and Art Criticism* 52, no. 4 (1994): 383-406, 390. See also her "Intention, Supervenience, and Aesthetic Realism," *British Journal of Aesthetics* 38, no. 3 (1998): 179-293, 290.
40 Marcia Eaton, *Merit, Aesthetic and Ethical* (New York: Oxford University Press, 2001), Chapter 3, "The Nature of Aesthetic Properties," 41.

Sibley thinks that critics get us to perceive aesthetic qualities by mentioning or pointing to non-aesthetic features. For example, a critic might say "This line gives it vitality." However, contra Sibley, when something like this is said, the reference to the line is not directed to something non-aesthetic. If it were, it could not support an aesthetic attribution. Perhaps it *seems* that "line" refers to something non-aesthetic since someone who does not see the line aesthetically might look in the same place as someone who does and that person may seem to be talking about the same thing. Perhaps it would be better for the perceiver to say "If you saw this line aesthetically you would see how it gives the painting vitality." However, when he or she says "This line gives it vitality" he or she is *not* saying, "If you looked at this line *non*-aesthetically you would see how it gives the painting vitality." Yet, this is precisely what the dependence theorist thinks he or she is saying. Or consider a case in which one person says a wall looks great and says this is because it has a colour she loves and because of the way it makes the wall contrast with other walls around it: isn't she just drawing attention to a physical feature of the wall? My answer is no. She is basing one aesthetic attribution on something else aesthetic, i.e., the attractiveness of the colour, particularly in its context (i.e., in relation to the colours of the other walls).

Thus, I would argue, contra Sibley and contemporary supervenience theorists, that aesthetic judgments are *never* supported by reference to non-aesthetic features. The point is similar to Hume's idea that we cannot derive "ought," or value statements, from "is," or factual statements. It is based on a claim about word-meaning. If I say that this house is beautiful partly because it is a big house, and this is at all convincing, I am using *big* in an aesthetic sense. Mere bigness (in some non-aesthetic sense) is not enough to provide a reason for aesthetic goodness in a house. Using the term *big* in this instance draws on our experiences of other things as "big" in an aesthetically positive way. An example of this is that the Nilotes of Southern Sudan take a strong aesthetic interest in their cattle, and one of the most important aesthetic features, for them, is the bigness of the cattle.[41]

John Searle has questioned Hume's position, claiming that you *can* derive ought from is.[42] The problem with Searle's strategy is that he imports norma-

---

41 See Jeremy Coote, "'Marvels of Everyday Vision': The Anthropology of Aesthetics and the Cattle-Keeping Nilotes," in *Anthropology, Art, and Aesthetics*, ed. Jeremy Coote and Anthony Shelton (Oxford: Clarendon Press, 1994), 245-73, 254.
42 Hume, *Treatise*. John Searle, "How to Derive 'Ought' From 'Is'," *Philosophical Review* 73, no. 1 (1964): 43-58.

tive material into his "is" dimension. He rightly says that promising something entails obligation. But the institution of promising is already normative, and oddly, Searle proves this himself through his analysis of the concept of "promise." Similarly, one cannot argue from the fact that incest tends to increase genetic disease to the immorality of incest. Of course, one can derive a hypothetical ought from something that is. For example, you can claim that if you want to decrease genetic disease it is a good idea to avoid incest. But this is not morality.

Since Sibley insisted that aesthetic terms like "delicate" can also have non-aesthetic uses, he should also have admitted that so-called non-aesthetic terms, like "big" could have aesthetic uses. He should have realized that the reason that critics can get us to see aesthetic properties by pointing out certain non-aesthetic features in works of art is that those so-called non-aesthetic features are really aesthetic. The critic leads us from something aesthetic and simple to something aesthetic and complex. Aesthetic concepts cannot be applied according to a rule because the reasons offered in support of aesthetic concept attributions, although they may appear to be directed to describing non-aesthetic qualities, are actually describing aesthetic qualities, albeit often low-level ones. Supervenience theorists might think they avoid this argument since if A supervenes on B then A cannot be derived from B, and so the issue is not one of derivability. However, Sibley's theory is not about derivation either. The problem remains that supervenience theorists assume that something can be appealed to that is underneath the aesthetic: that the aesthetic is based on something non-aesthetic, although not reducible to it.

Recently we have seen an attempt to defend supervenience theory by broadening the supervenience base to include contextual factors.[43] Nick Zangwill seeks to go beyond narrow non-aesthetic properties such as intrinsic primary properties to allow in relational properties such as historical ones as part of the supervenience base. Yet as soon as one is willing to broaden the supervenience base there is no reason why the broadening needs to be limited to a narrow conception of context. Context may also include not simply the context of the work's immediate production and reception but also the context of its ongoing production (as in production of instances of the work as in various productions of plays) and reception. However, once this happens (and I would have no

---

43 Nick Zangwill, *The Metaphysics of Beauty* (Ithaca: Cornell University Press, 2001). See especially Chapter 3, "Aesthetic Supervenience Defended."

problem with it) the whole point of supervenience theory, which is to ground aesthetic judgments objectively, is lost.

Moreover, when Zangwill says that "[s]omething can be elegant in virtue of its smooth and curving lines, but not any smooth curving lines will determine elegance; they have to be smooth and curving in exactly that way"[44] he almost concedes the point, as the exact way is aesthetic, and hence the appeal to something non-aesthetic (i.e., something calculable) fails. There is no reason to go along with him in saying that "nonaesthetic properties are responsible for aesthetic properties"[45] if he can give no instance, as he admits, of knowing that a thing has a non-aesthetic property and then being able to infer from that that it has an aesthetic property. Recognizing this, he says that supervenience theory is a "framework principle," i.e., an "a priori presupposition of aesthetic thought."[46] This implies that one could not think about aesthetic matters without presupposing supervenience theory, which I have shown is false.

Rejecting supervenience opens the field of aesthetics dramatically. It is noteworthy that Zangwill thinks that his theory gets us back to "the good old days" in which "aestheticians did not worry about daintiness, dumpiness, elegance, balance, and the rest."[47] My theory encourages the good new days in which aestheticians can talk about a wide variety of aesthetic properties once relegated to the non-aesthetic realm. We are not committed, as Sibley was, to saying that certain terms used to describe features of works of art, terms like "darker" or "straight," are strictly non-aesthetic terms. In opening up the field of aesthetic terms, we reveal the vast domain of the everyday aesthetic that often underlies the traditionally-conceived set of aesthetic terms. This also has implications for aesthetics generally, including the aesthetics of art.

CONCLUSION

Aesthetic experience is one of the central concepts of aesthetics. In this chapter I developed my own view of aesthetic experience, one that does not limit the concept to art objects. Rather, I defined aesthetic experience in terms of experience of objects with aura. Aura is a phenomenological quality I find common to all aesthetic experiences. I developed the notion of aura not by

---

44 Zangwill, *Metaphysics*, 45.
45 Zangwill, *Metaphysics*, 39.
46 Zangwill, *Metaphysics*, 39.
47 Zangwill, *Metaphysics*, 41.

defining it in terms of necessary and sufficient conditions but by characterizing it broadly, defining it in a rough way, and then giving a series of metaphors that limit possible misinterpretations. This view is quite different from recent theories of aesthetic experience, in particular those of Carroll and Levinson. Moreover, although aura theory is like Iseminger's in being phenomenological, it shares with Carroll an interest in aesthetic properties. It can do this because it is phenomenological in the Husserlian sense, i.e., in that it brackets the objective/subjective distinction that Iseminger accepts. I then gave seven advantages to aura theory. One advantage is that it allows us to know whether a term is being used aesthetically. Something standing in the way of everyday aesthetics is supervenience theory or the idea that aesthetic designations depend on non-aesthetic truths. This would have the effect of limiting the extension of aesthetic terms required for an everyday aesthetics. However, supervenience theory, at least as applied in aesthetics, is insupportable. In the next chapter I will look at specific examples of aesthetic terms in relation to everyday aesthetics.

CHAPTER 5

A Bestiary of Aesthetic Terms for Everyday Contexts

Part of the fun of everyday aesthetics is working one's way through the vocabulary of praise and disgust to explore terms not often discussed in the aesthetics literature. Most of these terms have applications with the fine and popular arts as well. However, they are often neglected because they are seen not to be very serious. Philosophers' interest in these terms is different from that of lexicographers. Although a dictionary might sometimes be a starting point for investigation, the main philosophical interest is in seeing how reflection on such terms might shed light on traditional problems in aesthetics and sometimes more generally in philosophy itself. I here propose something like a bestiary of such terms, drawing out whatever lessons their investigation might have. This process was initiated at the end of first chapter and will be pursued beyond the current chapter as we look into the aesthetics of neatness and messiness and of the everyday sublime in the final two chapters.

Each of these terms has many uses only some of which are aesthetic. As I observed in the last chapter, determining whether the use is aesthetic is a matter of determining whether the object to which the term is applied is experienced as having aura. Many terms can be used either positively or negatively. However, most have a tendency towards one direction or the other, for example "neatness" tends to positive and "messiness" to negative. Most positive terms have negative correlates if not actual opposites, for example "beautiful" and "ugly," "graceful" and "graceless," "bright" and "sombre." There are also terms that denote purely non-aesthetic experience, for example "dull," "boring," and "ordinary." In most uses of such terms nothing aesthetic is implied. They are the concern of aesthetics only in that aesthetics must talk about them. The matter is different for the negative. Negative aesthetic terms, and negative aesthetic use of any term, pose an interesting problem for aura theory. In the last chapter I suggested that the ugly would be aesthetic insofar and to the extent that it combined pleasure and pain. However, what of ugliness that provokes only displeasure? Is such ugliness outside the realm of the aesthetic in the same way that the boring is? Well, it could be argued that even the most unpleasant form of ugliness has a quality of heightened experience. It seems to go beyond itself, to have a kind of aura. Although pleasure may be absent there may be a certain fascination present.

Perhaps this issue will be resolved further when we get into discussion of individual aesthetic terms. Let us proceed now to our bestiary. The list of terms that follows is by no means exhaustive. I have mainly focused on ones that have posed interesting problems in aesthetics. The point is to have some philosophical fun in the new field that has been opened up.

FUN

Two candidates for the set of aesthetic terms are "fun" and "funny." "Fun" has almost never been mentioned as a term of aesthetics. An exception is in the work of philosopher John Morreall, who argues for the aesthetic importance of humour.[1] Fun things might best be seen as a subset of things that are liked or pleasant. The word "fun" is strongly associated with jokes and jocularity, but you can have fun without laughter. Morreall notes that babies do most things because it is fun to do so. The concept is also of great importance in the aesthetic lives of children and teens, and continues as a somewhat less important aspect of adult aesthetic experience.

Artist and art critic Julian Bell has some interesting things to say about "fun." Not surprisingly, Bell (whose uncle was the famous critic Clive Bell) is more interested in application of the term in the arts than in everyday life.[2] Bell says that what we call fun includes images that we cannot take seriously.

---

1   John Morreall, "Humor and Aesthetic Education," *Journal of Aesthetic Education* 15, no. 1 (1981): 55-70.
2   Julian Bell, *What is Painting: Representation and Modern Art* (New York: Thames and Hudson, 1999), 200.

These include works we might call "pretty" and others that try to be art but fail. Although Bell is right that "fun" is sometimes a put-down in the visual arts, he fails to see that sometimes we call successful works of art fun, for example some cases of deconstructivist architecture, and certain films.

Yet one of the main reasons "fun" is not studied in aesthetics is that it is not generally considered a valuable term of praise for art. Nor do we use it to refer to the aesthetic phenomena of nature. Although one can certainly have fun in nature, as in skiing, fishing, or just taking a walk, one does not refer to a mountain and a river as fun except in relation to these activities. The term "fun" is applied mainly to activities, for example play, amusement, and entertainment, although it may also be applied to things, for example jokes. There are shocking uses of the term, as when Vittorio Mussolini, the Italian dictator's son, thought that the look of a bomb falling in the midst of horsemen was "exceptionally good fun."[3] Regardless of their morally abhorrent nature, all of these applications of the term take place within the domain of everyday aesthetics.[4] Although aestheticians seldom discuss the concept of fun, it is not totally neglected. For example, two writers for a consumer studies journal see it as central to our understanding of consumption.[5]

There is a problem with such double terms as "looks fun" and "sounds fun." Unlike "looks good" and "sounds good," these may just be predictions of aesthetic and other delights to come, rather than evaluations of something immediate. To say that something "looks fun" is to say "it looks like this will be fun in the future" or "it looks like it would be fun if I did it too." Actually, "looks good" can have this predictive meaning too. The difference is that "looks fun" is probably merely predictive, whereas "looks good" can be directly evaluative as well.

Perhaps "fun," just by itself, is an aesthetic quality. It is a quality of an activity that involves pleasure. However, as we have seen, "giving pleasure" is not enough for something to be aesthetic. Fun probably only fits the broadest definition of the aesthetic, the one that defines beauty as pleasure gained in the mere appre-

---

3   Emmanuel Chapman, "Beauty and the War," *The Journal of Aesthetics and Art Criticism* 2, no. 6 (1942): 61-67.
4   See Johan Huizinga, *Homo Ludens* (Boston: Beacon Press, 1955) and Hilde Hein, "Play as an Aesthetic Concept," *The Journal of Aesthetics and Art Criticism* 27, no. 1 (1968): 67-71 for further comments on "fun."
5   Morris B. Holbrook and Elizabeth C. Hirschman, "The Experiential Aspects of Consumption: Consumer Fantasies, Feelings, and Fun," *The Journal of Consumer Research* 9, no. 2 (1982): 132-40.

hension of something. Someone, however, might argue that the term "apprehension" implies some sort of understanding, which fun does not require, and may even inhibit. Yet, if we do not insist on this interpretation of "apprehension," the sentence "That amusement ride was fun" might well be an aesthetic judgment based at least on the minimalist definition derived from Aquinas.

But can it meet a more robust definition of the aesthetic like Dewey's, Beardsley's, or most importantly, my own concept of aura? Based on my last chapter, my own view would be that when the term is applied in such a way that the object of the experience has aura in my sense, then it is aesthetic. Certainly to say that something or some experience is fun can mean that it has a heightened significance, that it is more alive, that it seems to emanate meaning, and so forth. However, this would require distinguishing between "fun" used in a very ordinary way and "fun" used to express something special.

Fun is attacked by Marxist aesthetician Theodor Adorno as not even a form of pleasure. On his view, it is a simulacrum of pleasure, a form of escapism promoted by the culture industry.[6] Perhaps Adorno had his own very narrow sense of "fun" in mind since the point does not correspond to the usual uses of the term. Chimps clearly have fun when they play, and this implies that fun is not dependent entirely on the culture industry. A child who swings on a swing is having fun, but this activity equally does not seem something promoted by the culture industry. Nor is fun that depends on the culture industry necessarily a bad thing. (And how does one tell a simulacrum of pleasure from the real thing, anyway?) However, Adorno may be giving us a hint at how to distinguish between "fun" applied in a non-aesthetic way, and "fun" applied aesthetically. Perhaps non-aesthetic fun includes mere escapism promoted by the culture industry.

Fun is more important as an aesthetic concept for some countries or regions than others. Yi-Fu Tuan writes that the "American aesthetic appears at times to be driven by a sense of fun," and he refers specifically to a "folksy fondness for the extremes, the eye-catching, the amusing, and the grotesque."[7] He is no doubt thinking of such oddities in American vernacular architecture as buildings in the shapes of ducks, dinosaurs, and hats. Yuriko Saito judges the act of opening a Japanese package as especially fun-filled. In doing so, she treats fun as an aesthetic value.[8]

---

6   For the last, see Erica Weitzman, "No Fun: Aporias of Pleasure in Adorno's Aesthetic Theory," *German Quarterly* 81, no. 2 (2008): 185-202.
7   Tuan, *Strange*, 144.
8   Yuriko Saito, "Japanese Aesthetics of Packaging," *The Journal of Aesthetics and Art Criticism* 57, no. 2 (1999): 257-65.

Fun has been a strongly positive aesthetic quality for many artists in their art practice. As Bell observes, the Cubists' making collage from newsprint, the Dadaists' appropriations, Mondrian's allusions to jazz, Pollock's references to child's play in his action paintings, and Rauschenberg's use of junk-yard materials, all are oriented in some way to fun. Indeed, Pop Art, for example in the work of Roy Lichtenstein, seems mainly to be about fun, both in subject matter and in the way it works with materials. Bell refers to late twentieth-century painting as "a progressive encroachment of the realm once considered as art by materials one considered as fun."[9] Likewise, Northern Californian artists over the last fifty years have often focused on fun. Examples include Roy De Forest with his joyous colourful dogs and Wayne Thiebaud with his bubble-gum machines. Architecture also often takes fun as a topic or motif: Art Deco and Postmodern Architecture are salient examples.

Some might have a problem with "fun" as an aesthetic term since it does not seem much like such classic and paradigmatic aesthetic terms as "beautiful" and "sublime." A response to this would be to say that aesthetics has levels: "fun," "pretty," "clean," and "ordered" are relatively simple, surface-oriented aesthetic concepts, whereas "beautiful," "sublime," "elegant," are more complex and multi-layered.

The concept of "fun" makes us think of the amusement park and the world of games. This leads us to other everyday aesthetic qualities related to this world, for example "thrilling," and "exciting." They can be applied to a wide variety of things beyond the amusement park. For example, one might find the new fall fashions thrilling, and a four-year old will usually find a birthday party exciting. We also use these terms in the contexts of fine arts and natural beauty appreciation.

TRAGIC

Göran Hermerén in his elaborate classification of aesthetic terms does not mention "fun," but does include "funny." He ties that concept with "moving," "tragic," "comic," and "shocking" as "reaction qualities."[10] This collection works as well for everyday aesthetics as for art aesthetics: we often find everyday events tragic, moving, comic, or shocking.

---

9   Saito, "Packaging," 204.
10 Göran Hermerén, "The Variety of Aesthetic Qualities" in *Aesthetic Quality and Aesthetic Experience*, ed. Michael H. Mitias (Amsterdam: Rudolpi, 1988), 11-23.

However, this is problematic. Let's focus on the terms "tragic" and "shocking," although similar points could be made about the other "reaction qualities." If you say that something in everyday life is tragic, you are expressing a kind of sadness, an experience of pain. There is nothing particularly pleasurable to a person with ordinary moral sensibilities in contemplating an *actual* plane crash or a young person's death, and those few who do find such contemplation pleasurable do not generally refer to the phenomenon as "tragic." Whether or not a tragic event is going to be tragic in the aesthetic sense will depend on whether it has aura as I defined it, whether for example it fascinates.

Of course anything can be perceived aesthetically, including tragic events, but the question is whether the term "tragic" can be an aesthetic term when applied in everyday life. I will argue that it can be. First, a framework for its application is provided by Aristotle. Although Aristotle developed his concept of tragedy in relation to tragic plays, many of the ideas he uses may also be applied to tragic events in a way that is aesthetic.[11] For example, we can speak of a tragic event as having a beginning, middle and end, as being an organic whole, as having a protagonist who suffered from hubris, and so on. Although many non-dramatic tragedies fail initially to have these qualities they often take them on as they are remembered or recounted later. We might speak of a story that someone tells about a tragic event as itself tragic, and by this we mean that it has an aesthetically tragic quality. (The event may have an aesthetically tragic quality, but stories about the event may have this in even greater degree.) Indeed, the very existence of "tragic" as an aesthetic quality within certain art forms, most notably in tragic plays, is based ultimately on a prior existence of this quality in non-art phenomena, especially in stories, whether told publicly in news media or privately amongst friends. A story we tell about a tragic event is an imitation of an action, many of the elements of which can be matched to Aristotle's parts of tragedy, for example that it is made up of incidents that are serious, that the agents have a certain character that compels them to act in certain ways, that decisions are expressed in speeches that manifest thought, and that the recounting may involve catharsis of pity and fear. It is not uncommon for people to speak of the life of Lady Diana, for instance, as a tragedy, and to find accounts of her life fascinating because of this. Spectacle may even be an element of a tragic event. There is, for example, the spectacle of a terrorist

---

11 Aristotle, *The Poetics of Aristotle*, trans. Preston H. Epps (Chapel Hill: The University of North Carolina Press, 1970).

attack. There is also spectacle in natural disasters and disasters that are the result of human error. Although this use of "spectacle" does not fit Aristotle's notion of spectacle as the business of the stage designer and costume-maker, it does fit the more contemporary idea of spectacle as grand display.[12]

SHOCKING, FRIGHTENING AND SAD

The term "shocking" is similar to "tragic" in that to call something shocking literally is usually not to make an aesthetic attribution. "Shocking" is generally a term of moral disapproval. However, it is also often used as a term of aesthetic approval with respect to pulp fiction and movies. Here, "it will shock you!" is high praise. It is also often used as a term of aesthetic disapproval with respect, for example, although perhaps ironically, to someone's clothing ensemble.

"Frightening," similarly, is a term of aesthetic praise mainly within the context of fiction. However, it does have everyday applications. A Halloween mask might be praised aesthetically because it is frightening, or better, because it looks frightening, but not if real fear is aroused.

A somewhat similar point can be made about the term "sad." Yet it is hard to imagine a context in which "those flowers look sad" would be aesthetic praise when directed to actual flowers. This is true even though sentences like "the music was so sad" or "that story was sad" can be examples of positive aesthetic judgment in the arts. On the other hand "looks sad" can be a term of aesthetic disapproval, as of a poorly put together Christmas display. It can also be a term of aesthetic approval when applied to certain types of dogs in a dog show. It is not an aesthetic claim however to say a dog looks sad and mean that one thinks that the dog actually is sad (as when its owner has left him home alone).

The opposite of sad, "happy," can also be an aesthetic property, as when we say that certain colours are a "happy combination" or when we say "look at that happy child" and are drawing attention to pleasure that can be taken in the child's look.

SEXY AND SENSUOUS

If "looks great" is an aesthetic quality, then so too is "looks sexy," as well as "smells sexy," "feels sexy," and "sounds sexy." We can add some other items to

---

12 Thanks to my students Amy Diep and Vanessa Estrada for their comments on this.

this list, like "erotic," and "romantic," as in "feels erotic," or "sounds romantic." Consider the wife who comes home to a candlelit dinner and exclaims "How romantic!" True, there are many other factors that go into this exclamation.[13] However, it is, at least in part, an exclamation in response to a certain display that pleases the senses and the imagination, i.e., pleases in the apprehension of it.

One could even say that there is a broad sub-field of everyday aesthetics: the aesthetics of sex.[14] This field covers not only the aesthetic qualities of sexual activity but also the issues surrounding sexual attractiveness. The idea that sexual love is in response to beauty is quite common, going back long before Plato. Freud thought that "the conception of the 'beautiful' is rooted in the soil of sexual stimulation and signified originally that which is sexually exciting."[15] This of course was contrary to Plato's view, as expressed through Socrates' dialogue with Diotima in the *Symposium*, that sexual attraction was only the first stage on the ladder of love which reaches towards Beauty itself. Many of the same qualities featured as aesthetic in the arts are also found to be aesthetically attractive in potential sex partners, for example grace, delicacy, elegance. In both areas certain lines, colours and shapes are praised. Writers on these matters have often worried over whether the appreciation is purely sexual or aesthetic (Clive Bell rejected beauty as an aesthetic quality because he thought it was associated with sex.[16]), although how one separates the two is not clear.

The aesthetics of sex brings to our attention various qualities that have to do specifically with the sense of touch. For example, the term "gentle" is usually aesthetically positive in the domains of sex and of touch in general. A gentle touch may give us pleasure simply in its apprehension. "Gentle movements" and "gentle manners" also come to mind.

A related term is "sensuous." It emphasizes that the sense qualities of the object, whether of sight, sound, smell, taste, or touch, provide a kind of rich pleasure: "What a sensuous experience, to bite into this apple!" "Sensual" is similar. However, as Berleant observed in 1964, although the sensuous is often

---

13 John Austin, *How To Do Things with Words*, ed. J.O. Urmson (Oxford: Clarendon, 1962).
14 For an early discussion see Hugo G. Beigel, "Sex and Human Beauty," *The Journal of Aesthetics and Art Criticism*, Special Issue on Symbolism and Creative Imagination, 12, no. 1 (1953): 83-92.
15 Sigmund Freud, *Three Contributions to the Theory of Sex*, accessed Aug. 2, 2011, http://www.gutenberg.org/ebooks/14969.
16 Bell, *Art*.

(reluctantly) accepted in aesthetics, the "sensual," which is more related to bodily pleasures, particularly the sexual, is not.[17] He rightly sought to allow the sensual as well as the sensuous into aesthetics.

DELICIOUS, TASTY, YUMMY

We should also mention some features of the aesthetics of food. The term "tastes good" has already been mentioned. The term "delicious" generally marks the height of culinary praise, whereas "appetizing" accounts for a low-level gustatory pleasure. A number of other terms are found in this region, for example, "tasty," "mouth-watering," and "yummy." Some are appropriate for specific foods: for example, that a steak is "tender." Although some food may be a form of art, and thus come under the aesthetics of art, most would come under everyday aesthetics, although again, this is a matter of controversy.[18]

EXPRESSIVE PROPERTIES

Another area of everyday aesthetic properties is that of expressive properties, properties that refer directly to feelings. Hermerén lists "sad," "melancholy," "gay," "somber," "solemn," "serene," "joyous," and "sentimental" as expressive qualities.[19] He mentions how these qualities, which tend to designate emotional states of persons, also designate properties of works of art and natural objects. To this I would add that they can designate *aesthetic* properties of persons (as in "looks sad" where the emphasis is on visual appearance rather than internal state). They can also designate aesthetic properties of non-art non-natural objects, as in "the summer vacation was joyous." Although usually pejorative in art contexts, the term "sentimental" can be used positively in everyday life when referring to things that we value aesthetically because of their pleasurable reference to family or personal history. I will discuss serenity and peacefulness later.

---

17 Arnold Berleant, "The Sensuous and the Sensual in Aesthetics," *The Journal of Aesthetics and Art Criticism* 23, no. 2 (1964): 185-92.
18 See Carolyn Korsmeyer, *Taste* for a thorough study of this. Also interesting is Meredith Schwartz and Khadija Coxon, "Gender and the Everyday Aesthetics of Food," no date of publication, accessed Jan. 18, 2010, http://thedepartmentofaesthetics.org/GenderandtheAestheticsofFood.pdf.
19 Göran Hermerén, *The Nature of Aesthetic Qualities* (Lund: Lund University Press, 1988), 123.

PRETTY AND PLEASANT

There are other low-level aesthetic qualities that often are ignored partly because of the prominence of their more famous cousins, and partly for other reasons. For example "pretty" is a very frequently used aesthetic term, although virtually never as a term of praise in fine arts magazines. Indeed, it is often used as a put-down. The pretty is often, for example, associated with kitsch, as when Bouguereau's paintings were considered kitsch because of his pretty girls. The association of pretty with kitsch may be related to one of the usages of the term to mean "superficially attractive," as in "pretty phrases." "Pretty" is seldom discussed in aesthetics, although Sibley saw both it and "lovely" as very general aesthetic terms that people with only moderate aesthetic sensitivity could apply.[20] This is probably right, although Sibley's account does not capture the surface-oriented quality of "pretty" or the way that it can be a put-down, as in stressing that something is not beautiful.

The absence of discussion of prettiness is odd given that it may be one of the most frequently used aesthetic terms.[21] We use it to characterize houses, gardens, clothes, ornaments, snap-shots, phrases, music, children, pets, napkins, and a host of other things. Its dictionary meaning is "pleasing or attractive to the eye [or the ear], as by delicacy or gracefulness."[22] There is a heavily gendered dimension to the term in that girls and women are more commonly called pretty than boys and men, who, when attractive, are called handsome, except in some homosexual and transvestite contexts.

In his discussion of prettiness Jared Moore wrote: "any man would be proud to be called 'handsome,' but highly resent being referred to as 'pretty'; whereas any woman would be delighted with either epithet."[23] This comes from a period prior to the rise of feminist culture-criticism (1948). Francis Sparshott, writing in 1963, similarly comments that "pretty" is "applied only to more or less feminine and pettable things; men are called pretty only in derision," and notes that the word "handsome" "suggests vigour rather than pettability."[24]

---

20 Sibley, "Concepts."
21 An early observation of this absence is found in Jared S. Moore, "The Sublime, and Other Subordinate Esthetic Concepts," *The Journal of Philosophy* 45, no. 2 (1948): 42-47.
22 "Pretty," Dictionary.com. *Dictionary.com Unabridged (v 1.1)*. Random House, accessed July 13, 2009, http://dictionary.reference.com/browse/Pretty.
23 Moore, "Sublime," 47.
24 Francis Sparshott, *The Structure of Aesthetics* (Toronto: University of Toronto Press, 1963), 72-75, 74.

This classification of women with pets is degrading to women and would not be considered acceptable today. However, "pretty" is still commonly used on a daily basis, hopefully without these associations.

Prettiness plays a more important role in the aesthetic life of children than in that of adults. For example, a psychological study of children's reactions to pictures showed that half of fourth grade children gave prettiness as their reason for selecting a picture as their favourite. This percentage went down for later grades, with 23% of fifth graders responding similarly.[25]

Sparshott speaks of the pretty as part of a trio that includes as its other members the sublime and the beautiful. This would give it much more importance than it has today. Such a move would require clearly distinguishing the pretty from the beautiful. Along these lines he observes that it is understandable to say that a kitty is pretty and not beautiful, and that the *Mona Lisa* is beautiful but not pretty. He then puts forward the idea that a thatched house may be pretty because it evokes dreams of a grandmother's life whereas the *Taj Mahal* is beautiful because it evokes nothing connected with everyday life.

Sparshott thinks that the beautiful/pretty distinction is between what demands serious attention and what does not. To be appreciated, a kitten does not have to be scrutinized as intently as the *Mona Lisa*. The pretty arouses stock responses or is inherently trivial, whereas the beautiful is relatively free from association with the everyday. Although one could say that the *Mona Lisa* also arouses a stock response in the average viewer, Sparshott is right that to view it appropriately one should scrutinize it intently. He concludes that there is no sound reason to discuss the term "pretty" and that the distinction between the pretty and the beautiful may be ultimately indescribable. However, the idea that there is no reason to discuss the pretty is odd since Sparshott must have thought he had a sound reason to discuss it himself. Nor is it clear that philosophers need special reasons for discussing terms that interest them.

In general, aestheticians associate the pretty with the pleasant and the merely enjoyable, and oppose it to the beautiful. Kenneth Dorter, in describing Plato's views in the *Ion*, writes "Beauty in art ... is not equivalent to prettiness or pleasantness. We might call a great tragedy or grotesque painting beautiful, while not

---

25 Eunice Hammer Waymack and Gordon Hendrickson, "Children's Reactions as a Basis for Teaching Picture Appreciation," *The Elementary School Journal* 33, no. 4 (1932): 268-76. See also, Michael J. Parsons, "A Suggestion Concerning the Development of Aesthetic Experience in Children," *The Journal of Aesthetics and Art Criticism* 34, no. 3 (1976): 305-14, 312.

claiming that either is in any normal sense pleasant...."[26] Ron Moore similarly distinguishes the pleasures of beauty from simple enjoyments: "the pleasure we feel in responding to the beauty of a nightingale song is not a simple enjoyment akin to the relief that comes from scratching a mosquito bite."[27] Instead he sees beauty as a complex awareness that "transcends mere pleasantness to be transformative."[28] Richard Shusterman also distinguishes pleasure from the pleasant, to the disadvantage of the latter, referring to fun and pleasantness as "banally light, easy, and self-indulgent."[29] Allen Carlson, when talking about the aesthetic of environmental buildings and architecture, insists that it not be restricted "to questions about whether the relationships are simply 'pleasing to the eye' or 'pretty'" as this would exclude concern for values expressed.[30] The exclusion of the pretty and the pleasant from aesthetics is quite common even today, as is the assumption that they are aesthetically degraded.

Regardless of their negative press in the halls of academe "pretty," "pleasant" and similar terms, such as "charming" and "attractive," have particular relevance to the aesthetics of everyday life. It is possible that the concept of the pretty has, in part, been downgraded in our society for sexist and homophobic reasons. Adultist (only children care about the pretty) and classist (concern about the pretty is low-class) reasons may also play a role. The pleasant may have been neglected more because it is associated with easy and non-reflective pleasure. Although the pretty and the pleasant can be less rewarding than the beautiful and the sublime, and it is plausible that interest in these qualities can direct us away from more valuable experiences, they should not therefore be neglected. At the very least they provide an important contrast to the more central concepts of aesthetics which cannot really be understood without them.

THE CUTE AND THE DECORATIVE

John Morreall argues that even though the term "cute" is not important for the arts and is a second-class aesthetic property, it is nonetheless important

---

26 Kenneth Dorter, "The Ion: Plato's Characterization of Art," *The Journal of Aesthetics and Art Criticism* 32, no. 1 (1973): 65-78, 76.
27 Moore, *Natural Beauty*, 84.
28 Moore, *Natural Beauty*, 76.
29 See Richard Shusterman, "Interpretation, Pleasure and Value in Aesthetic Experience," *The Journal of Aesthetics and Art Criticism* 56, no. 1 (1998): 51-53.
30 Carlson, *Landscape*, 77.

for humans more generally.[31] Drawing from work by Konrad Lorenz, he argues that our positive response to cuteness evolved as the result of the necessity of adult protection for mammalian, particularly human, babies. Cute dolls exaggerate features (for example round protruding cheeks) that evoke this response.[32]

Morreall however is not pro-cuteness in every respect. He and co-writer Jessica Loy associate cuteness with kitsch, and insist that there is something objectionable about Walter and Margaret Keane paintings of big-eyed girls, widely thought paradigms of kitsch in the 1960s. Morreall and Loy write that, "[k]itsch is perfectly suited to most people's passivity, short attention span, and shallow understanding, for it promises them immediate gratification requiring no special background knowledge or activity."[33] This is a fairly typical account of kitsch.

Robert Solomon, however, has defended cuteness, even in art, and he does this in connection with his defence of kitsch.[34] His view, generally, is that there is nothing harmful in expressing what he calls "sweet emotions" or experiencing them in response to works of art. He even thinks it is valuable to re-experience these child-like emotions as an adult as long as the context is appropriate. His thoughts can apply not only to art but to cute decorative items found around the home, for example garden gnomes.

When kitsch is admired, the appropriate terms are taken from the aesthetics of everyday life: e.g., "cute," "cuddly," "charming," "pleasing," "thrilling," "pretty," "colourful," "joyous," "sad-looking," and "beautiful." (Think of late-night television shows that sell ceramic "collectibles.") By contrast, kitsch-haters often use words like "sentimental" and "banal" to describe kitsch.

Ruth Lorand, by contrast to Solomon, associates the cute with "the insignificant," and argues that cute objects cannot be beautiful, although they can be pretty, lovely or decorative. She believes that great art, instead, illuminates basic human issues.[35] Although Lorand may be right about this, the point does

---

31 See John Morreall, "Cuteness," *British Journal of Aesthetics* 31, no. 1 (1991): 39-47.
32 John Morreall and Jessica Loy, "Kitsch and Aesthetic Education," *Journal of Aesthetic Education* 2, no. 4 (1989): 63-73.
33 Morreall and Loy, 68.
34 Robert C. Solomon, "On Kitsch and Sentimentality," *The Journal of Aesthetics and Art Criticism* 49, no. 1 (1991): 1-14. Also, see his *In Defense of Sentimentality* (New York: Oxford University Press, 2004). For a famous attack on kitsch, see Clement Greenberg, "Avant-garde and Kitsch," originally *Partisan Review* 6, no. 5 (1939): 34-49, accessible at http://www.sharecom.ca/greenberg/kitsch.html.
35 Ruth Lorand, "Beauty and Its Opposites," *The Journal of Aesthetics and Art Criticism* 52, no. 4 (1994): 399-406, 404.

not in itself drain cute, pretty, lovely or decorative objects of aesthetic value. Decoration, for example, can increase significance. It can be an example of what ethnologist Ellen Dissanayake calls "making special."[36] Dissanayake's work in evolutionary aesthetics is strongly supportive of continuities I have found between the aesthetics of art and the aesthetics of everyday life. For Dissanayake, art derives from the same sources as everyday life, and depends on the same physiological factors. Art, she argues, is just one form of "making special." If Dissanayake is right, making something pretty or lovely, for example by way of decoration, *is* significant and in a way that, although different from art, is continuous with it.

When we turn to non-Western cultures, the distinction Lorand favours tends to dissolve. Consider bicycle decoration in Northern Nigeria.[37] After studying these decorations, Elisha Renne and Dakyes Usman have concluded that the dichotomy between everyday objects and traditional artworks is artificial.[38] Traditional art in Northern Nigerian culture shares an aesthetic sensibility with the embellishment of everyday objects among Westerners. Like Dewey, Renne and Usman wish to stress continuity between everyday life and fine art.

In contemporary Japanese culture, cuteness is considered valuable to an extent that may be quite surprising to Western eyes. Adult women, called "Peter Pans" were known in the 1990s to dress in cute outfits.[39] Cute kitty cartoons are ubiquitous in popular Japanese culture, and cuteness (*kaiwasa*) is widely regarded as an aesthetic concept. Recently, however, there has been a reaction against this and a New York City art show called "Bye Bye Kitty!!!" has featured the work of younger Japanese artists who reject the "cute" aesthetic.[40]

Dewey understands the decorative in terms of a hunger the eyes have for light and colour, a need which is fulfilled by wall-paper, rugs, and tapestries as well as such natural phenomena as changing sky colours and flowers.[41]

---

36 Dissanayake, *Homo Aestheticus*.
37 Elisha P. Renne, and Dakyes S. Usman, "Bicycle Decoration and Everyday Aesthetics in Northern Nigeria," *African Arts* 32, no. 2 (1999): 46-51.
38 Renne and Usman, 46.
39 Karal Ann Marling, "Letter from Japan: Kenbei vs. All-American Kawaii at Tokyo Disneyland," *American Art* 6, no. 2 (1992): 102-11.
40 "Bye Bye Kitty: Japanese artists challenge 'cute' esthetic," The Associated Press, *CTV News* (March 17, 2011), accessed June 8, 2011, http://www.ctv.ca/CTVNews/Entertainment/20110317/bye-bye-kitty-japanese-art-110317/.
41 Dewey, 124.

Moreover, it is not limited to the everyday; there are decorative elements and aspects of works of art as well. Dewey also distinguishes between good and bad decoration, arguing that when decoration is isolated and external, as in cake-decoration, it is "empty embellishment."[42] He also observes that the decorative qualities of flowers in a room add to expressiveness when harmonious with furniture and handled sincerely.[43] In short, we may safely state that "decorative" is a positive aesthetic attribute when applied to everyday phenomena, although less often perhaps when applied to art.

Drawing from Solomon, Dissanayake, and Dewey, I have been arguing for a role for cuteness and decoration in aesthetics. Contra Lorand, they can be significant. This is not to say that such things as cuteness are always valuable. They can for example lead people to fail to recognize the value of richer, deeper, and more difficult aesthetic properties.

THE TASTEFUL

Consider, also, "tasteful," as applied, for example, to a house, garden, gift, or item of apparel. The tasteful is not to be confused with something that is beautiful, although that which is beautiful can be tasteful. The tasteful is that which shows "good taste." It is culturally emergent and constantly changing; turtlenecks may be tasteful one year and not the next. "Tasteful" often has to do with the quality of an object that is according to certain norms of appearance and is not garish.

Although "tasteful" is sometimes used in relation to the arts it is central to home decoration, clothing, and food preparation. It is also often associated with quality of materials and workmanship, as well as good principles of formal organization and colour coordination. Thus it can only be afforded by those who have the money for quality craftsmanship, and the time to attend to such matters. This is not to exclude the possibility of referring to some items, arrangements and behaviours as tasteful within traditional or tribal societies even though the people are not rich by our standards.

Because of the cost of high-quality work and because of upper-class needs for self-legitimating symbols, the tasteful is often associated with wealth.[44] This

---

42 Dewey, 127.
43 Dewey, 128.
44 See Daniel Cottom, "Taste and the Civilized Imagination," *The Journal of Aesthetics and Art Criticism* 39, no. 4 (1981): 367-80.

is not to say, however, that the tasteful is exclusively an upper-class concern. Architects, for example, have occasionally tried to design buildings that are both tasteful and cheap. And, in the nineteenth century a lower-class home or farm could be considered tasteful if it embodied such things as neatness, convenience and beauty.[45] Thus the aesthetics of the tasteful is closely associated with the aesthetics of fashion not only for the wealthy but also for the rest.

The tasteful is also opposed to content that is jarring, disturbing or extreme in some way. One can have a taste for the war scenes of Goya, but it may not be tasteful to have these in one's dining room.

Finally, the tasteful is associated with adulthood. Lucien Rudrauf captures its adult-oriented nature when he writes that "the child is enraptured by the beauty of flowers, butterflies, and shells, and proceeds gradually, if he is well gifted with sensitive and intellectual faculties, toward a knowledge of the formal world which is more and more tasteful and correct."[46]

Related to the quality of the tasteful are such qualities as "artistic," "creative," "poetic," "imaginative" and "expressive." These are often attributed to things that are not works of art, for example to hats, pillows, hairstyles, and car decoration. They might be metaphorical, as in "poetic," or literal, as in "this decorated room is imaginative and expressive too!"

SPARKLES AND SHINES

When I was a child I watched Mister Clean swirl through the kitchen to transform it into something that sparkles and shines. Today, we associate these qualities with extremes of cleanliness. To that extent, we also sometimes reject them as aesthetically unimportant—nothing more than a reminder of the silliness of the 1950s. Yet sparkle and shine are qualities that pervade our lives aesthetically. Moreover, they are *generally* thought to be positive (at least in the West). Consider some of the kinds of things that can be admired for sparkle and shine. First, there are things that literally sparkle, that is, in the sense that they actually give off sparks: fires, sparklers, and fireworks, when they are not dangerous, are pleasurable to watch. If, as I have argued, Aquinas is right that beauty is that which gives us pleasure in the apprehension (with apprehension understood to

---

45 Jan Jennings, "Cheap and Tasteful Dwellings in Popular Architecture," *Perspectives in Vernacular Architecture*, 5, Gender, Class, and Shelter (1995): 133-51, 139.
46 Lucien Rudrauf, "Perfection," *The Journal of Aesthetics and Art Criticism* 23, no. 1 (1964): 123-30, 123.

include a contemplative element on the subject side and aura on the object side, phenomenologically speaking), then these things are beautiful. Moreover, something need not literally produce sparks to literally sparkle: stars sparkle only in appearance and yet this is considered part of their beauty. Similarly, torchlight parades and city lights sparkle in the distance. Jewels, particularly diamonds, sparkle, and again, this is part of why we value them aesthetically. This is also true for glass, gold and silver. Shine also plays a role in everyday aesthetics. It is associated with products made out of the abovementioned materials, as well as steel, aluminum, porcelain and plastic. A beautiful kitchen shines with these materials, hence the need for Mr. Clean. An important part of the attraction of new products is their shine: the shiny new car, for example. As Crispin Sartwell puts it, our attraction to what glitters and shines "is obvious, nor should it be dismissed as tasteless or childish."[47]

"Sparkles" and "shines" seem to indicate another kind of aesthetic quality from the ones I have been discussing. For one thing, they are not directly evaluative. I include them because, as I have argued, correct aesthetic term attribution is not based on reasons that are non-aesthetic in nature. Someone might say, for instance, that something looks good because it sparkles. This claim does not base something aesthetic on something non-aesthetic. Rather "sparkles" here is taken in its aesthetic sense, and in its positive aesthetic meaning.[48]

NICE

"Nice" is an important, perhaps even a central, quality in everyday aesthetics: "nice tie," "nicely written," "nice walk," "nice night," "nice feeling." "Sounds nice," "looks nice," and "feels nice" are also positive aesthetic qualities. "What do you think of the sound of the fountain in my garden?" "Nice." This is an aesthetic judgment, although at a very simple level. Its opposite is "nasty." "Nice" can refer to something appealing or agreeable. It can also be a matter of showing delicacy or refinement. "A nice piece of craftsmanship" is craftsmanship that shows skill.

---

47 Crispin Sartwell, *Six Names of Beauty* (New York: Routledge, 2004), 35. See Chapter 2 "Yapha: Hebrew, glow, bloom" and specifically his discussion of fireworks, 46-50, and jewels, 50-51.
48 For more on this, see my article, "Sparkle and Shine," from which this material was taken.

Of course, as with other terms, there are non-aesthetic uses of "nice." Someone might be referred to as nice simply because well-mannered. An old-fashioned usage refers to a morally upright person as nice, as in "she's a nice girl." Sometimes we speak of subtle distinctions as "nice." The word has a long history and many obsolete meanings, including "foolish" and "stupid," going back to the Latin *nescius* for "ignorant." I will, however, only be concerned here with contemporary aesthetic uses.

Some philosophers situate the nice and the nasty (its opposite) outside of aesthetics. Nick Zangwill does this by associating "nice" with Kant's concept of the agreeable.[49] This is based on the idea that judgments of niceness are wholly subjective and judgments of beauty are wholly objective, or at least subjectively universal, as Kant put it. I do not think that the nice and the beautiful are as far apart as Kant and Zangwill imply. If I say that a house looks nice I might well expect others to agree with me every bit as much as I do when I say that it is beautiful. I cannot just randomly say that things are nice. Moreover, people may rightfully disagree with me that, for example, a room is nice. Kant says that when we say that something is agreeable we should say "it is agreeable to me." However we don't often say "it is agreeable to me," and there is a reason for this. It is because we expect others (or at least, others who "count") to find it agreeable too. Kant is also wrong about beauty. When I say that something is beautiful, for instance the shadows of a flight of birds against a wall at sunset, I may not require that everyone agree with me in the way Kant expects me to. I may only expect or hope that the person I am saying it to will agree. The distinction between the nice and the beautiful may, then, be more a matter of degree than one of subjectivity vs. objectivity.

There is conflict between the lovers of art and lovers of niceness in everyday life. What the average person might see as nice may well be abhorrent kitsch to the art sophisticate. Thus, within the artworld, the term "nice," as with "pretty," can be a put-down when applied to a work of art (a case of damning with faint praise). "Nice" may be in opposition to "powerful" and "interesting." "Nice" *Musak* often replaces what music-lovers would consider true music. And yet what is merely nice, or intended to be nice, can be painful to some. Think of listening to music by Kenny G. (the stage name of saxophonist Kenneth Gorelick) in an otherwise agreeable coffeehouse. It is not that the coffeehouse fails to play powerful and interesting music, but that it plays music that is so insipidly "nice" that it is actually painful to the ears. Yet others find it enjoyable.

---

49 Nick Zangwill, "Aesthetic Realism I," in *Oxford Handbook of Aesthetics*, 71.

Assuming that niceness is an important quality in everyday aesthetics, lovers of the arts might insist on a radical separation of the aesthetics of everyday life from the aesthetics of art. Admittedly, the pleasures of niceness are generally at a low level of intensity compared to the pleasures of beauty. However, niceness is not limited to the everyday: works of art are just as likely to be merely nice as to have more dramatic aesthetic qualities. Also, none of this makes the quality of niceness less important than other aesthetic qualities, if importance is measured in terms of the pleasure we take in life. We need to have our surroundings and the objects we use look, sound, taste, feel and smell nice, and this forms a background against which everything else aesthetic happens. For example, we expect an art gallery to look nice: if it does not, we are distracted from the art. We can recognize the importance of niceness as an aesthetic quality if we think of how much more important it is, generally speaking, to have nice than to have beautiful clothes: the latter are only needed for special occasions and are otherwise usually inappropriate.

When we say that a person is nice it is not generally a direct judgment of aesthetic quality, although "looks nice" is. Rather, a person who is nice is someone who is pleasant to be around: someone who does nice things. It may be a moral quality, as when it implies kind-heartedness, although somebody can be deeply moral and not particularly nice. Perhaps nice people are basically moral individuals who are also engaging or charming in some way.[50] Also, the judgment of niceness is usually based not only on personality ("pleasant," "agreeable," "not abrasive") but also on personal appearance ("clean," "neat," "handsome," "beautiful," "lovely"). The aesthetics of the person is a broad and complex domain of everyday aesthetics that has hardly been touched by philosophers, although the aesthetics of personal presentation has been discussed by such philosophers as Novitz and Naukkarinen.[51]

Consider the common exclamation: "What a nice day!" Any survey of everyday aesthetics should include the aesthetics of "the day." Some days are good, aesthetically, and some are not. Typically, we refer to an aesthetically bad day as "dreary" or "depressing." A good day can be "beautiful," "pretty," "lovely," or "pleasant." The reference may be to the skies, or more broadly, to

---

50 There is a parallel issue with respect to moral and aesthetic beauty. See Guy Sircello, *A New Theory of Beauty* (Princeton: Princeton University Press, 1975), Chapters 24-26 for a good discussion.
51 See Novitz and Naukkarinen.

the weather.[52] However, sometimes it can refer retroactively to the pleasures of a day already experienced: "We had a nice day today, didn't we?" When people say, "Have a nice day!" they are expressing (albeit, often in a purely *pro forma* way) the wish we enjoy the events of the day to come.

COZY AND COMFORTABLE

Furniture, clothes, relationships, fireplaces, restaurants, hotels, homes, cabins, and home decoration can all be cozy or comfortable. Although these terms are not indexed in the *Encyclopedia of Aesthetics* they are used on a regular basis to signify our sensual pleasure in things and can also be used to designate aesthetic properties.

In 1969, Beardsley made a strong distinction between having an aesthetic experience, which he calls a "glorious state," and feeling "merely comfortable."[53] However, although being comfortable is not a matter of "having an aesthetic experience" in the glorious sense of that phrase, it is still aesthetic in the sense of providing a kind of sensuous pleasure that carries with it some degree of aura. Recently, Scruton has noted that when a carpenter says that a doorframe is "just right," and is asked why, he may reply that it "has a comfortable, serene, peaceful, or homely look." He observes that these characterizations are often metaphorical and that they "situate the object in the current of human life, endowing it with a moral or social significance."[54] This would give these qualities, including comfort, greater aesthetic significance than Beardsley would allow. Cynthia Rostankowski has taken an explicit position in favour of comfort as an aesthetic concept. She argues that "it is relevant to multiple sensory perceptions, is a value term, is indicative of a desirable property or condition, and is both subjectively experienced and objectively understood."[55] She finds the concept of comfort to be particularly important in contemporary culture of childhood as manifested in some children's books.

"Comfortable," comes from "*comfortare*," a Latin term meaning *to greatly*

---

52 For an excellent discussion of the aesthetics of weather, see Yuriko Saito, "The Aesthetics of Weather" *The Aesthetics of Everyday Life*, 156-76.
53 Beardsley, "Experience," 4.
54 Scruton, "Search," 246.
55 Cynthia Rostankowski, "The Aesthetics of Comfort in Neil Gaiman's Coraline," paper given at a conference *Metamorphic Spaces 2008 in Children's Literature and Culture*, University of Jyväskylä, Finland, Jan. 17-19, 2008. Abstract accessed June 23, 2010, https://www.jyu.fi/en/congress/metamorphoses2008/programme/abstracts/workshopabstracts.

strengthen. However, it has more to do today with providing a feeling of support, ease, relaxation, or contentedness. Whatever is comfortable eliminates hardship, trouble, pain, anxiety, and concern. It encourages calm, relief, well-being, peace, and restfulness. "Discomfort" and "uncomfortable" are the negative correlates. Something comfortable is pleasant. Like cosiness, comfort is also associated with warmth, hence the term "comforter." "Cozy," of Scottish and perhaps Scandinavian origin, is associated with snugness, warmth, and being comfortably sheltered. Hence "snug" and "warm" are related aesthetic terms.

The concept of comfort has evolved over time, and has become increasingly important in our lives. As John E. Crowley has argued, a culture of comfort arose in eighteenth- and nineteenth-century Europe along with the development of the middle class.[56] Crowley finds the term "comfort" associated with domestic enhancements that favour "privacy, cleanliness, warmth and light."[57] A more recent development is the idea of comfort food, which the *American Heritage Dictionary* defines as "[f]ood that is simply prepared and associated with a sense of home or contentment."[58]

The most prominent place comfort has played in philosophical aesthetics has been in the aesthetics of architecture and interior decoration. Architecture has traditionally taken an interest in comfort. Take for example the role that comfort played in the work of architect Julia Morgan. Central to Morgan's aesthetic was the concept of developing a feeling which was unique to the site. She believed buildings should have a certain personality that would resonate in the experience of the users. She sought a *particular* feeling, one that she associated with the work of her mentor; California arts and crafts architect Bernard Maybeck. Russell Quacchia, in a recent book on Morgan's work at Asilomar Conference Grounds in Pacific Grove, California, describes this feeling in terms of concepts of warmth and comfort. He quotes critic Allan Temko's claim that, among the buildings by Morgan, these had the most "warmth, strength and feel for the land."[59] The term "warmth" here is closely associated with comfort.

---

56 John E. Crowley, *The Invention of Comfort: Sensibilities and Design in Early Modern Britain and Early America* 2nd ed. (Baltimore: The Johns Hopkins University Press, 2003), 292.
57 Crowley, ix. I have already mentioned cleanliness as an aesthetic property and will discuss it later in my chapter on neatness and messiness.
58 "comfort food," *The American Heritage Dictionary of the English Language, Fourth Edition* (Boston: Houghton Mifflin, 2004), accessed Nov. 7, 2008, Dictionary.com, http://dictionary.reference.com/browse/comfort food.
59 Russell Quacchia, *Julia Morgan, Architect and the Creation of the Asilomar Conference Grounds* (Bloomington, IN: Xlibris, 2005), 189.

Most recent discussions of comfort in architecture centre on whether it is legitimate to overcome the need for comfort to achieve other goals.[60] Witold Rybczynski argues that modernist architecture rejects comfort, and that this is a mistake. By contrast, David Goldblatt describes how Peter Eisenman, a leading deconstructivist architect, rejected the aesthetics of comfort and function in order, as Eisenman put it, to "let other voices speak."[61] By "other voices" Eisenman probably means alternative perspectives concerning lived space. Rejection of comfort can, Eisenman believes, help express a power that has been *repressed* by an "externalized" daily life, thus opening architectural creativity. This strategy is exemplified in his design for the *La Guardiola House* in which there were windows in the floor, and in which one would have to overcome obstacles to get from one room to the next. (Not surprisingly, the house was never built.) As Goldblatt observes, Eisenman calls for a dislocation of the architectural self (by means of, for example, use of chance in the creative process) to achieve a deep exploration of meaning. This was precisely *not* Julia Morgan's direction at Asilomar.

There is much to be said for deconstructivist architecture, but we should remember that this is just one pole of legitimate architectural experience, the other of which has not been represented strongly in recent architectural writing, and which may even be seen by some as a kind of kitsch. However, just as Robert Solomon argued for the value of the sweet sentiments represented by kitsch, one could say a word for the feelings of comfort, functionality, harmony, and simplicity advocated by Morgan.[62]

PEACEFULNESS, SERENITY, TRANQUILITY AND STILLNESS

These terms (and such related ones as "still," "stillness," "quiet," "undisturbed," "relaxing," "restful," and "soothing") are often used in relation to the aesthetics of art, nature, and everyday life. A house can be peaceful, a person's expression serene, an afternoon tranquil. I suppose that these terms would fall under what Hermerén calls "emotion" or "expressive" qualities mentioned earlier, although he doesn't name any of them.[63] He does mention "sereneness" in his encyclopaedia article on aesthetic qualities.[64]

---

60 Witold Rybczynski, *Home: A Short History of an Idea* (New York: Viking, 1986).
61 David Goldblatt, "The Dislocation of the Architectural Self," *The Journal of Aesthetics and Art Criticism* 49, no. 4 (1991): 336-48.
62 Solomon, "Kitsch."
63 Göran Hermerén, *Nature*, 106.
64 Göran Hermerén, "Qualities, Aesthetic," *Encyclopedia of Aesthetics*, Vol. 4, 97-99.

These terms play an especially important role in music. Jenefer Robinson speaks, for example, of music expressing such emotional qualities as sadness and serenity.[65] Peter Kivy argues that musical works can only express emotions that do not have intentional objects, of which serenity is one.[66] Daniel Kaufman speaks of the second movement of Vaughan Williams' *London Symphony* as "a great piece of music because of its quiet tranquility and deep soulfulness."[67] Aestheticians of painting sometimes use these concepts too. For example, John Gilmour refers to the harmony of one of Cezanne's paintings as containing "a feeling of meditation, freedom and peacefulness."[68] Earlier, these terms were often associated with Classicism, as in the paintings of Claude Lorrain (1604-82). Schopenhauer recognized that works of art can express moods, such as those of peace.[69]

Contemporary painting and sculpture have not much emphasized the properties of peacefulness and serenity, and one might say that these concepts are today more strongly associated with kitsch. However, they continue to have application to everyday life, as when we speak of a peaceful scene, room, look, or smile and mean it aesthetically (i.e., as something to be contemplated). A segment of time may also have these qualities, for example a "relaxing afternoon" or a "serene day."

These qualities are not stressed nearly as much in the West as in the East. The *rasa* tradition in India gives them particular attention. Although serenity was not one of medieval aesthetician Bharata's original eight emotions, it was eventually added to the rasa tradition.[70] As Richard Shusterman has observed, the direct experiential quality of rasa has been seen as unworldly and the pleasurable experience it gives as restful or tranquil.[71]

---

65 Jenefer Robinson, "The Expression and Arousal of Emotion in Music," *The Journal of Aesthetics and Art Criticism* 52, no. 1 (1994): 13-22, 13.
66 Peter Kivy, *Music Alone* (Ithaca: Cornell University Press, 1990), 175-77.
67 Daniel A. Kaufman, "Normative Criticism and the Objective Value of Artworks," *The Journal of Aesthetics and Art Criticism* 60, no. 2 (2002): 151-66.
68 John C. Gilmour, "Improvisation in Cezanne's Late Landscapes," *The Journal of Aesthetics and Art Criticism* 58, no. 2 (2000): 191-204, 199.
69 Carroll C. Pratt, "Abstract vs. Realistic Art," *The Journal of Aesthetics and Art Criticism* 33, no. 4 (1975): 403-05.
70 V.K. Chari, "Poetic Emotions and Poetic Semantics," *The Journal of Aesthetics and Art Criticism* 34, no. 3 (1976): 287-99.
71 Richard Shusterman, "Definition, Dramatization, and Rasa," *The Journal of Aesthetics and Art Criticism* 61, no. 3 (2003): 295-98. Here he is referring to Pravas Jivan Chaudhury, "The Theory of Rasa," *The Journal of Aesthetics and Art Criticism* 24, no. 1 (1965): 145-49. Shusterman also references G.B. Mohan Thampi, "'Rasa' as Aesthetic Experience," *The Journal of Aesthetics and Art Criticism* 24, no. 1 (1965): 75-80.

However the differences between West and East should not be overemphasized. Pravas Chaudhury, for example, argues for a close connection between at least one Romantic poet and the Indian perspective. Keats, he contends, would have admitted the Asian view that in the poetic mind the objects are contemplated so that the mind may enjoy unity and serenity.[72] Other Eastern traditions also emphasize these qualities. For example, it is said that in the martial art of Taijiquan (Tai Chi Chuan), peaceful harmony is felt and expressed in every movement.[73] Serenity also often comes up with reference to Japanese gardens.

We may conclude that peacefulness, serenity, tranquility and stillness can all be positive aesthetic qualities not only in art and nature but also in everyday life, for example in a room, a backyard garden, or a time of day. They can also be aesthetic qualities in persons we perceive, as for instance in the woman's graceful movements as she walks across a lawn.

TERMS OF VERY HIGH VALUATION

What about terms of very high valuation? May they be found in everyday aesthetics? Where do we place phrases like "looks great" and "sounds fantastic"? Similarly, how do we classify such terms as "wonderful," "awe-inspiring," "marvellous," "exquisite," "amazing," "extraordinary" and "perfect" when used in conjunction with such sense-related terms as "looks," "sounds," and "feels"? Again, these may be combined in double terms, as in "looks amazing" and "sounds wonderful." For that matter, what about "beauty," and "beautiful"? Is beauty too rare to be considered "everyday"? If it is, then the example of the video of a fluttering plastic bag falls out of everyday aesthetics.

Such terms are more likely applied to works of art and to natural phenomena than to a made-up bed or a cleaned room. However, they may be just as readily applied to a vase, a moustache or a pair of shoes. Although we are more likely to say that a painting or a landscape is marvellous than a household appliance, it really depends on the appliance. Many of these terms, for example "perfect" and "fabulous," are often used when talking about fashion.

---

72 Pravas Jivan Chaudhury, "Keats and the Indian Ideal of Life and Poetry," *The Journal of Aesthetics and Art Criticism* Supplement to the Oriental Issue: The Aesthetic Attitude in Indian Aesthetics, 24, no. 1 (1965): 207-11.
73 Sophia Delza, "The Art of the Science of T'ai Chi Ch'uan," *The Journal of Aesthetics and Art Criticism* 25, no. 4 (1967): 449-61.

There are aesthetic high-points in everyday life. We mark these with lofty praise, although perhaps sometimes with irony or exaggeration. We say that someone "looks great" or "fantastic" in a certain outfit, or that a dinner was "wonderful." Moreover, craft objects sometimes transcend the ordinary. I once had the pleasure of trying on some very expensive Bally shoes. These were marvellous things: so soft, malleable, beautifully proportioned and finely worked. They seemed to go far beyond ordinary shoes.

More problematic are the phrases "deeply moving" and "powerful." Although these are terms of high praise in the aesthetics of art, it is difficult to come up with examples of their application in everyday aesthetics. One example might be when we find a memorial service or a wedding ceremony deeply moving. Yet, although we may be deeply moved by seeing someone rescued on the TV news, or by the victory of a favoured candidate, it is arguable that this is not an aesthetic experience. "Powerful" is similarly difficult. Whereas we might speak of a powerful painting, "powerful" tends to be literal and non-aesthetic in everyday life. A powerful shower, for example, is one that produces a forceful spray. It would be strange to speak of powerful flower-arrangements, dinner parties, or present-wrappings. Nonetheless, when we do speak of real-life experience as "deeply moving" or "powerful" (for example, we might say that witnessing child-birth was deeply moving and that the experience was a powerful one) we do so in much the way we speak of a theatrical performance as having this quality. The analysis would be similar to that of "tragic" above.

There is an argument against terms of very high valuation in everyday aesthetics. As we saw in discussing Haapala and Saito, one way to talk about everyday aesthetics would be to stress that which is ordinary. One might for example distinguish between major and minor league aesthetic phenomena, keeping the everyday to the latter category. In the aesthetics of music, Stan Godlovitch distinguishes the local and little from the great and big, suggesting that "it is out of place to judge with the same ear the struggles of the Red Deer Civic Orchestra and the effortless perfection of the Berlin Philharmonic." He then asks whether this can also be done in appreciation of nature. My appreciation of a short glimpse of Coyote Creek over a bridge on my walk to work would be an example of small-scale appreciation of nature—nature in the little league.[74] Applying this thought to everyday aesthetics we might say, similarly,

---

74 Godlovitch does not actually advocate this view but brings it up as a possibility. "Evaluating Nature Aesthetically," *The Journal of Aesthetics and Art Criticism* 56, no. 2 (1998): 113-25.

that my appreciation of student fashions would be small-scale in relation to the major league of high fashion. The idea here would be that the everyday would be limited to the minor leagues. On this view, once experience becomes extraordinary it is no longer a part of the everyday.

The major league/minor league distinction is nice, but it does not sink the idea of terms of very high valuation in everyday aesthetics. As I have argued, once we talk about the everyday in terms of aesthetics we are talking about the ordinary becoming extraordinary, and so everyday aesthetics cannot be limited to the ordinary. Nor is it required that an aesthetic experience be a low-level one to count as part of everyday life. Aesthetic terms of very high valuation are often appropriate descriptors of everyday experience, although some applications are relatively rare.

SACRED AND SPIRITUAL

Consider now such terms as "sacred," "spiritual," and "holy." No one denies that sacred experience often has an aesthetic dimension. There are certainly sacred arts. We also speak of sacred spaces. However, is there a use of "sacred" in everyday aesthetics? (I first broached this issue when discussing Sartwell's theory of everyday aesthetics.) At first it would seem that the sacred would be limited to religious contexts. Yet an atheist can use "sacred" or "spiritual" in aesthetic contexts without making a religious commitment. It has been said that Frank Lloyd Wright created sacred qualities in his spaces despite his religious skepticism. However, whether the sacred can find a place in the aesthetics of everyday life is open to question. The closer the term "everyday" is to the ordinary, the mundane, and the banal the further it seems from the sacred. Ronald Hepburn believes that one is being profane when one treats something that merits reverence as common and "robustly everyday."[75] He says this in referring to a comment of Gadamer's that the sale in an antique shop of pieces that still have some traces of intimate life is profane. Here, the sacred is considered as distinct from the everyday. The idea is that objects with a sacred aura

---

75 Ronald Hepburn, "Restoring the Sacred: Sacred as a Concept of Aesthetics" (Lahti, Finland: International Institute of Applied Aesthetics Series vol. 6, 1999), 166-85, 177-78. This is also found in his *The Reach of the Aesthetic* (Aldershot, UK: Ashgate, 2001), 124-25. Hepburn's is a good discussion of the role that the concept of the sacred can play in aesthetics. In the end, he prefers terms like "mysterious" and "wonder" that are not as closely tied to traditional religious belief as "the sacred."

should not be treated as aesthetic commodities. However, ironically, the point simply proves that some objects of everyday ("intimate") life have a sacred aura. So, although it might be crude to sell them, the appreciation may still be aesthetic. In sum, concepts related to the sacred may be applied to everyday life, but only in special circumstances, and with recognition that the original meaning of sacred terms implies something apart from the everyday.

Concepts of the sacred are more often used (outside strictly religious situations) in the contexts of high art and pristine nature than in everyday life contexts. Some, however, wish to see aesthetic possibilities in everyday life that go deeper. For example, although Benjamin was generally in favour of the loss of aura in the age of mechanical reproduction, he often talked about the ephemera of our urban worlds as though they were sacred.[76]

Some writers, following Heidegger, encourage us to experience the world poetically as something sacred, although with no commitment to a creator God. Berleant has extended the concept of "an aura of reverence" not only to certain works of art and natural environments but also to such things as gardens. He seems to favour transforming the mundane into the sacred, even referring to a neighbourhood square as a sanctified place.[77] It is hard to imagine neighbourhood squares that could be called "sanctified" as much as they might be valued for their aesthetic qualities. Yet, "sacred" and "spiritual" can be used metaphorically to refer to everyday aesthetic phenomena, especially things that have great personal or group value.

REACTION QUALITIES

Another set of terms that may be called aesthetic includes "interesting," "engaging," "absorbing," and "fascinating." These have been called "reaction qualities" since they require a subject who is engaged, absorbed, or fascinated in or by the aesthetic object.[78] They may be applied to everyday aesthetic phenomena as well as to works of art and to natural phenomena. A flower arrangement, a costume, or a well-laid fire can be interesting, engaging, absorbing or fascinating in the aesthetic senses of these terms. A word needs to be said about "fascinates." I used it earlier to help explain aura, and so on my view there is a sense in which everything aesthetic fascinates. However, there is also a narrower use of the term

---

76 Benjamin, "Work."
77 Berleant, *Environment*, 76.
78 Göran Hermerén discusses these in "Variety."

where fascination involves "irresistible attractiveness" which goes back to the Latin *fascinum*: spell. Following this usage, something can fascinate in a way that is irresistible as if one were under a spell. Obviously things that are cute, nice or pretty do not necessarily fascinate in this way. However, sometimes they do, and so this would then be an additional everyday aesthetic quality.

There are also terms of aesthetic disapproval that go along with these, for example "boring," "depressing," and "distressing." The usual use of these terms does not indicate an aesthetic experience, but rather lack of aesthetic experience. However, they may still have aesthetic use. A scene may be depressing because it looks bad in a way that is at the same time interesting or engaging. That is, it may (although this would be rare) be depressing and have aura.

GENERAL TERMS OF AESTHETIC APPROVAL: UNIFIED, ELEGANT, GRACEFUL, DELICATE

Many terms apply to art, nature *and* everyday life: for example, "unified," "elegant," "graceful," and "delicate." Unity is classically considered a quality that makes works of art good. It is related to such other commonly-mentioned qualities as "coherent" and "complete," and, less directly, to the qualities of "symmetrical" and "balanced." All of these can equally well apply to the aesthetics of everyday life, although in a different way than to art. One can have a deep debate over the unity of a painting by Picasso. For example it might be argued that *Demoiselles d'Avignon* is unified in some ways and not in others. By contrast, determining whether a vegetable garden has unity, and determining the nature of that unity, may be a simple matter.

Three other traditional aesthetic terms that may be applied generally are "elegant," "graceful," and "delicate." Although these terms are often used in the aesthetics of art, they are sometimes even more appropriate for everyday aesthetics. The Japanese see this and exploit it more readily than European cultures. Sei Shōnagon lists a white coat worn over a violet waistcoat, "a rosary of rock crystals," and "a pretty child eating strawberries" as elegant. All of her examples are items of everyday life, or at least they were for the Japanese aristocracy of the tenth century.[79] Even though we might not understand

---

79 See Barbara Sandrisser, "On Elegance in Japan," in Higgins, ed., 628-38. Higgins's textbook *Aesthetics in Perspective* was groundbreaking in containing several articles relevant to the aesthetics of everyday life. Sandrisser's article is included in a section of that book titled "Popular Culture and Everyday Life."

completely how all of them can be considered elegant (as Barbara Sandrisser observes, the child eating strawberries might be more appropriately called charming), we get the basic idea.

Sandrisser has noted that, in the West, the term "elegant" has been used not only as a positive aesthetic term for something chosen carefully, but also as a negative term for something fastidious and foppish. It has a long history with some reversals, and is currently unpopular, although I recently had a discussion with a design professional who saw it as the primary aesthetic quality in his discipline. Sandrisser finds something parallel to our appreciation of elegance in various Japanese concepts, for example *mono no aware*, which can be translated as "sensitivity to the poignant—sad—beauty of things." She also connects this interest in elegance with everyday life insofar as it evokes aesthetic pride in the Japanese based on their traditional appreciation of "the grace and dignity inherent in everyday life."[80]

Beauty is the most general of aesthetic terms. Our experiences of beauty might not be typically everyday or ordinary, although I have mentioned examples earlier of everyday applications of this term, e.g., the cultivated flower and the plastic bag fluttering in the wind. Scruton uses the term "minimal beauty" to apply to "an unpretentious street, a nice pair of shoes, or a tasteful piece of wrapping paper."[81] This usage has the advantage of recognizing that something can be both everyday and beautiful.

POSSIBLE OBJECTIONS TO THIS APPROACH

It might be argued that my strategy has increased the field of aesthetic terms too much. The term "old" for example would not seem to be an aesthetic quality under any circumstances. Yet, it *can* be under some (relatively rare) circumstances, for example with reference to antiques when the term is not being used simply literally. Similarly, aesthetician of music Ted Gracyk has recently claimed that "fast" can become an aesthetic term in some contexts with respect to Rock music.[82] Nonetheless, it is still useful to distinguish between terms that are directly classifiable as aesthetic and the much broader collection of terms that merely have aesthetic uses.

---

80 Sandrisser, "Elegance," 633.
81 Scruton, *Beauty*, 12.
82 Ted Gracyk, *Listening to Popular Music: Or, How I Learned to Stop Worrying and Love Led Zeppelin* (Ann Arbor: University of Michigan Press, 2007), 37, 88, and 202.

Many would oppose the idea that terms like "pleasant" or "nice" should be called aesthetic at all. Ron Moore observes that the history of aesthetics is full of efforts to keep aesthetic experience separate from the merely pleasant. He himself insists that being moved aesthetically is more than being pleased.[83] He specifically wants to exclude such things as the spontaneous pleasure attending the smell of popcorn or a drink of cold water on a hot summer day. His main idea is that aesthetic experience has to be more complicated. On his view scientific knowledge could contribute to making it more complicated, but also imagination could, as long as the comparisons are apt.[84]

Three points could be made in response. First, although Moore is right that the separation between mere pleasure and aesthetic pleasure is constant in the history of aesthetics, it is difficult to find cases of the former. Even pleasant things may be contemplated, for example, thus raising them above the level of "merely pleasant." What is pleasant is not necessarily "merely pleasant." Second, pleasure attending the smell of popcorn may actually be quite complex, involving early life associations and other contextual features. Third, it is not clear that complication is always required for aesthetic experience, otherwise we wouldn't sometimes see "simple" as an aesthetic property.

Moore might reply that the complication he is referring to has to do mainly with what is required to savour an experience. Time and reflection are needed, and this would not usually be available in the popcorn or the warm water case. He is right to distinguish between experiences that involve savouring over time and those that do not. However, the distinction may be more problematic than he suggests. Through poetry and other art forms, we have learned that what is appreciated as pleasant and simple in the short term can also be savoured as complex by way of the medium of art. Reading a poem about taking a bath can draw attention to several aesthetic qualities in that experience and may even unify these qualities into an aesthetic whole. My position here is that experiencing the arts is one way we experience the subject-matter of the arts, and that subject-matter is often everyday experience. Even if the term "aesthetic" were to be limited to complex experiences savoured over time I would want to stress that the simple can become complex when mediated by art.

In a move that would counter much of what I have been saying in this book, Robert Stecker argues that appreciation of nature is not usually based on per-

---

83 Moore, *Natural Beauty*, 147.
84 Moore, *Natural Beauty*, 148.

ceiving an aesthetic property, for example the property of stillness. (I assume he would apply this to everyday aesthetics as well.) He thinks that when we appreciate a lake's stillness we are not appreciating the aesthetic property of stillness: we are just appreciating a complete lack of movement. He thinks an aesthetic property is not involved in appreciating a lake's stillness since taste is not needed. In this he follows Sibley's idea that taste (i.e., a special sensitivity) is required for recognizing aesthetic properties, but not for recognizing such merely physical properties as stillness.[85]

Yet, one can say that a chair is graceful, be right about it, and even be fairly well justified, without having taste in the sense of a special sensitivity when it comes to chairs. Virtually everyone who knows English knows how to use the word "graceful" and how to apply it to chairs, even though some connoisseurs of chairs may have very different and very precise criteria for using that term. So taste is not required for perceiving aesthetic properties. Moreover, one can also be aware of the physical property of stillness without apprehending it aesthetically. Although two people can see that nothing in the lake is moving, one might see the aesthetic quality of stillness while the other might notice stillness only in the sense that he or she perceives a lack of movement. If the first says "Look how still the lake is!" in a way that shows pleasure, he or she will likely be referring to the aesthetic property of stillness. Imagine that the second person thinks that the first is just referring to the non-aesthetic fact of stillness, and replies, "Yes, I see it. So what?" There has obviously been a misunderstanding. Similarly, if I appreciate the smoothness of a stone, and this appreciation is enhanced by my knowledge of the geological forces that produced the smoothness, I am appreciating the aesthetic quality of "smoothness." I am not, contra Stecker, appreciating some abstract science-based quality of malleability.

Stecker probably holds this position because he believes that it is not necessary for general-value properties such as beauty to be based on perceiving other aesthetic properties. He says that his appreciation of flowers is mainly connected to a pleasure he gains from closely observing their shape and colour, i.e., he directly perceives non-aesthetic properties of colour and shape and sees them as beautiful. So there is no need for other aesthetic properties. However, someone could closely observe the colour and shape of the flower and experience no delight at all. And if you called out to such a person with delight saying "Notice the colour and the shape of those flowers!" there would

---

85 Stecker, 29.

be a misunderstanding. Such an exclamation is an attempt to call attention to *the aesthetic nature* of the colour and the shape. If you say "great colour" or "great shape" you are referring to an aesthetic quality, and these become aesthetic quality terms. That is why I do not think Stecker can replace aesthetic properties with "formal, sensuous, and meaning properties of an object valued for its own sake."[86] Stecker is also basing his position in part on a conviction that aesthetic properties are based on non-aesthetic properties, an idea which I criticized in the last chapter.

The next four possible criticisms of my position developed so far are ones with which I have some sympathy and need to address in a way that is more accommodating. The first is that I place too much emphasis on terms and the qualities to which they refer. It may be argued that everyday aesthetics is not limited to appreciation of aesthetic qualities. Just as the practice of interpretation is important in the appreciation of art, so too interpretation plays a role in everyday aesthetics. Semioticians and cultural theorists have long been interested in the ways that people express themselves through their purchases, collections, and displays. Such theorists might be critical of my approach for downplaying meaning and interpretation.

A follower of Dewey's aesthetics might raise a similar criticism. As Dewey is one of the originators of everyday aesthetics and one of the heroes of this book it is important to pay attention to possible criticisms from his direction. Dewey, in *Art as Experience*, goes deeply into the basis of everyday aesthetics and provides a clear understanding of the continuity between everyday aesthetic experience and art. As he sees it, the live creature faces daily tensions which it attempts to resolve. Resolution of such tensions in a culminating moment brings about harmony which then sets the stage for new tensions and new resolutions. Experience is not passive but rather is closely tied to action. Happiness occurs when we are "fully alive" and have "heightened vitality." Being most alive is, for Dewey, a heightened aesthetic state. The live creature achieves this when its present moment is rich with connections to both past and future. Aesthetic experience happens, he says, when the past is carried into the present, and when the present seems full of potentiality in relation to the future. Dewey, then, sees everyday aesthetics not just in terms of objects having properties which are relatively passively perceived, but in terms of the life of the creature interacting with its environment. For Dewey, aesthetic experience

---

86 Stecker, 29.

is just experience at its best. It has a kind of heightened significance and, for humans, this means that it is saturated with conscious meaning. In experience, the senses come together to tell a larger story. Thus, Dewey would reject any separation of the semiotic from the aesthetic dimension of everyday aesthetics, or from any domain of aesthetics.

Dewey would also not rigidly separate everyday aesthetic from religious experience or from quasi-religious experience as in our experience of the sublime. He believed that immediate sensuous experience may absorb into itself spiritual meaning. The point here is that the sensible surface of things is never just surface. Ritual, for example, immediately enhances experience. It is closely related to the sublime, which plays an important role in Dewey's aesthetics, as when he concludes his second chapter of *Art as Experience* with a discussion of sublime experiences. I will pursue this issue in the last chapter of this book.

Another criticism could come from the direction of existentialism. It may be argued that in order to talk about the aesthetics of everyday life one must situate it within the typical life-story of humans. All humans die and, as the existentialists put it, we all exist as beings-towards-death: we are conscious that we are going to die. Surely, how we approach our everyday experience is related to this. The poignancy of the impermanent, so much remarked in Japanese aesthetics, but also often present in Western aesthetics, would be impossible without the presence of suffering and death. It is commonly thought that everyday aesthetic experience must be related only to the superficial: to the pleasant, the pretty, the cute, and so forth. These are important elements in everyday aesthetics. However, in agreement with Nietzsche, these critics would argue that what underlies all experience is the reality of suffering and death. Although everyday aesthetics is concerned with what Nietzsche referred to as the Apollonian, it cannot avoid the Dionysian, which itself is a response to what Nietzsche called "the wisdom of Silenus," i.e., the feeling that life after the death of God is worthless.[87] (Nietzsche's answer to this is saying "yes" to life: an affirmation of life and of the possibility of self-transcendence in a world without God.[88]) The existentialist and the Nietzschean would insist that the tragic dimension of human existence shapes our lives. All other stories told are related by us to the story we tell ourselves about our own lives: hence our ability to appreciate tragedy as a fine art. Moreover, as beings-towards-death

---

87 Friedrich Nietzsche, "The Birth of Tragedy," in *Basic Writings*.
88 Nietzsche, "Thus Spoke Zarathustra," in *The Portable Nietzsche*.

we humans develop life projects, and these projects are constructed in terms of a narrative that takes into account the various stages in life. Everyday aesthetic experience is always coloured by the place one finds oneself in, i.e., in one's implicit autobiography. Failure to take account of these realities would sink an aesthetics of everyday life.

Finally, the theory so far might be criticized for not sufficiently considering the extent of the aesthetics of everyday life within the animal kingdom as a whole. It would seem that wherever there is consciousness, pleasure, and some degree of selection there is aesthetic experience. It would be grossly anthropocentric to see humans as the only participants in aesthetics. The science of biology and the theory of evolution guarantee that the faculties humans possess have some parallels or analogs among the other species. It is plausible that, as Darwin thought, man is pleased by the same colours, forms, and sounds as many other species.[89] Preferences in mate selection are often based on such features as symmetry, vibrant colour and complexity, which we also value. Charles Hartshorne provides good evidence that, even for birds, singing can be enjoyable in itself and that nearly every characteristic of human music is also found in birdsong.[90] Ben-Ami Scharstein also stresses continuities between human and non-human aesthetics in his *Of Birds, Beasts, and Other Artists*.[91] And, as Wolfgang Welsch has suggested, perhaps human aesthetics developed from animal aesthetics.[92]

Whereas I resisted the criticisms I imagined coming from such philosophers as Moore and Stecker, I accept these criticisms from semioticians, Dewey, the existentialists and biologically-oriented aestheticians as useful pointers to future work in everyday aesthetics.

---

89 Charles Darwin, *The Works of Charles Darwin, Volume 21: The Descent of Man, and Selection in Relation to Sex (Part One)* (Princeton: Princeton University Press, 1981), 63.
90 Charles Hartshorne, *Born to Sing: An Interpretation and World Survey of Bird Song* (Bloomington: Indiana University Press, 1992). For a more up-to-date version of the same view, see David Rothenberg, *Why Birds Sing: A Journey into the Mystery of Bird Song* (New York: Basic Books, 2005).
91 Ben-Ami Scharfstein, *Of Birds, Beasts, and Other Artists* (New York: New York University Press, 1988).
92 Welsch, "Animal." Cf. criticism of Welsch's article in the same journal: Stefán Snævarr, "Talk to Animals: A Short Comment on Wolfgang Welsch's 'Animal Aesthetics,'" *Contemporary Aesthetics* 2 (2004), accessed Oct. 25, 2007, http://www.contempaesthetics.org/newvolume/pages/article.php?articleID=251. See also Jan Baptist Bedaux and Brett Cook, *Sociobiology and the Arts* (Amsterdam: Rodopi, 1998).

CONCLUSION

I have argued in this chapter that a fruitful way to explore the aesthetics of everyday life is through discussion of aesthetic terms. It turns out that most of these are applied throughout the field of aesthetics. However, some have special importance for everyday life. There are also certain terms that, although applicable across the field of aesthetics, have been neglected because of an overemphasis on the aesthetics of art. These include "neat," "messy," "looks good," "smells nice," "pleasant," and "cozy," among others. I observed an interesting conflict between the aesthetics of everyday life and the aesthetics of art, where certain terms that appear positive in one appear problematic in the other, for example "nice," "pretty" and even "beautiful." This conflict between the aesthetics of art and the aesthetics of everyday life may be part of the reason for the neglect of the latter. I concluded with a discussion of some of the possible criticisms of this approach by semioticians, Dewey and the existentialists. In the next chapter I will consider further possible and actual criticisms of my project as a whole.

CHAPTER 6
Criticisms Actual and Possible

In this chapter I will address various criticisms that either have been raised or could be raised against the theory of everyday aesthetics offered so far. This is a continuation of the project of addressing criticism that I began in the last chapter. These criticisms could take the form of a series of challenging questions: How does one evaluate everyday aesthetic phenomena? What about situations in which everything is experienced as aesthetic, for example when someone achieves Buddhistic enlightenment or when someone suffering from bipolar disorder is immersed in manic appreciation? Can everyday aesthetic experiences be considered aesthetic if they do not rise to the level of what Dewey calls "an experience"? Doesn't the aesthetics of everyday life aestheticize the world in a way that distorts reality or is morally problematic? Finally, related to the problem of aestheticization, is the version of aesthetics of everyday life favoured here guilty of an over-optimistic or not sufficiently socially-conscious view of the world?

HOW DOES ONE EVALUATE EVERYDAY AESTHETICS?
Some would argue that there is no such thing as everyday aesthetics since there is no basis for objective evaluation within this realm. By contrast, although there are debates over whether objectivity exists in evaluation of art, at least there are many good arguments in favour of a standard of taste in that domain. Also, whereas people often believe that disputes between art appreciators should be resolved, there is a tendency to shrug off disagreements concerning everyday aes-

thetics as matters of personal taste. You may find a street scene tawdry whereas I find it attractive: why see a conflict here that needs resolution? In addition, the aesthetics of everyday life lacks, for the most part, the equivalent of art critics, although it is noteworthy that this does not distinguish it from the aesthetics of nature. Although there are differences between the aesthetics of art and everyday aesthetics I will argue that they are not sufficient to show that there are no principles of evaluation in everyday aesthetics.

So, how should we go about evaluating everyday aesthetic objects and experiences? Some believe that the objections I raised earlier to supervenience and non-aesthetic dependence theories leave no room for objectivity here. There is an alternative to relying on such theories, however. It is to base evaluation on whatever socially accepted criteria need to be followed in applying the appropriate aesthetic predicate. The most important of these predicates will be the most general, and the most general aesthetic predicate of all is "beautiful." It is here that contest is most likely to occur, just as it is in art and nature. For example people may disagree over whether something is a beautiful home, garden, dress or baby. Some may argue that beauty is unrelated to everyday life, that it is a quality that distinctively applies to the non-everyday. Granted, beauty is something special. Yet we do speak of the beauty of friends, conversations, papers, lives, mouths, dresses and lawns. "Beauty" is an essentially contested concept (to use Gallie's term again), and we draw from different theories of beauty to make our competing claims. Whereas the standard approach in philosophy is to assume that one theory is correct and that the others are not, I prefer a more pluralist approach. When looking at theories of beauty, some are most appropriate for some phenomena whereas others work better for other phenomena. For example, we might use the concept of harmony, central to the Pythagorean notion of beauty, to describe the aesthetic quality of a Sunday drive, or Hume's concept of delicacy of taste to guarantee a good judge's evaluation of a glass of wine, or Kant's notion of a free play of imagination and understanding to justify attribution of beauty to a display of shadows on a wall. If so, then the recommended approach to evaluation in everyday aesthetics is eclecticism, at least when it comes to beauty. Other predicates related to what I have called low-level experience are probably going to generate less conflict. Nonetheless, people do have differing notions of what counts for neatness, prettiness, niceness, cuteness and so forth. As with beauty, resolution of debates over these follows traditional social channels.

"Beauty" has long been seen not simply as one term of aesthetic value among many (in which case it is contrasted to "pretty," "sublime," "delicate," and so forth) but also as a term for aesthetic excellence in general. On this view the various aesthetic properties are examples or types of beauty. When we say that something is graceful or sublime we are saying that it has a sort of beauty. It is this latter sense that makes the various historical efforts to define beauty (Pythagorean, Humean, Kantian, etc.) useful for our purposes. One might even argue that any positive aesthetic quality taken to its highest qualitative point amounts to beauty. For example, we commonly say that someone is so pretty, charming, graceful, or elegant, as to be beautiful. We might even say that something is so comic as to be beautiful. The term "sublime," however, goes in the other direction: we say "it is so beautiful as to be sublime" not "it is so sublime that it is beautiful." So it is not the case that *every* positive aesthetic quality taken to its highest point equals beauty.

Pythagoras and the Pythagoreans are the first Greek philosophers to provide us with an actual aesthetic theory. The central idea of the Pythagoreans with regards to aesthetics was harmony. However, unlike contemporary aesthetic theories, Pythagoreanism did not limit this idea to the arts: it covered all aspects of the world including the cosmos and the soul. For example, when the Pythagoreans said that no art comes about without proportion they used the word *techné* which refers not only to the arts but to all crafts. The Pythagoreans understood proportion in terms of specific numerical ratios, for example the golden mean. So, on their view, all of the crafts arise through number.

Two even more fundamental aesthetic qualities than harmony and proportion were introduced by the Pythagoreans: order and unity. One might call the correlated properties of "ordered" and "unified" pre-aesthetic in that they are very simple and they contribute to more complicated aesthetic properties. Although order is not always pleasing, for we can find it boring or dictatorial, generally speaking we prefer it to disorder and we often get pleasure from its contemplation. Unity is also often aesthetic, as we explored when discussing Beardsley. Although one meaning of unity is oneness, and it is difficult to see how oneness itself can be beautiful, unity can also characterize a complex whole, for example when diverse parts are ordered within the whole. Unity can be found in every aspect of life and is not limited to the arts.

The concept of harmony was probably invented by the Pythagoreans. Harmony for the Pythagoreans is not the same as peacefulness. The term originally comes from the Greek words *harmos* (joint) and *harmozein* (fit together). When two things are joined in a functional way we may speak of harmony. However, the Pythagorean idea of harmony goes beyond what the word's etymology implies since it also incorporates the ideas of order and unity, and of course pleasure in the apprehension of it.

The idea of harmony was closely associated with that of symmetry which in turn was associated with beauty. The Pythagoreans believed that order and proportion (symmetry) are beautiful and useful, and that things are beautiful because of number, which is to say, proportion. In the same paragraph in which Aristotle sets forth the Pythagorean belief that the principles of mathematics are the principles of all things, he says that for them the whole of the universe is a proportion (*harmonian*) and a number.[1]

It is clear that the Pythagorean principles of harmony, symmetry, proportion, order and unity apply to aesthetics in general, not just to the aesthetics of art, and that these properties, when perceived, generate aesthetic experience. These ideas are as relevant to home decoration and personal beauty as to fine art painting. However, the concepts of harmony, symmetry and order are not sufficient by themselves to answer the question of evaluation in everyday aesthetics. More is needed.

A Humean approach to everyday aesthetics is also plausible.[2] Whereas Pythagoras focused on good-making properties, Hume turned to "the good judge." A Humean would require that one evaluate the items of everyday aesthetics in the way a good judge would. A good judge is someone who has delicacy of sentiment based on considerable experience with the matter under consideration including practice making comparative judgments. The good judge should also avoid prejudice as much as possible and should have good sense. Hume thinks that the good judge is able to perceive "certain general principles of approbation of blame" in particular, qualities that are "calculated to please."[3] He gives one example of such principles when he says that the poet Ariosto "charms by the force and clearness of his expression, by the readiness and variety of his inventions, and by his natural picture of the passions...."[4] Thus a good judge would be able to appropriately apply such aesthetic terms as "forceful," "clear," "inventive," and "natural."

A Humean approach will work in any case in which there are connoisseurs. There are, for example, connoisseurs for every class of things that people col-

---

1 Aristotle, *Metaphysics*, trans. Hugh Tredennick (Cambridge, MA: Harvard University Press, 1933), I, V, 33.
2 Hume, "Standard," 592-606.
3 Hume, "Standard," 596.
4 Hume, "Standard," 595.

lect, and people collect all sorts of things, from matchbooks to telephone poles. Moreover, there are all sorts of connoisseurs for tastes and smells. However, the Humean approach cannot apply everywhere. It is useful to distinguish between those cases in which we are willing to defer to a connoisseur, or think that connoisseurship is relevant, and those in which we tend to ignore issues of connoisseurship. For example, although there are connoisseurs of feline beauty I do not see myself needing to defer to them when I say that a cat is pretty or cute.

Some might argue that where we have connoisseurs we have an art-form. For example, whereas many would consider taste in food to be a matter of everyday aesthetics, others would classify gourmet food as an art-form. We do not need to decide here whether gourmet taste falls within everyday aesthetics. The important point with respect to evaluation is that these matters can be handled in much the same way that Hume handles taste with regard to literary works.

Hume himself makes his point about literary taste by way of an analogy to taste in wine. He refers to the former as a mental and the latter as a physical taste. However, I doubt that there is a great difference between taste in wine and taste in paintings that can be explained by making a physical/mental distinction. Following Hume, we can argue that something is good in the way wine or food is if it is judged as such by the good judge, the good judge having the characteristics Hume classically gave, i.e., lack of prejudice, practice in making judgments, experience in making comparisons, good sense, and delicacy of taste. The only problem left would be to answer Hume's various critics, and since this issue is shared with the aesthetics of art, we need not go into this in detail here.

Nick Zangwill thinks it problematic that the virtues and vices Hume cites in relation to the fine arts may equally apply to our ability to be pleased by food.[5] So he doubts that the virtues Hume finds in the good judge can explain how our judgments of beauty or ugliness can be correct. Yet, I would argue that there is no big distinction between a wine connoisseur and a painting connoisseur. Both may make claims to correctness. Both may use the terms "beautiful," "lovely," "awful," and so forth. Both can be good judges in Hume's sense.

Zangwill bases his attack on a misunderstanding of Hume's argument. When discussing the central notion of delicacy of taste, Zangwill equates delicacy with the simple capacity to make subtle sensory discriminations. However, for Hume, delicacy of taste is a matter not simply of discriminating but of judging the various elements discriminated. Sancho's first cousin's ability

---

5   Zangwill, "Realism," 73.

to taste the leather allows him to qualify his otherwise positive judgment of the wine. Moreover, delicacy of sentiment just is what the good judge achieves through practice with the objects in question. Hume observes that before such practice taste cannot perceive all the ways each item is excellent. It cannot perceive the beauties and defects of each part.[6] The only thing wrong with this is that Hume is overly optimistic about the possibility of precise knowledge in criticism (whether of mental or physical objects).

In his response to Hume, Zangwill only gives us vague talk about how judgments of beauty are more "robust" and have higher "normative aspirations" than judgments of niceness. He seeks radically to separate art from everyday life and judgments of beauty from judgments of niceness. This is partly because he thinks judgments of niceness follow the philosophy of "anything goes." Yet, it is not true that anything goes in judgments of niceness. If I say that a passage of writing is a nice piece of prose, my pronouncement will be evaluated by others on the basis of certain standards, their own perceptions, and their evaluation of my status as a good judge. Although there are differences between judgments of niceness in everyday contexts and judgments of beauty in great works of art, this is more a matter of complexity than of some grand distinction between the subjective and the objective. Moreover, Zangwill ignores the fact that there are judgments of beauty in everyday life. In short, his rejection of what Hume refers to as "the great resemblance between mental and bodily taste" is unfounded.

What about people who collect and cherish objects and appear to be able to distinguish between better and worse examples, and yet these objects are considered to be of poor taste or of little value to others, especially to art experts? That is, what about people who value kitsch? Hummel figurines (ceramic items first produced in 1935 by the Goebel company based on drawings by Sister Maria Innocentia Hummel) are widely considered to be kitsch, but are also collectible, some going for sale on eBay for as much as $6000.

We can resolve the problem of evaluation here by talking about different levels. Let us first assume that Hummel figurines exist in a tradition of connoisseurship, although not a sophisticated one, and that there are good judges in this tradition. Here, the Humean approach is relevant to evaluation. However, there can be a second level of discourse in which the tradition itself may be evaluated. This is where we get the criticisms of certain domains of everyday aesthetics as cheapening the human spirit and distracting the appreciator from higher-

---

6   Hume, "Standard."

quality aesthetic experiences. Similar considerations enter in at the level of fine arts. One can be a connoisseur of Bouguereau's nineteenth-century paintings of charming little girls. However, another level of evaluation may question whether his saccharine images are worthy of consideration as art.

Some people may believe that an interest in the aesthetics of everyday life implies a belief that there is no distinction in principle between the value of a Rembrandt and that of a Hummel figurine. I do not see why that would be implied. Even lovers of these figurines will probably admit that Rembrandt's *Night Watch* has greater aesthetic value. To say that there is an aesthetics of everyday life is not to say that the pleasures we gain from kitsch are equally valuable to those we gain from fine art.

Also, the relationship between kitsch and fine art is not just on an evaluative scale: it is also interactive. It has long been the practice of fine artists to draw on kitsch and similar everyday life material for their own work. These sources of inspiration provide a base for some of our more complex aesthetic experiences. Jeff Koons is one example of a contemporary artist who takes objects from everyday life, including figures that would be considered kitsch, and transforms them in a way that enters them into the artworld, giving them more complexity and value. A case in point is his "Michael Jackson and Bubbles" (1988) made of gold-covered porcelain and representing the musician with his pet chimpanzee.

Just as with the Pythagorean idea of harmony, Hume's idea of the good judge is also not sufficient alone to evaluate everyday phenomena aesthetically. Some items are best evaluated simply in terms of how well they serve their function. However, as mentioned earlier in my critique of Carlson and Parsons' approach to everyday aesthetics, it is not clear that evaluations of functionality are completely outside the domain of connoisseurship. Often what we call functionality is really more the look of functionality, and looks can have connoisseurs. Also, there are aspects of our everyday lives in which functionality is not clearly an issue, but connoisseurship is. For example, within the fashion industry there are very specific needs with respect to the look of a model, and there are people who are paid well to find the women and men who meet these standards. These standards are quite different from what would meet the function, for example, of maximum gene survival. Biological functionality is clearly not a criterion for beauty in choice of fashion models. To reply that they meet the function of being fashionable would be to beg the question since "fashionable" is a culturally determined and changeable aesthetic property that falls outside the domain of functionalism.

There are even areas in which neither Pythagorean, Humean, nor functionalist criteria are relevant but in which Kant's idea of disinterested beauty is. A free play of the imagination and understanding in the appreciation of such objects as sunsets and shadows sometimes better serves our purposes than ideas of symmetry, connoisseurship or "looking fit for its function." Assume that Kant is right that in proclaiming a sunset beautiful I expect others to also see it as beautiful. This does not imply that I am or must be a connoisseur in sunsets. That which is conducive to free play of imagination and understanding might be considered valuable in the realm of everyday aesthetics. For example, I might find the way laundry flaps in the wind beautiful because it causes my mind to go into the kind of free play Kant describes.

So the answer to the criticism that everyday aesthetics would have no principles of evaluation is that an eclectic set of evaluations based on various theories of beauty and taste may be applied. Each of the traditional theories discussed is most applicable to a particular range of objects. These authors tended to see their theories as universally true. However, the theories just do not apply universally. I should also add that the list of theories of beauty useful for the eclectic approach is open-ended: perhaps there are items best evaluated according to theories derived from Beardsley or Heidegger, for example. Finally, eclecticism is still bound within the general theory that for "beauty" to be applicable the object must be perceived as with aura. This is a necessary, although not a sufficient condition for beauty. A sufficient condition for good application of the term would be needed to determine whether it or another aesthetic property term should be used.

ZEN BUDDHIST MONKS, THE AESTHETIC ATTITUDE, LSD AND MANIC-DEPRESSION

The Zen Buddhist monk, the aesthetic attitude theorist, the psychedelic drug user and the manic-depressive together pose another problem for the theory I have offered. Each is capable of transforming everyday experience into something extraordinary in a way that seems to destroy the distinction between the aesthetic and the non-aesthetic. Zen monks who have achieved satori seem to dissolve the distinction between the aesthetic and the spiritual: for them even a crack in a rice bowl can have great aesthetic/spiritual significance. Aesthetic attitude theorists pose a similar problem when they say that anything can be experienced aesthetically. Psychedelic drug-users and manic-depressives in their manic phase need no special attitude or theory to experience everything as aesthetic, and that too is a problem.

Archie J. Bahm describes Zen as "aesthetic experience in which one appreciates whatever is for what it is or as it is."[7] He says that this experience is "direct, intuitive, concrete, spontaneous, and dynamic." Quoting from Daisetz Suzuki, he denies that Zen is mere subjectivism, for it is a frame of mind that can respond immediately to what comes to it from the outside. Here, the realm of aesthetic experience seems to have no limits.[8]

Also, consider Wordsworth's idea of a utopia in which even the average man could transfigure the commonplace, appreciating mere real things instead of art objects.[9] George Leonard associates this idea with Arthur Danto's experience in the 1960s when facing Warhol's *Brillo Boxes*.[10] Unfortunately, this misconceives Danto since he stresses a great difference between the work by Warhol, which has been transfigured into the artworld, and ordinary boxes in a warehouse. Indeed Danto's point is the opposite of Warhol's, who wanted to break down barriers between fine art and the everyday. However, Leonard has found in Wordsworth, and perhaps in Warhol, something similar to the Zen Buddhist's experience of satori. John Cage is another artist who seems, as Leonard observes, to turn everything into an aesthetic object, particularly in his composition *4'33"*. The point of the piece, which I described in Chapter One, was to notice the aesthetic qualities of ambient sounds during the performance, including what are commonly called noises. This too, has a Zen-like quality, of which Cage himself was quite aware.

Similarly, those who have argued that there is such a thing as "the aesthetic attitude" have sometimes claimed that *anything* can be appreciated under that attitude, and hence become aesthetic. Jerome Stolnitz, writing in 1961, famously defined the aesthetic attitude as "disinterested and sympathetic attention to and contemplation of any object of awareness whatever, for its own sake alone."[11] He went so far as to allow aesthetic appreciation of "dull, unexciting things like supplies stacked row upon row in a warehouse" (anticipating

---

7   Archie J. Bahm, review of *Zen and Japanese Culture*, by Daisetz T. Suzuki, *The Journal of Aesthetics and Art Criticism* 19, no. 2 (1960): 238-39, 238.
8   Leonard, 147-62.
9   Leonard, 57.
10 The reference is to Arthur Danto, "The Artworld," *Journal of Philosophy* 61, no. 19 (1964): 571-84.
11 Jerome Stolnitz, "On the Origins of 'Aesthetic Disinterestedness,'" *The Journal of Aesthetics and Art Criticism* 20, no. 2 (1961): 131-43.

Warhol's *Brillo Boxes*). He also quotes an earlier writer as saying that although his normal attitude towards a littered street market on a Sunday morning is to avoid it, he has sometimes experienced it impersonally so that, although remaining ugly, it has gained a new coherence and clarity.[12] Stolnitz thinks that experiences like this tend to support the view that *all* objects can be aesthetic. Paul Ziff similarly argued in 1979 that "anything that can be viewed is a fit object for aesthetic attention" even objects which some cannot bear to view.[13]

Whereas Stolnitz saw the aesthetic attitude as detaching things from the everyday, I think that it can only have value if it involves detaching everyday things from mere ordinariness. Nor can I take Stolnitz seriously when he says that "[t]o perceive disinterestedly is to make oneself a pure, unflawed mirror, prepared to receive without distortion [quoting from Archibald Alison], 'all the impressions, which the objects that are before us can produce.'"[14] No human can be an unflawed mirror. At best, we can act as if we were.

Later, in 1979, Stolnitz recognized the value of avant-garde art in transforming our perception of ordinary things, writing that their "depictions and assemblages of utensils, commercial products, and industrial detritus (junked automobiles) do not tell against disinterested perception. They solicit such perception."[15] He added that "[t]his art proceeds by divorcing objects from their quotidian settings" and from our practical selves: "Only then do we see [such objects] perhaps for the first time, for what they are." Although this approach places too much emphasis on detachment from the practical setting in which the object exists, and is too optimistic about seeing objects for what they really are, it does capture ways in which art can enhance our experience of the objects of everyday life.

What Monroe Beardsley calls "the LSD problem" is similar to the problem of the Zen Buddhist monk. It is also probably directed against philosophers like Stolnitz and Ziff, and artists like Cage.[16] Beardsley's intuition was that although it might seem possible to appreciate a pile of dung aesthetically while

---

12 E.M. Bartlett, *Types of Aesthetic Judgment* (London: George Allen & Unwin, 1937), 211-12.
13 Ziff. I will explore Ziff's ideas on this later.
14 Stolnitz, "Origins," 138.
15 Jerome Stolnitz, "The Artistic and the Aesthetic in Interesting Times," *The Journal of Aesthetics and Art Criticism* 37, no. 4 (1979): 401-13, 411.
16 Monroe Beardsley, "The Aesthetic Point of View," in *Contemporary Philosophy of Art: Readings in Analytic Aesthetics*, ed. John W. Bender and H. Gene Blocker (Englewood Cliffs, NJ: Prentice Hall, 1993), 384-96.

under LSD, this experience should be discounted as illusory. A psychiatrist once described his experience of Beethoven's *Eroica* as causing him to simultaneously feel insatiable longing and total gratification. Beardsley replied that this *proves* he was on LSD, presumably because such an experience is impossible. But this example does not confirm Beardsley's conclusion that for an object to have aesthetic value it must provide aesthetic gratification only when *correctly* experienced. Would he hold that Van Gogh incorrectly experienced his small bedroom when he painted *Bedroom in Arles* (1888)? Van Gogh's experience might well be just as unusual as that had by someone under LSD. Yet it seems strange and unfair to call his experience somehow incorrect.

In short, the argument Beardsley uses to exclude LSD experiences as aesthetic appears to also exclude the transformative experiences that artists have during the creative process. Can this be justified? Wouldn't it make more sense to say that, although someone might make incorrect inferences under LSD, the experience is still aesthetic? Beardsley thought we would be forced into saying that *everything* has equally high aesthetic value if we accepted that everything can provide intense aesthetic gratification under some circumstances. However, it is not clear that this follows. As Ziff argued, the idea that no one thing is more fit for aesthetic attention than anything else is not inconsistent with the idea that some things are more aesthetically valuable than others in some respects.[17]

There is a solution to the problem of how to approach the aesthetic attitude and its accompanying concept of disinterestedness which I already raised in a previous chapter. Peggy Brand, a feminist aesthetician, argues that although disinterestedness is "a masculinist approach to the experiencing of a work of art, it is still a possible and appropriate, useful mode of experiencing art, including feminist art...."[18] Brand is particularly interested in aesthetic perception of the nude, which traditional theorists believed could be perceived in a disinterested fashion. Feminists prior to Brand tended to argue that perception must always be "interested," and perception of the female nude always guided by male sexual or power interests. Brand breaks with these feminists, not out of any sympathy for the older masculinist view, but because she believes that controversial feminist art needs sometimes to be viewed in a disinterested fashion in order to undercut conventional viewing habits. For her, disinterestedness

---

17   Ziff, 30.
18   Brand, 163.

can serve feminist needs. Instead, she favours toggling between interested and disinterested attention. She likens this to the switch between seeing the Jastrow Duck-Rabbit figure as a rabbit or as a duck. Toggling from interested attention to disinterested attention, and then back again to interested attention, allows for a richer overall aesthetic experience. The point is not necessarily tied to feminist issues. Theodore Gracyk applies it much more broadly to any subject matter that "challenges our existing interests."[19]

This strategy may also be applied to everyday aesthetics. One can look at an everyday streetscape from a disinterested perspective, focusing on sensuous and design features, and then switch to a perspective that takes into account history and context. One can follow Stolnitz in isolating the object from the flow of experience and from its interrelations with other things, and then toggle to a non-isolated form of perception.[20] I have been arguing that taking the aesthetic attitude is taking an attitude that allows objects, environments or events to have aura. Although either disinterestedness or interested perception alone might do this, toggling between interested and disinterested perception is more likely to heighten significance. The toggling approach may be applied to all types of aesthetics: of art, of nature and of everyday life.

The idea of toggling is not unique to Brand and Gracyk. Mexican aesthetician Katya Mandoki proposes a similar idea when she recommends swinging between identification and distancing, a swinging she finds both in a painter providing detailed views alternating with overall views, and with the viewer's tendency to look at paintings both from close up and from a distance.[21] This alternation may also be applied to the appreciation of the phenomena of everyday life.

Toggling allows viewers not to be tied to rigid context-based forms of perception. Contemporary aestheticians tend to expect that viewers base their perception of aesthetic phenomena on understanding of how those phenomena fit into specific and standardized contexts. Parsons and Carlson, for example, require that one view a spoon in terms of whether or not it has the look of serving its proper function. They see the matter as a choice between Stolnitz's

---

19 Theodore Gracyk, "A Different Plea for Disinterest," in *Aesthetics: A Reader in Philosophy of the Arts*, 502-08.
20 Stolnitz, *Aesthetics and Philosophy of Art Criticism* (Boston: Houghton Mifflin, 1960), 35.
21 Katya Mandoki, *Everyday Aesthetics: Prosaics, the Play of Culture and Social Identities* (Burlington, VT: Ashgate, 2007), 22.

disinterestedness approach and their interestedness approach. In doing this they fail to recognize the value of toggling.

Before going on to the last example we should dispel a possible confusion. The Zen experience of satori is in many ways not in the same category as an LSD experience. For one thing, Zen enlightenment, unlike the LSD experience, requires great discipline and a gradual growth in self-knowledge. Also, although Zen enlightenment is sometimes described in a way that implies an extremely intense aesthetic experience, it is possible that the language of aesthetics is not appropriate to it. For example, Zen adepts often refer to a sense of oneness with the object, which excludes the distancing often associated with the aesthetic. There are, of course, aesthetic theories that do not stress distancing, for example Berleant's "aesthetics of engagement."[22] But even these do not give us an experience comparable to that described by Zen monks.

Also, the world of Zen monks, including the monastery and the physical accoutrements of Zen practice, is far from aesthetically indiscriminate. Many Japanese art forms, for example the Art of Tea, in which there is much room for subtle discrimination and connoisseurship, have been strongly influenced by Zen sensibility. The existence of these forms seems inconsistent with the idea that *all* things become aesthetically charged in the moment of Zen enlightenment, although one could still argue that they are only preliminary exercises that become unnecessary after enlightenment.

Shinkei, a Zen monk and poet (1406-75), emphasized the Japanese concept of *yugen* as a refined beauty that can only be appreciated by the heart. He advised, as Andrew Tsubaki puts it, "paying attention to inconspicuous objects such as white, single-petalled plum blossoms blooming among bamboos, or the moon revealed through the gaps of the clouds." Shinkei was not, however, interested in red, double-petalled blossoms.[23] Zen aesthetics appears, then, to be highly selective.

It is also arguable that we should speak not so much of the *problem* as of the *promise* of Zen. The Zen ideal of satori, in which everything is potentially appreciated, could be an ideal for everyday aesthetics. Yuriko Saito speaks of the Zen commitment to egalitarianism, which she sees as "embodied in the aesthetic elevation of the mundane and the ordinary, practiced in particular

---

22 Arnold Berleant, *Art and Engagement* (Philadelphia: Temple University Press, 1993).
23 Andrew T. Tsubaki, "Zeami and the Transition of the Concept of Yugen: A Note on Japanese Aesthetics," *The Journal of Aesthetics and Art Criticism* 30, no. 1 (1971): 55-67, 60.

by the tea ceremony and haiku."²⁴ She observes that the tea ceremony elevates such things as washing hands and boiling water to artistic heights and that haiku takes objects which may seem vulgar as its objects, concluding that, for Zen aesthetics, value is not limited to the noble and elegant.

My final example of a type of experience that might challenge my theory by making all experience aesthetic is that of someone who suffers from manic-depression. In the manic phase of this illness the individual is said to experience everything as having heightened significance.²⁵ As psychologist Oliver Sacks observes, mania changes not only thought and affect, but sensation. One manic-depressive describes his experience in the manic phase in this way: "My hearing appears to be more sensitive, and I am able to take in many different sound-impressions at the same time.... If I were to be allowed to walk about freely in a flower garden I should appreciate the scents far more than usual ... Even common grass tastes excellent, while real delicacies like strawberries and raspberries give ecstatic sensations appropriate to a veritable food of the gods."²⁶ He also says that while he was in his manic phase faces would "glow with a sort of inner light," showing characteristic lines with extreme vividness.²⁷ The depressive phase, which usually follows, is described by the same writer as one of "misery, dejection, and at times of appalling horror."²⁸ In the manic phase he could be described as seeing everything with positive aura, whereas the depressive phase involves the negation of all aesthetic experience. Although it could be argued that my theory of aesthetic experience is too broad because it includes manic experience as aesthetic, I would reply that we are simply talking about the nature of aesthetic experience, not about the value of any particular type of aesthetic experience.

Although it appears that many famous authors, musicians and artists were bipolar, or at least had manic episodes, it is also clear that the manic state is dangerous. It encourages irrational beliefs and actions, and is often followed by equally intense depressive episodes. If mania was the only method by which this kind of heightened sensation could be achieved then the personal cost

---

24 Yuriko Saito, "The Japanese Aesthetics of Imperfection and Insufficiency," *The Journal of Aesthetics and Art Criticism* 55, no. 4 (1997): 377-85, 382.
25 Oliver Sacks, "A Summer of Madness," *The New York Review of Books* (Sept. 25, 2008): 57-61.
26 Sacks, 59 quoted from John Constance, pseud. *Wisdom, Madness and Folly: The Philosophy of a Lunatic* (New York: Pellegrini and Cudahy, 1952).
27 Sacks, 59.
28 Sacks, 58.

would be too high. Zen practice suggests less dangerous ways of achieving a similar effect, as do the experiences of artists and those who can experience the world with the eyes of an artist. Manic experience may sometimes be aesthetic: but not everything aesthetic is valuable overall.

Taking the aesthetic attitude towards an object is one way to appreciate it aesthetically. This idea has been opposed by those who believe that the only proper appreciation involves understanding the historical context of the thing under consideration. Historical understanding has its value, but its overemphasis has deprived us of the value of disinterestedness. The solution is to follow the toggling theory put forth by Brand, Gracyk and Mandoki. Only by swinging between the two perspectives can a fuller and richer experience be achieved. Zen Buddhist practice poses an interesting problem: someone who achieves satori seems to experience everything as aesthetic. LSD and the manic state pose similar problems, although there are also differences. None of this in the end is a real problem for aura theory which allows that an experience may be aesthetic even though pervasive throughout life or even though dangerous to one's survival.

The problems we have raised here, with the Zen Buddhist monk, the aesthetic attitude theorist, the LSD taker, and the manic-depressive have shown that the aesthetics of everyday life *ordinarily experienced* needs to be distinguished from the aesthetics of everyday life *extraordinaryly experienced*, i.e., as experienced under one of these special states. However, the distinction should not be taken as rigid. As we shall see in the next section, any attempt to increase the aesthetic intensity of our ordinary experiences will tend to push those experiences in the direction of the extraordinary.

HOW PERVASIVE IS THE AESTHETIC IN ORDINARY EXPERIENCE?

A possible criticism of everyday aesthetics is that it confuses the aesthetic with the pleasant. There have been many attempts to make or firm up a distinction between the merely pleasant or pleasurable and the aesthetic. Carolyn Korsmeyer, for instance, has argued, following Nelson Goodman, that the aesthetic necessarily contains a cognitive dimension not found in the merely pleasurable.[29] Cognitive content is achieved when properties are

---

29 Carolyn Korsmeyer, "Food and the Taste of Meaning," in von Bonsdorff and Haapala, *Aesthetics in the Human Environment* (Lahti: International Institute of Applied Aesthetics, 1999), 90-105. See Nelson Goodman, *Languages of Art* 2nd ed. (Indianapolis: Hackett, 1976).

"exemplified." Exemplification happens when an object possesses a property and also refers to its label, as when a blue tailor's sample refers back to or exemplifies "blue." At the same time, Korsmeyer is willing to expand our notion of what can be viewed aesthetically. She believes, for example, that food may be approached aesthetically insofar as it sometimes has meaning and frequently exemplifies its properties. If we can do this with food then perhaps we can do it with many other kinds of everyday objects. If we could just figure out what makes a property exemplified we could separate pleasures which are aesthetic from ones that are not—that is, if we follow Korsmeyer in accepting Goodman's view of the aesthetic. However I find Goodman's concept of exemplification too thin insofar as it consists only of a combination of property possession and referral to a label without any phenomenological component or pleasure dimension that could make it criterial for aesthetic experience.

Before we pursue this issue further we need to ask what kind of thing is "the aesthetic"? Is it a natural kind, like water? Or is it a cultural kind, like "America" or, perhaps, "art"?[30] If it is a cultural kind, then does it change with history and context (which, I would argue, is the case with cultural kinds)? Philosophers sometimes treat it as a natural kind when they imply that they have found some new fact about it. This would be like finding out that neutrinos were more pervasive than we thought. Alternatively, they may simply be asking us to expand the meaning of the term, to see things as aesthetic that we did not before, hence treating "aesthetic" more like a cultural kind term. Perhaps, instead, the aesthetic is *like* a natural kind in some yet-to-be-specified way, and so should be looked at much like we look at natural kinds. I treated it as a cultural kind earlier when I defined it in terms of the experience of aura. That definition was not intended to capture a natural kind like *gold*, but something that is real, cultural and evolving. However, sometimes it may be useful to think of it as *like* a natural kind. For instance, one can speak of discovering something about it, although that discovery is relativized to cultural and historical context. Although it is true that writers like Irvin and I seek to expand the meaning of "aesthetic," we are not claiming that we have discovered the *right*

---

30 I argue for the idea that art is a cultural kind in "Rigid Designation in Defining Art," *The Journal of Aesthetics and Art Criticism* 45, no. 3 (1987): 263-72. See also Dickie, *Art and Value*, 18-24.

use of the concept.³¹ Rather we believe that something new and valuable is captured by this extension.

One could similarly ask whether "ordinary experience" is a natural or a cultural kind. If it is a cultural kind it is both humanly created and historically conditioned. On this view, what is considered part of ordinary experience in one place or time is not in another. It could be added that the very concept "ordinary experience" is "essentially contested" like "art" and "beauty."³² That is, there are competing theories of ordinary experience even within particular times and places, just as there are for "aesthetic experience." If both "aesthetic" and "ordinary experience" name cultural kinds, then their mutual relations will shift and evolve historically and culturally. However, as with other cultural kinds and other essentially contested concepts, this does not mean that one cannot present and defend definitions of them, or gain some value from the ensuing debates.

Opponents of everyday aesthetics might also argue that the approach to these terms that I and others advocate violates ordinary language, and that, although ordinary language is not sacrosanct, we have not given them reason to follow us.³³ Many would argue that such experiences as that of lazy relaxation in bed on a Sunday morning, or of petting one's cat, cannot have an aesthetic quality.³⁴ They would wonder why we wish to extend the term "aesthetic" to such experiences, when its more central meaning has to do with experiences of nature and fine art. They might say that the term is highly charged in value, as for instance in its association with strong experience of works of art, and that everyday phenomena cannot hold this charge. I would reply that this argument is based on dubious assumptions about what language can do, about what is necessary, and about what is historically contingent. "Aesthetic" has an evolving meaning. For example, it had a much broader meaning in the eighteenth century than in the nineteenth and twentieth, and seems to be gaining a broader meaning again.

One potential criticism of everyday aesthetics could come from one of its friends. Dewey might argue that without conscious enjoyment and some "pervasive quality" or something like "unity" there cannot be aesthetic experience in the sense of "an experience" and that everyday aesthetic phenomena fail

---

31 Soucek in his criticism of Irvin limits her to this option and changing the topic in his "Resisting the Itch to Redefine Aesthetics: A Response to Sherri Irvin," *Journal of Aesthetics and Art Criticism* 67, no. 2 (2009): 223-26, 226.
32 Gallie, "Contested."
33 Brian Soucek argues this for example, 226.
34 The example of petting one's cat is from Sherri Irvin's "Pervasiveness."

to achieve this. However, as I argued earlier, there are a number of ways in which phenomena could be considered aesthetic, and this is not limited to "an experience." Also, Aquinas's definition of the aesthetic in terms of pleasure in the object's apprehension, taken together with that of Baumgarten in terms of sensuous cognition, allows for a broader conception of the aesthetic than that of Dewey or of more recent aestheticians.

This is not, however, to extend the aesthetic to include all that is pleasurable: for example, it does not include pleasure taken in one's child receiving a prize, or even pleasure in a warm bath. For an experience to be aesthetic there must be a contemplative or reflective element present, and a dimension of aura in the object experienced. Also, much depends on how we interpret "pervasive quality" and "unity." If "pervasive quality" can be taken to imply what I have called "aura" then there is no inconsistency between Dewey's theory and my own, and we have already discussed more compatible interpretations of "unity" when discussing Beardsley.

Although Dewey's concept of "an experience" was one of the originating ideas of everyday aesthetics,[35] and is still of considerable value, it cannot cover all aspects of that field. "An experience," as Dewey saw it, might be the culminating moment or highest point in everyday aesthetics. However, some ordinary aesthetic experiences do not involve every aspect of "an experience" as he understood it. There exist what I have called pre-aesthetic experiences that provide low-level aesthetic pleasure. The experience of pleasure in perceiving a neatened room is an example. There might be a sense of consummation here but not the pervasiveness of one quality Dewey requires. More importantly, Dewey fails to discuss transitional states that fall between experiences with minimal aesthetic quality and "an experience." We may posit a continuum that goes from the pre or proto-aesthetic, through experiences that are aesthetic but not examples of "an experience," to ones that do meet that high standard. The pre-aesthetic refers to what I have called low-level aesthetic properties such as "pretty" and "pleasant," or what Scruton calls "minimal beauties." The "proto-aesthetic" refers to what comes prior to actual aesthetic experience in evolutionary or childhood developmental terms. When Dissanayake speaks of the infant as having innate preferences for certain treatments of sights, sounds and movements she says that these are not quite aesthetic, but "proto-aesthetic."[36]

---

35 Crispin Sartwell says so in "Everyday."
36 Ellen Dissanayake, "In the Beginning: Pleistocene and Infant Aesthetics and Twenty-First Century Education in the Arts," *International Handbook of Research in Arts Education*, ed. Liora Bresler, Chapter 53, Vol. 2 (2007): 783-98.

Sherri Irvin has recently argued that even scratching an itch can be an aesthetically positive experience.[37] Although this act generally speaking is not aesthetic, it *can* be when it has some reflective or contemplative dimension. Petting one's cat, another example of Irvin's, may fall into a category further up the continuum (aesthetic, but not "an experience") insofar as it has some, but not all, of the features of "an experience." For example, it can be pleasurable, have a beginning, middle and end, and have a pervasive quality, but involve no consummation.

Any experience can be heightened through re-contextualization. One can frame it in such a way as to make it more complex phenomenologically, and this would move in the direction of making it aesthetic in the fullest sense. As I have suggested, art, for example a poem about an itch, can help carry out this transformation. As Irvin has argued, itches are appropriate objects of aesthetic experience if they contribute aesthetically to more complex experiences of which they are parts.[38] In short, anything can be experienced aesthetically, although not everything *is* so experienced, and not everything experienced aesthetically is experienced on the same level of the continuum.

As part of an attack on Irvin's theory, and on everyday aesthetics in general, Brian Soucek has argued that itches and scratches cannot be aesthetic since they are mere brute sensations, having little meaning, and because they are not publicly accessible, and thus can provide no grounds for objective evaluation.[39] There are four objections to this. First, it is not clear that any sensation is merely a brute one, if by that is meant having no meaning content, associations, or larger context. Second, whereas some itches and scratches have little meaning content, others may be rich in meaning or layers of experience. For example, there is a Vietnamese art of ear-picking that has an erotic dimension based on a form of tickling or scratching that is focused on parts of the ear that are extra-sensitive.[40] Third, although itches are not publicly accessible, neither are our personal experiences of art. My Mona-Lisa-as-experienced is inevitably going to be different from yours. Fourth, lack of public accessibility does

---

37 Sherri Irvin, "Scratching."
38 Sherri Irvin, "Scratching," 26.
39 Soucek.
40 John Boudreau, "Vietnamese clients wax poetic over ear picking," *San Jose Mercury News* (MCT) (January 27, 2011), reprinted in *The Seattle Times*, accessed June 29, 2011, http://seattletimes.nwsource.com/html/health/2014054475_ear28.html.

not invalidate all knowledge. We do not really doubt people when they say that scratching an itch gives them pleasure: after all, it has done the same for us!

To elaborate on the first point, I would argue that there really are no brute colours and thus there really is no pleasure in brute colours. The notion of a brute colour is of something abstracted completely from real experience. A colour is always experienced in some context and hence, insofar as it is influenced by that context, it is complex. The pink post-it I see before me as I write is contrasted to the black computer-screen frame on which it sits, which in turn is situated in relation to the colours on the screen and also to the grey printer to the right. Moreover, my experience of the post-it is influenced by associations and expectations. One could of course set up a psychological experiment in which colours were relatively isolated. However, this would not represent how we generally experience them. To see them as brute and to see pleasure in them as non-aesthetic requires abstracting them from all contexts.

One way to assure that there is a distinction between aesthetic and non-aesthetic pleasure is to say that some types of pleasure can never be aesthetic. This is Soucek's strategy: to say that itches belong to the class of brute sensations which can never be aesthetic. I have questioned whether there are brute sensations. But what of the wider strategy of finding a type of experience that can never be aesthetic? This strategy will fail as well. Even the smell of dung can be aesthetically positive given the right context. However, although any type of pleasure can be aesthetic this is not the case for any particular pleasure in any context. Based on my argument of Chapter Three, I would say that the dividing line between the aesthetic and the non-aesthetic is not between brute pleasures and ones that are more complex, but between pleasures associated with aura and ones not so associated.

Although I have defended Irvin so far, we part ways when she seeks to guarantee the possibility of objectivity for aesthetic judgments of itches and scratches by basing such judgments on knowledge of the non-aesthetic phenomena on which they are based.[41] I argued earlier against the non-aesthetic dependency thesis of which this is an example. Irvin holds that a child learns what things are graceful by figuring out what accounts for their being graceful at the non-aesthetic level.[42] I disagree. One learns how to use the term "graceful" when one is able to see something as graceful, i.e., as having aura of that sort. Objectivity on my

---

41 Sherri Irvin, in her reply to Soucek, "Aesthetics and the Private Realm," *The Journal of Aesthetics and Art Criticism* 67, no. 2 (2009): 226-30.
42 Irvin, "Private," 229.

view cannot be guaranteed by reference to non-aesthetic qualities but must be grounded on the innate tendencies to appreciate harmony and symmetry captured by the Pythagoreans, the judgment of Humean good judges, the free play of imagination and understanding observed by Kant to attend things that have a look of purposiveness, the Japanese concept of *yûgen*, or on one of the other traditional aesthetic theories that fits this particular phenomenon well.

The question at the beginning of this section was "How pervasive is aesthetic experience?" The answer is that it is quite pervasive; and yet there are limits. Not everything that is pleasant is aesthetic. This is true even though "pleasant" is a term of everyday aesthetics. Something more is required than mere pleasantness for aesthetic status. Korsmeyer's suggestion that what is required is exemplification in Goodman's sense is helpful, but the idea of exemplification is thin and fails to capture what I have called aura. Dewey's idea of a pervasive quality also helps, especially if reinterpreted in the direction of aura. However his concept of "an experience" is really more of an ideal than a criterion.

THE PROBLEM OF AESTHETICIZATION

One complaint about everyday aesthetics is that in blurring the distinction between art and life it makes things more beautiful than they really are: it aestheticizes them. This can happen, but there is no reason to believe that it must. Take kitsch, for example. Someone who disapproves of Hummel figurines might believe that such things are taken by their admirers to be more beautiful than they really are. On this view the admirers have aestheticized the figurines. Yet this assumes that each thing has an objective beauty-ranking so that we could clearly determine that someone *is* seeing it as more beautiful than it really is. The problem with this, as many aestheticians have seen, is that beauty is at least in part a matter of *how* one sees things. Beauty, as Hume would say, is in the experience, not in the object. Yet, as we have seen, Hume does not then throw out the notion of a standard of taste, i.e., the good judge who has trained through practice and comparison, who has delicacy of sentiment, who lacks prejudice and also has good sense. So we could say, following Hume, that Hummel figurines might be taken to be more beautiful than they really are (for example, as beautiful as a Rembrandt) by people who are not good judges in Hume's sense. They would be like people who considered a third-rate writer to be superior to Milton. However, these figurines could also be appreciated in a modest way as having certain low-level aesthetic properties.

In this case they would not be taken as more beautiful than they are, and good judges could not justly complain about their appreciation. There might even be good judges or connoisseurs of Hummel figurines. In short, Hummel figurines are aestheticized only if taken as beautiful in the way a great fine art painting is, or as having certain complex or sophisticated aesthetic properties.

Although "aestheticization" does not yet appear in dictionaries, "aestheticize" does. It tends to mean either the act of depicting something in an idealized or art-like manner or the act of making something aesthetic. However theorists often define the term so as to make it relevant to changes in contemporary culture. Naukkarinen, for example, defines it as "the notion that more and more things get absorbed into the aesthetic sphere, and that aesthetic matters are becoming increasingly important in our daily li[ves]."[43] The idea is that we increasingly choose things (e.g., products) based on aesthetic, rather than other more appropriate criteria—religious, political or economic, for example. There is considerable anecdotal and some statistical evidence for this claim.[44] Whether it is true is a matter for sociologists to determine. However, the claim also often has a normative dimension. "Aestheticization" usually has negative connotations: so the claim may also be that our increasingly choosing things based on aesthetic qualities is bad. Is this true?

In his introduction to *The Aesthetics of Everyday Life* Jonathan Smith worries that my own theory might "lend intellectual support to the commercial aestheticization of everyday life that one finds in advertisements."[45] It is not that people are making too many choices based on aesthetics that worries him but that they are making too many choices based on the aesthetic qualities of advertisements. Or perhaps he believes that every aspect of our everyday lives is too dominated by aesthetic choice, and that the prominence of advertising is a sign of this. If aestheticization of everyday life is understood in one of these ways, and if the aesthetics of everyday life did lend intellectual support to this, then this would be a good criticism of it.

Many scholars have raised problems with the aestheticization of such things as politics and war. Walter Benjamin warned of the aestheticization of politics; an example would be that the Nazis made their political activities appealing by making them look beautiful. Benjamin was also concerned that aestheticization promotes

---

43 Naukkarinen, 203.
44 See especially Postrel.
45 Jonathan M. Smith, "Introduction," in *Aesthetics of Everyday Life*, x.

a false aura.[46] Alternatively, aestheticization can be seen as a matter of focusing on aesthetic properties when one should be focusing on political or ethical ones. Someone might speak of aestheticization of architectural works meaning that he/she objects to seeing architecture primarily in terms of aesthetic properties and not primarily in terms of political and social context. Monuments can aestheticize brutalities and horrors, making them less pressing by being more attractive. Here aestheticization looks like a kind of seduction that leads to political or ethical error. Aestheticization could also involve the extreme of seeing things such as murder and death as beautiful, as did the Italian Futurists.

Those who believe that aestheticization is a bad thing probably think of it as an attempt to place aesthetic above other values, for example religious or moral values. Jane Bennett, however, has argued that aestheticization need not be opposed to other values: it does not have to be reduced to fascism, hedonism, or indiscriminateness.[47] She does not see aestheticization as giving something more aesthetic value than it should have but as caring about sensuous experience in a disciplined way. She even thinks that this kind of caring has positive implications for ethics. She sees the attack on aestheticization as an over-reaction to the aestheticization of violence.[48]

Jean Baudrillard, however, is more negative about aestheticization of everyday life, describing it as a matter of *everything* coming to be seen as art. This causes such concepts as beauty and ugliness to become meaningless and art to no longer be transcendent. For Baudrillard, the image has become the new reality, and aesthetics, which governs the image, comes to govern everything.[49]

By contrast, cultural theorist Mike Featherstone maintains a neutral attitude towards aestheticization.[50] For him, aestheticization of everyday life takes

---

46 Nicholas Rennie, review of Lutz Koepnick's *Walter Benjamin and the Aesthetics of Power* in *The German Quarterly* 75, no. 2 (2002): 224-25 alerts us to this. See also Wolfgang Welsch, *Undoing Aesthetics*, trans. Andrew Inkpin (London: Sage, 1997), Chapter 1, "Aestheticization Process," for a thorough analysis of the different meanings of aestheticization, and my "Aestheticization, Artification and Aquariums," *Contemporary Aesthetics* (forthcoming) for elaboration of my own position.
47 Jane Bennett nicely defends Foucault against charges of aestheticization by Terry Eagleton, Sheldon Wolin, and Christopher Norris in "'How is It, Then, That We Still Remain Barbarians?': Foucault, Schiller, and the Aestheticization of Ethics," *Political Theory* 24, no. 4 (1996): 653-72.
48 Bennett, "Barbarians," 657.
49 Jean Baudrillard, *The Transparency of Evil* (London: Verso, 1993).
50 Mike Featherstone, *Consumer Culture and Postmodernism* (London: Sage, 1991). See especially his chapter, "The Aestheticization of Everyday Life," 65-82.

different forms: the avant-garde attempts, among Dadaists, Surrealists, and others to destroy boundaries between art and life; the importation of art into such things as advertising; the project of turning life into a work of art, as found in Nietzsche; and, most importantly, the rapid flow of signs and images which saturate everyday life, what he refers to as the "aestheticization of everyday life through the figural regimes of signification" which he finds central to postmodernism.[51] Unlike Benjamin and Baudrillard his discussion does not include a value dimension.

It appears that Featherstone, and other culture theorists concerned about aestheticization, are talking about a narrower domain than that covered by such writers as Carlson, Irvin, Saito, Berleant, Scruton and myself. The rapid flow of signs and images characteristic of our time would be only one part, albeit an increasingly important one, of the overall field of everyday aesthetics. It would relate mainly to the experience of people addicted to web-surfing and media consumption, although admittedly we all see many signs and images as we drive down urban streets, leaf through magazines and shop in malls. However, it is hard to see how appreciating the neatness of one's room, the tastiness of a home-cooked dinner, or the look of one's garden as a function of this proliferation of signs.

When Smith speaks of the commercialization of everyday life that one finds in advertisements he is probably referring to the fact that things that we consume every day are generally portrayed in commercials with heightened or exaggerated aesthetic properties: colours are more intense, sounds are louder, and the look of newness is intensified. This is also often true for the products that are advertised. They, too, typically display intensified colours, sounds, and smells. They also seek to exemplify the properties of newness and good taste (or at least taste that meets the standards of the targeted consumers). If a product is agreeable, pleasant or cute it is more likely to be purchased. Smith must believe that the commercial aestheticization of everyday life in advertisements and in products is a bad thing, as he assumes that giving intellectual support for it is bad. Commercialization is probably thought bad because it encourages consumers to revel in shallow pleasures at the expense of ones that are deeper and more fulfilling. I wouldn't want to lend intellectual support to that!

Advertising, with some exceptions, forces itself on our consciousness in any way that will encourage us to purchase a product. It encourages us to

---

51 Featherstone, 70.

associate products with things we value, with aspirations, and with lifestyle choices. It does this typically by trying to get us to see purchasing of a certain product as necessary for our identity or well-being. If featuring or enhancing aesthetic properties of products will help sell them then advertisers and product-designers will do so. Also, since advertising is usually directed to people with a common run of taste, when it does focus on aesthetic qualities, it usually stresses the ones that are easy to understand and appreciate. Of course, this might not be the case for advertising directed to connoisseurs, for example, of fine wine.

How could everyday aesthetics lend intellectual support to these practices? Perhaps it is thought that in promoting appreciation of the properties that advertising uses for its own purposes, it also promotes advertising itself. Yet the everyday aestheticians I have discussed tend to promote unmediated appreciation of everyday phenomena rather than appreciation of those phenomena by way of advertising. And although I promote mediated appreciation, it is through the arts not through advertising. Moreover, most everyday aestheticians encourage complex and sophisticated responses to everyday phenomena, not the shallow and quick responses that increase probability of purchase. Although everyday aesthetics recognizes the centrality of advertising in our everyday lives, this is not the same as supporting it.

Let us take it that Smith's "aestheticization" is treating something as having valuable aesthetic properties when doing so entails social harm. The "commercial aestheticization of everyday life" then is the trend over the last couple hundred years, motivated by commercial interests, to emphasize relatively superficial aesthetic properties in a way that is detrimental to human flourishing. Smith's implicit claim appears to be that the act of analyzing aesthetic phenomena outside the arts, and the analysis of aesthetic properties not generally featured in the arts, will lend support to this tendency. However, this does not follow. Perhaps paying attention to these properties would help us to *understand better* the power of advertising. Although understanding the power of advertising could be used to enhance that power, it could also be used to diminish it.

Perhaps it is thought that paying attention to everyday aesthetics draws attention away from the value of art. Yet why would that be the case if, as I have argued, the various arts themselves devote so much attention to the everyday? Perhaps the problem is that legitimizing the use of the aesthetic predicates mentioned in previous chapters would destroy the difference between art and kitsch.⁵² The argument, I suppose, is that aestheticians of everyday life say that such predicates as "comfortable" and "cute" are sometimes used legitimately, and that this makes a Hummel figurine as valuable as a Rembrandt. Yet no one has actually made this inference. The greatness of Rembrandt's paintings is not diminished by recognizing that the cuteness of a Hummel figure is an aesthetic property.

John Dewey would argue that the problem of aestheticization is a function of current unacceptable social conditions. Although Dewey is vague about those conditions, his thinking is consistent with that of Karl Marx about alienation and exploitation of the worker within the capitalist system. Thus, his description of the everyday aesthetic experience contains within it an implicit ideal of a world in which social conditions are such that humans are more fully alive and happiness is possible for all. His point is similar to that of William Morris who argued for a socialist transformation in which the processes and products of industry are fully realized through reanimation of earlier craft traditions. I agree with Dewey, Morris, and the culture critics we have discussed that our society could be improved by changing social conditions, increasing social democracy and personal autonomy, and downplaying commercialization.

A different type of critic of aestheticization is Martin Jay.⁵³ He thinks that works by such artists as Marcel Duchamp and John Cage seek to dissolve the distinction between art and everyday life, and that, as the title of his essay indicates, this is "drifting into dangerous waters." In particular, if everything can be aestheticized there is a danger that we will engage in the kind of aestheticization of cruelty characteristic of the Futurists, and worse, the Nazis. He believes that "uncoupling the aesthetic experience from the art object," when connected with emphasizing subjective response to objects, leads to "indiscriminate elevation of all objects to potential works of art"⁵⁴ and finally to "de-materializing" reality.

Yet treating all things as potential aesthetic objects or as potential works of art does not in itself imply de-materialization. Nor does it imply acceptance of

---

52 This has been argued by Christopher Stevens in "Revising Aesthetics' Place Amongst the Disciplines: Aesthetic Values, Moral Obligation, and Everyday Aesthetics," National Meeting of the American Society for Aesthetics, Los Angeles (Fall, 2007).
53 Martin Jay, "Drifting into Dangerous Waters," in *Aesthetic Subjects*, ed. Pamela R. Matthews and David McWhirter (Minneapolis: University of Minnesota Press, 2003), 3-27.
54 Jay, 14.

unethical forms of appreciation, as for example appreciation of murder. With respect to the first point, often when we speak of seeing something aesthetically we speak of seeing it as it is in itself independently of our subjective interests. Nor is it clear that drawing attention to the aesthetics of everyday life must have a negative impact on art. This is somewhat like the absurd view that gay marriage would have a negative impact on heterosexual marriage.

Critic Michael Fried once criticized an account by artist Tony Smith of a sublime experience had while driving at night on the New Jersey Turnpike as importing theatre into art and thus destroying art's unique nature. Jay similarly thinks that interest in this kind of aesthetic experience involves "erosion of the work of art."[55] However, it is not clear how this would be the case. Jay's worry that Duchamp's readymades and similar works contribute to the "promiscuous re-enchantment of the entire world"[56] fails to see that only some things are re-enchanted. The changes are piecemeal, not global. That every object is potentially a "legitimate occasion for aesthetic experience" does not mean that every object is that *right now*.

I agree with Jay that the aesthetics of the everyday owes something to the "natural supernaturalism" of the Romantics in which the natural world was infused with the numinous meaning formerly reserved for the transcendent world. As he observes, "[n]ow the everyday, the commonplace, could be understood as glowing with immanent significance" filling the vacuum left by the death of God.[57] He writes that for Carlyle, Ruskin and John Cage "[e]ven the sublime, which had been reserved for awesome and unfathomable experiences in the eighteenth century, could now be applied to the commonplace, just as long as the aesthetic sensibility of the beholder was capable of appreciating it in this manner."[58] I will explore this idea in Chapter 8. Whereas Jay tends to think this is a bad thing I think it is good.

At the end of his essay Jay, I think correctly, presents Dewey's concept of aesthetic experience as a way of avoiding the privileging of subject over object that he thinks leads to aestheticization of immoral acts. He also thinks Dewey's effort at democratizing aesthetic experience may, every bit as much as naturalist supernaturalism, lead to an "indiscriminate levelling of the distinction between artwork and lifeworld through the projection of the qualities of the former onto

---

55 Jay, 15.
56 Jay, 16.
57 Jay, 16.
58 Jay, 17. Jay is attacking Leonard's *Light*.

the latter."[59] Of course, democratization can be taken too far, and levelling can be indiscriminate: but I don't think this criticism can be made of Dewey's ideas.

From Walter Benjamin's perspective one could argue that, with the elimination of aura in art and with the attack on tradition and religious cults, the everyday becomes more significant. Whereas Benjamin's discussion mainly has to do with transformations both in fine and in popular art, the important aspect of his "The Work of Art" article for everyday aesthetics has to do with how everyday perception is changed in the age of mechanical reproduction. In discussing this, he makes us aware that any study of everyday aesthetics must take into account changes in modes of perception that accompany changes in modes of production. Benjamin remarks on the freeing transformation that film brings to everyday experience: "[our] taverns and our metropolitan streets, our offices and furnished rooms, our railroad stations and our factories appeared to have us locked up hopelessly. Then came the film and burst this prison-world asunder ... With the close-up, space expands; with slow motion, movement is extended."[60] He was perhaps unwarranted in his conviction that the new media would produce a revolution in perception, new dimensions of knowledge, and an opening up of free agency which would in turn encourage a social revolution. However, even if this sequence never meshed together that well (and film techniques were easily incorporated into works with capitalist messages), it may still be the case that with the age of mechanical reproduction we see our bars, streets, offices and rooms differently. It is even arguable that because of mechanical reproduction we now have a freer way of perceiving these spaces and that this might, under some conditions, be conducive to other forms of freedom. Benjamin goes on to say that the camera, with its many technical resources, helps us to understand such familiar routines as reaching for a lighter.[61] What he failed to mention, surprisingly, is that as we become more aware of these simple acts we also become more aware of them aesthetically.

Another important change brought about by mechanical reproduction is in what actually comes within the field of daily experience, both visually and aurally. Benjamin remarked on the increase in number of non-art reproductions in his own time, for example pictures in magazines. Today, we would speak of the increasingly pervasive presence of images on TVs, computer screens, and hand-held electronic devices. We also live in a world of increasing dominance of recorded

---

59 Jay, 21.
60 Benjamin, "Work," 236.
61 Benjamin, "Work," 237.

over live sound. So the changes in ways of seeing and hearing (more variety and greater quantity) and in what is seen and heard (more images and sound segments, electronic and otherwise) makes for a different world of everyday aesthetics than that of, for example, one hundred years ago, or even thirty years ago.[62]

THE PANGLOSSIAN PROBLEM

Katya Mandoki has accused contemporary aestheticians of everyday life of suffering from what she calls the Pangloss Syndrome (named after the over-optimistic character in Voltaire's *Candide* who famously said "all is for the best in the best of all possible worlds") because of neglect of such things as aesthetic violence. She says they have excluded "all phenomena that are not positive and useful in their supply of pleasure and nice thoughts."[63] This, she argues, is why such things as "the disgusting, the obscene, the coarse, the insignificant, the banal, the ugly, [and] the sordid" have been neglected in aesthetics. In particular she believes that what she calls "aesthetic poisoning" has been neglected. Cruelty, she argues, is not only a moral but an aesthetic category. She attacks Yi-Fu Tuan who, although he succeeds in seeing beauty in everyday life, fails to see "the twilight that surrounds it and the darkness into which it sinks when aesthetic violence is exerted."[64] She also criticizes Arnold Berleant for failing to see that aesthetics is not necessarily a remedy for violence since it may equally be a constituent of it.[65]

These criticisms are to some extent warranted. There is a tendency in everyday aesthetics to encourage readers to enjoy all the positive aesthetic properties around us while at the same time not addressing the issue of all the ugliness we must experience on a daily basis. This, by the way, cannot be said of Saito's book, which came out the same year as Mandoki's.[66] As we saw, Saito is particularly concerned with the ugly messes of our world and our urge to clean them up. To be fair, traditional aesthetics has addressed the ugly to some extent, although more in relation to the aesthetics of art than to everyday life.[67] And since the time

---

62 See Scott McCracken, "The Completion of Old Work: Walter Benjamin and the Everyday," *Cultural Critique* 52 "Everyday Life" (Autumn, 2002): 145-66, and Rita Felski, "The Invention of Everyday Life," *new formations* 39 (Winter 1999-2000): 15-31, 26.
63 Mandoki, 37.
64 Mandoki, 83.
65 Mandoki, 98.
66 Saito, *Everyday*.
67 One example of interest in ugliness is Lorand, "Beauty and Its Opposites."

of Aristotle, aestheticians have puzzled over why things like human tragedy may be appreciated when put on stage: the much-discussed "paradox of tragedy."

Mandoki's criticism should be taken to heart. Such thinkers as Marx, Morris, Ruskin, and Dewey all were concerned about the moral implications of everyday aesthetics, and so should we be. This would imply recognition of aesthetic pain in everyday life, for example in the way that we may feel oppressed by the assault of advertising or, more importantly, the alienating lack of aesthetic satisfactions experienced by workers in Mexican maquiladoras and on Chinese factory floors.

CONCLUDING COMMENTS

In sum, although a number of criticisms may be raised against my version of the aesthetics of everyday life, most can be answered. Many have to do with the dividing line between the aesthetic and the non-aesthetic. Most of these criticisms may be answered by reference to the continuum I have described between low-level and high-level aesthetic experience. Generally it has been the low-level experience that has been neglected through the neglect of everyday aesthetics. In the chapter that follows I will elaborate on a specific set of low-level features in some detail: mainly neatness and messiness.

By contrast, neglect of higher-level experiences has characterized most writers on everyday aesthetics itself. In their eagerness to declare independence from the aesthetics of art they have generally downplayed the intimate relationship between the domain of art and that of everyday life. They have often wrongly downplayed the importance of moments when the ordinary becomes extraordinary. Instead, they have focused on the ordinariness of the ordinary and on mere functionality or "looking fit for its function." By contrast I have found the first two of these to be not aesthetic at all: they constitute the region of the banal and the boring, whereas "looks fit for function" is just one of many aesthetic properties. The emphasis I place on the extraordinary in the ordinary is not however intended to deny the importance of negative aesthetic properties such as ugliness and messiness, or the need to overcome or eliminate what has these properties.

In my final chapter I will return to the higher-level properties and will consider everyday aesthetics and the sublime. I have already touched on this idea in the current chapter through discussion of the challenges and promise of Zen Buddhist aesthetics, the aesthetic attitude applied universally, LSD, and manic-depression.

CHAPTER 7
Everyday Surface Aesthetic Qualities

In the literature of aesthetics there are numerous lists of aesthetic qualities. These lists almost invariably leave off entire sets of items.[1] One of these sets will be the topic of this chapter. The items in their adjectival form are "neat," "messy," "clean/unclean," "dirty," "sloppy," "filthy," "ordered/disordered," (although something can be ordered in complex ways, I am referring to a certain low-level order, as in "I want these chairs lined up in an ordered fashion"), "cluttered/uncluttered," "cleared/not cleared," "blemished/unblemished," "attractive/unattractive" (again, something can be attractive or "look good" because it has other, grander aesthetic qualities: that is, it is beautiful, sublime, or elegant, but, as with "order," there is a kind of low-level attractiveness that I wish to refer to here), and "pure/impure." Noteworthy about these qualities is that they are found frequently in everyday life. Moreover, they are concerned not with the underlying structure or substance of things but with what might be called surface properties. By "surface" I mean what does not heavily influence underlying form or substance: this can either be actual physical surface or some other aspect of the object which may be dis-

---

[1] Consider the lists in the following well-known articles and books: Sibley, "Concepts"; Beardsley, "What is"; Kivy, *Speaking*; Ted Cohen, "Aesthetic/Non-aesthetic and the Concept of Taste: A Critique of Sibley's Position," *Theoria* 39, no. 1-3 (1973): 113-52 (reprinted in *Art and Philosophy: Readings in Aesthetics*); Roger Scruton, *Art and Imagination* (London: Methuen, 1974), 30-31; and Hermerén, *Nature*.

tinguished from underlying form or substance. I will call the listed group "everyday surface aesthetic qualities."

There is a problem with calling "dirty" a surface quality. Something can be dirty not just on the surface but through and through. However, we still tend to think of dirt as accidental to that which it covers or soils. So even if dirt is not literally on the surface alone it is still on the surface ontologically speaking. This leads us to a second difficulty. "Purity" and "impurity" do seem to refer to the entire substance and not just the surface. So perhaps *these* are not surface qualities. However, they are clearly related to the qualities I have mentioned and in particular to clean and unclean.

My thesis is quite radical. I am not simply arguing for the recognition of one or two neglected qualities. What we have here is *an entire class* of neglected properties. Yet, with the possible exceptions of Allen Carlson's discussion of roadside clutter and David Novitz's account of grooming, there has been almost no discussion of this class of properties in the aesthetics literature.[2] Novitz was mainly interested in the social implications of personal appearance and the dependence of aesthetic perceptions on socially held values, which is not my concern here. Purity and impurity have, of course, been discussed in relation to Aristotle's theory of catharsis.

Yuriko Saito's recent book, *Everyday Aesthetics*, has rectified this neglect to some extent. She rightly observes that since we all clean ourselves, the qualities discussed here are of universal interest, unlike the qualities of high art.[3] She also argues that our response to these qualities often includes action (for example, the action of cleaning up), which then makes inquiry into them all the more important. Saito usefully situates these qualities within the wider realm of what she calls "Everyday Aesthetic Qualities of Transience." She includes within this domain qualities of change in material objects and in ourselves that we view evaluatively: both changes that we welcome, for example "maturing," and ones that we evaluate negatively, as in "decay" and "get old."[4] She includes "messy" and "dirty" in the second category. Saito's overall emphasis is on our generally

---

2   Allen Carlson, "Environmental Aesthetics and the Dilemma of Aesthetic Education," *The Journal of Aesthetic Education* 10, no. 2 (1976): 69-82. David Novitz, *The Boundaries of Art* (Philadelphia: Temple University Press, 1992), Chap. VI: "Keeping up Appearances." There is also a reference in Hegel, when talking about Dutch art, to "this painstaking as well as cleanly and neat well-being" as one of the admirable features of the Dutch, "Art, Nature," 196.
3   Saito, *Everyday*, Chapter IV, 149-204.
4   Saito, *Everyday*, 149.

negative attitudes to such things as disorder, mess and filth. She stresses that we see objects as having an optimal state from which they decline, and she notes that terms like "decay" and "get dirty" reflect this. She finds application of such terms to be context-dependent: some objects in some contexts demand perfect organization, and others do not. She observes that disorder and clutter are sometimes expected and even found charming, for example in a Chinatown shop. Rather than favouring neatness over messiness, she calls for an appropriate balance between "total control over natural processes" implied by neatness/order and "wholesale submission" to such processes implied by messiness/disorder.[5] Although I like the idea of a broad domain of everyday aesthetic qualities of transience, I will focus on the narrower domain of everyday surface aesthetic qualities in this chapter. I should add that although such qualities as "decay" and "get old" are generally regarded negatively, this is not always the case. I also accept the idea of appropriate balance between neatness and messiness.

In order to establish such qualities as neatness and messiness as aesthetic a number of questions will need to be addressed. How do these qualities stand up against definitions of aesthetic quality that have been offered in the past? Do they really form a group, and what is it that holds the group together? Do everyday surface aesthetic quality terms refer to a different kind of quality in non-art contexts than they do in art contexts? What role do they play in artistic experience and evaluation? What is the difference between literal and metaphorical application of these terms, and how are they applied at different ontological levels? Finally, why have these terms and the qualities they represent been neglected? I will address the latter questions in this group first.

APPLICATION TO ART AND EVERYDAY LIFE CONTEXTS

Most discussions of aesthetic qualities begin with a discussion of art. Although many aestheticians insist that aesthetic qualities are not limited to the arts, even *those* thinkers generally take the arts as the primary focus of their discussion. This explains somewhat the neglect of everyday surface aesthetic qualities, since these are not primarily the qualities by which we praise works of art. However, some everyday surface aesthetic qualities, such as "neat," "clean," and "cluttered," do have application in the arts. In the visual arts, for example, we speak of clean lines, clean edges, muddy colour, neat construction, and

---

5   Saito, *Everyday*, 173.

cluttered space. Of course, the lines in a visual work are not literally clean: literal cleanliness has to do with the features of the work qua physical object. A painting is literally clean if it is free of dirt, dust, food particles, and such. Having clean lines is metaphorical. Thus something can be literally clean and fail to have clean lines, or have clean lines and fail to be literally clean.

Yet are we sure where the literal ends and the metaphorical begins? "Clean" could be taken to simply mean "clear or free of that which is unwanted," i.e., of impurities, adulterations, imperfections, blemishes, and other unwanted things. Cleaning off the table is often simply a matter of clearing it of materials irrelevant to the next project. "Clean" does not have to refer simply to absence of dirt. Absence of dirt is neither a necessary nor a sufficient condition for a room being clean, since a room may have a dirt floor. We even speak of clean dirt! It is true that cleaning a painting means getting dirt and other unwanted substances off the surface. However, this is not the only application of the term "cleaning" to painting. One can also speak of cleaning up the lines during the process of composition. It is just not clear that one meaning is literal and the other metaphorical. Moreover, *both* meanings of "clean," in this instance, are "aesthetic" in the sense that both have to do with perceptual properties that give or do not give pleasure.

This leads me to suggest that there are different *domains* in which everyday surface aesthetic quality terms may be applied. Cleaning off dirt from a painting is a matter of physical surface aesthetic qualities; cleaning up lines or colours within a painting is a matter of art surface aesthetic qualities. However, what about cleaning up the *composition* of a painting or a musical work? Composition seems to be well below the surface features of a work of art. Or is it? Ontological layers might be like the layers of an onion: even the inner ones can have their own surfaces. The features of the composition which are cleaned might still be considered surface features in that they are surface features of the composition. There is something that underlies those features, a more basic form of the composition, which is cleaned up. To say that something can be neatened or cleaned *implies* that there is something underlying that is worthy of neatening/cleaning. Someone might want to claim that the literal meaning of "clean" has nothing to do with perceptual properties—that something can be clean or not regardless of how it looks or smells. It would follow that since aesthetic qualities are perceptual then any aesthetic applications of the term "clean" would be secondary. Of course, there are cases in which something is unclean in a non-perceptual way, for instance, gold that has impurities or water that has bacteria. However, we learn the concept of cleanness as children by how things look and smell. This gives the perceptual meaning of "clean" a certain developmental primacy. Early training also brings us to value "neat" and "clean" over "messy" and "dirty."

Yet, interestingly, and despite early training, "messiness" is not necessarily a negative trait. That abstract expressionists' brush strokes are (or at least initially look) messy, and minimalists' brush strokes are (or at least initially look) neat, does not mean that abstract expressionism is worse than minimalism. Perhaps this is because the surface messiness of abstract expressionist paintings only hides an underlying order. Thus we might speak of de Kooning paintings as having clean edges or crisp lines even though they initially look messy. Part of the attraction of abstract expressionist painting may be due to this tension between surface messiness and underlying neatness.

The idea that messiness or disorder can be aesthetic, at least under special conditions, is not new. Dewey, for example, notes that the live creature demands novelty as much as order. If we do not get some novelty in our lives we find boredom.[6] However, he insists that the "disorder" that gives aesthetic pleasure is only disorder "by some external standard." This apparent disorder adds emphasis and distinction as long as it does not hinder cumulative development. If it were experienced as disorder it would make the experience displeasing. Disorder may provide a difficulty that can be overcome, which can in turn give rise to a more powerful aesthetic experience.

In a recent article, Arthur Danto has acknowledged the importance of messiness not only in late twentieth-century painting but also in aesthetics generally. Danto is inspired by the painter Robert Rauschenberg to take messiness seriously. He saw the Rauschenbergian aesthetic as almost opposite to that of Kant and Greenberg: "It is the aesthetics of grunge and mess, as exemplified in Rauschenberg's *Bed*, where he slathered paint over the bedclothes and quilt in which the material consists."[7] He observes the irony of applying paint in a messy abstract expressionist way to an object normally associated with cleanliness. He then defines grunge as "the aesthetic of disorder" which is promoted by rebellious adolescents. He notes, however, that taste for grunge can be developed, and can even be exploited.

Dirt has also been advocated in modern art as a possible object of aesthetic appreciation. In 1946, artist Jean Dubuffet asked, "Don't dirt, trash, and filth,

---

6   Dewey, 171-72.
7   Arthur C. Danto, "Embodied," 123-24. Also, see Saito, *Everyday*, 192.

which are man's companions during his whole lifetime, deserve to be dearer to him [than necklaces of pearls and fox furs] and shouldn't he pay them the compliment of making a monument to their beauty." In fact, Dubuffet displayed dirt materials in one of his exhibits.[8] Claes Oldenberg similarly said, "Dirt has depth and beauty. I love soot and scorching. From all this can come a positive as well as a negative meaning."[9] Oldenberg was known for taking pieces of trash shaped at a right angle and exhibiting them under the title, "Ray Guns." He originally made these items in plaster and papier-mâché but was later convinced that the world was full of these things and that all he had to do was pick them up from the street.[10]

Architecture provides another kind of case. Modernist architects claimed that their work, with its clean lines and uncluttered surfaces, was superior to the work of the eclectic schools that dominated the nineteenth-century. The notions of neatness and messiness have also played a role in the history of gardening, where French gardens are considered highly ordered and neat, whereas picturesque English gardens incorporated unkempt natural scenes.[11] Whatever the case it is certain that everyday surface aesthetic qualities are not only relevant to aesthetics in general but also to the various visual arts. Recently the idea has been applied even to textile arts.[12]

Stan Godlovitch applies the concept to music, as well, arguing that "Cleanliness has musical applications particularly in jazz and a propos playing style. Joe Pass is considered a 'dirty' player because many of his passages are 'dirty.' This means that he's pretty sloppy with tonal clarity and abides

---

8   Yve-Alain Bois mentions this in Yve-Alain Bois and Rosalind Krauss, "A User's Guide to Entropy," *October* 78 (Autumn, 1996): 38-88, 47.
9   Claes Oldenburg quoted in Barbara Rose, *Claes Oldenburg* (New York: Museum of Modern Art, 1970), 46.
10 Adam Trowbridge, blog, "Claes Oldenburg's 'The Ray Gun Wing'," "Collections and Archives as Creative Practice," accessed June 11, 2011, http://collectingseminar.wordpress.com/2008/11/02/claes-oldenburgs-the-ray-gun-wing/.
11 Stephanie Ross, "Gardens, Nature, Pleasure," *The Aesthetics of Human Environments*, ed. Arnold Berleant and Allen Carlson (Peterborough, ON: Broadview Press, 2007), 252-71.
12 Siri Homlong, *The Language of Textiles: Description and Judgement on Textile Pattern Composition*, Digital Comprehensive Summaries of Uppsala Dissertations from the Faculty of Social Sciences, 19 (Uppsala: Uppsala University, 2006), accessed July 17, 2007, http://74.125.155.132/search?q=cache:sjj23e1vgYgJ:www.diva-portal.org/diva/getDocument%3Furn_nbn_se_uu_diva-7216-1__fulltext.pdf+The+Language+of+Textiles:+Description+and+Judgement+on+Textile+Pattern+Composition&cd=6&hl=en&ct=clnk&gl=us.

buzzes and other distracting noises which come from a less than 'clean' execution. 'Clean' players give you all the notes crystal clear, well articulated, under control. Why is Joe Pass's playing accepted? Well, although, technically, dirty playing is sloppy playing and needs cleaning up, aesthetically dirty playing can have an appeal all of its own."[13] As Godlovitch argues, we would feel that something had gone wrong if Pass had cleaned up his act. Whereas Saito holds that "dirty" does not "seem to allow for positive appreciation, except in the metaphorical sense ... or in very specific situations,"[14] Godlovitch's example either shows this to be wrong or leads one to hold that it falls within the two exceptions.

Yet, where we find everyday surface aesthetic qualities most often discussed is in practical life: in the home, the yard, the workplace, the shops, personal attire, and personal grooming. Rooms become messy, cluttered. They must be cleaned, cleared, set straight, tidied up.[15] Kitchens and bathrooms can be unclean or filthy. Floors must be washed when dirty and unattractive. Shelves may be ordered or disordered. Desks can be cluttered. Schedules and organizational plans can be messy. Products can be presented neatly and attractively, or not. Clothes run from messy and dirty to neat and clean. People too can be messy or neat, clean or unclean. They are considered messy and unclean if their clothes, grooming, possessions, products or work stations have these qualities. Indeed, these are often the properties non-aestheticians are thinking of when they refer to the "aesthetics" of something. Moreover, as Elizabeth Burns Coleman argues, the ideas of neatness and messiness also play an important role in giving us a sense of place in the social hierarchy.[16]

A possible explanation of why everyday surface aesthetic qualities may have been neglected by aestheticians is gender socialization and stereotyping. The home and yard are traditionally the domains of the housewife and servant. There are househusbands and male servants, but most commonly this role goes to a woman. The office in its aesthetic dimension is traditionally

---

13 Stan Godlovitch: letter to me of Nov. 20, 1993. Lee B. Brown also defends the idea that "messy" can be a positive value in jazz in "'Feeling My Way': Jazz Improvisation and Its Vicissitudes—A Plea for Imperfection," *The Journal of Aesthetics and Art Criticism* 58, no. 2, Improvisation in the Arts (2000): 113-23.
14 Saito, *Everyday*, 164.
15 One of the best discussions of this is Melchionne.
16 Elizabeth Burns Coleman, "Aesthetics as a Cross-Cultural Concept," in *Before Pangaea: New Essays in Transcultural Aesthetics*, Special Issue, ed. Eugenio Benitez, *The Journal of the Sydney Society of Literature and Aesthetics* 15, no. 1 (2005): 57-78, 71.

the world of the secretary, again most commonly a woman. The teaching of personal grooming is traditionally the domain of the mother. The housewife, servant, secretary and mother are the ones who are generally concerned with the messy, the cluttered, the clean, and the neat. I am not suggesting that this is as it should be. Feminists have well argued that these activities should be shared equally between the sexes. Nor am I suggesting that men never engage in cleaning, neatening, dusting and so on. However, men who do have jobs which are primarily concerned with these activities, for example garbage men, often have low social status. (A possible exception is someone whose job is to clean up a corporate structure. However, that is not an example of concern for surface perceptual features.) This leads to the possibility that aesthetics has ignored everyday surface aesthetic qualities because of their association with "women's work" and low-status generally. If so, then recognition of the importance of these qualities should form a part of feminist aesthetics. Perhaps it is a form of sexism to think of these qualities as outside of aesthetics.

Women in our culture in the 1950s and the 1960s were taught to be obsessed with neatness and cleanness. Men of the same generation were encouraged to ignore these things, or delegate them to others while concentrating on matters that could gain them success in the business or professional worlds. Today it is possible for some of those same women to gain some aesthetic delight in observing clutter in their homes. I am not speaking here of the situation in which a woman thinks "Isn't it great that I no longer feel compelled to clean up," which would be merely consistent with tolerating clutter, but of the situation in which a woman, or a man for that matter, notices the clutter and perceptually enjoys it.[17] As I have suggested above, messiness and clutter are not necessarily negative aesthetic qualities, although they are usually cast in this role. Danto makes a similar point when he speaks of how a disordered room might be an expression of a feminist point rather than simply a manifestation of cultural background or a psychological condition. For him, order and disorder can carry semiotic charge.[18]

Another plausible explanation for the neglect of everyday surface aesthetic qualities is simply that aesthetics has been mainly associated with transcendent experience afforded by great works of art. Everyday surface aesthetic qualities have been neglected for the same reason as aesthetic qualities associated with

---

17 I owe this example to MaryAnn Shukait.
18 Arthur Danto, "Symbolic Expressions of the Self," in his *Beyond the Brillo Box* (New York: Farrar Straus Giroux, 1992), 56-57.

body decoration, kitsch, and the design of everyday objects. So, in conclusion, the reasons why these qualities have been neglected would include (1) art aesthetics has dominated the field, (2) the qualities and the activities with which they connected are traditionally associated with women and with lower-class jobs, (3) they do not seem particularly complex or interesting, (4) they are not associated with sophistication or connoisseurship, (5) they seem subjective and relative, (6) they are not associated with transcendent experience, and (7) they do not require complex skills to achieve, unlike such properties as balance and harmony (I will discuss this in the next section). Many of these issues have been discussed in previous chapters. Here I wish to stress that although many of these points are true, they do not individually or together justify continued neglect of everyday aesthetics. This is because they fail to take into account the continuities and connections between aesthetics of everyday life and the aesthetics of art, connections that are so great that the latter really depends on the former. The most important supposed reason for neglecting them is simply (8) they are not aesthetic qualities. I will now turn to that claim.

ARE THEY AESTHETIC QUALITIES?

But are the items I have listed really aesthetic qualities? As I noted in the beginning, they are virtually never mentioned in the main works on aesthetic qualities. Göran Hermerén's *The Nature of Aesthetic Qualities* distinguishes between five kinds (I will give two examples of each): emotion qualities ("sombre," "gay"); behaviour qualities ("bold," "nervous"); gestalt qualities ("unified," "disorganized"); taste qualities ("elegant," "delightful"); and affective qualities ("funny," "glaring"). It might be argued that although Hermerén does not mention them, everyday surface aesthetic qualities can simply be added to the category of gestalt qualities. Here is the rest of his list of gestalt qualities: "coherent," "tightly knit," "complete," "simple," "balanced," "harmonious," "integrated," "chaotic," and "consonant."[19] However, note that most of these qualities, i.e., "complete," "balanced," "harmonious," and "integrated," refer to structure. This is why they are called "gestalt" qualities. *The Oxford English Dictionary* describes "gestalt" as "an integrated perceptual structure or unity conceived as functionally more than the sum of its parts." Everyday surface aesthetic qualities border on the structural, and sometimes edge into it, but

---

19 Hermerén, *Nature*, 106.

they are mainly qualities of surface. That distinction is confirmed by the fact that one of the main functions of neatening and cleaning is revelation of underlying form or structure. For example, neatening up or cleaning a facade or a room may reveal an underlying structure with its own aesthetic properties. The architect and interior decorator are responsible for that structure, not the neatener or cleaner. However, this does not mean that "neatness" and "cleanness" are inapplicable to what architects and interior decorators do. As I have indicated, the architect and interior decorator are responsible for another domain or ontological layer to which the terms "neat" and "clean" may be applied.

It is arguable that neatening and cleaning *contribute* to a room being more balanced, harmonious, and integrated. Perhaps this happens not simply through revealing these properties but through clarifying them. However, again, that places everyday surface aesthetic qualities on another level than Hermerén's gestalt qualities, although related to them.

Hermerén's gestalt qualities are generally more complex (at least on a perceptual level) than everyday surface aesthetic qualities. Of course everyday surface aesthetic qualities may well be complex on other levels or in other respects, as has been argued by Saito. For instance, attributions of "neatness" in a particular sub-group of a particular culture may depend on complex social traditions. It is also arguable that these qualities are ontologically complex and therefore that an adequate philosophical analysis of them must be complex.[20] Gestalt qualities are more complex because they are structural, having to do with the inter-relation of parts along more than one dimension. Balance and harmony are special kinds of order that require complex skills to achieve. Think of what is needed to achieve harmony in a musical work. Harmony in music is a matter of combining parts, often from two or more different lines, to form an ordered and pleasing whole. The term "integration" is, in turn, closely related to "harmony": it is generally defined in terms of harmonious composition. Achieving balance, harmony or integration in a work of art or in a clothing outfit is quite different and considerably more difficult than simply creating order by "straightening up" or "putting away." Yet these are the typical actions involved in making something neat. By contrast, the term "chaotic," insofar as it refers to something which is utterly disordered, points us to a situation in which all structure is lacking. Although it is not as clearly a gestalt term as "harmony" and "integrated," it is also not an everyday surface aesthetic

---

20 Saito, *Everyday*, 153.

quality term since everyday surface aesthetic qualities require an underlying structure to be neatened, messed up, cleaned, or dirtied.

Cleanness is even further from Hermerén's gestalt properties than neatness. Something can be clean without having any of those properties, and something can have all of them and not be clean. Yet, like neatness, cleaning can reveal underlying structure. Cleaning up a building, sculpture or painting usually does this, as also cleaning a coat or a watch movement.

Someone might reply that aesthetics has to do *primarily* with art, and that although there are uses for everyday surface aesthetic quality terms in the artworld, they do not pertain primarily to art and are therefore not aesthetic terms. (This is a point I first raised in the Introduction.) It is true that these terms do not refer primarily to art. It is also true that qualities found primarily in art have a characteristic which everyday surface aesthetic qualities do not share: perceptual complexity. It is because of this complexity that we have professional critics in art and not in room neatness, although amateur critics of room neatness abound!

Sibley insisted that aesthetic terms or concepts are not limited to artistic discourse but may be used in everyday life.[21] However, like Hermerén, Sibley fails to mention any of the terms I have listed, even though he does include such unusual items as "flaccid," "weakly," and "washed out." Perhaps this is because everyday surface aesthetic quality terms are not found primarily in artistic discourse. Why not just say that some aesthetic qualities are found primarily in art, and others primarily in everyday life?

For Sibley, aesthetic concepts are (1) often based on, or linked to, appeal to non-aesthetic concepts, (2) perceptual: a matter of "noticing" and "seeing," (3) determined by taste perceptiveness, or sensitivity (by "taste" Sibley simply means the ability to discern the aesthetic qualities in things), and (4) not condition- or rule-governed. That is, they cannot be defined in terms of necessary and sufficient conditions—nor do they have sufficient conditions alone. Sibley also insists that we cannot derive the presence of these qualities from the presence of specific non-aesthetic qualities. Although I have raised criticisms concerning some of these points earlier, it is worthwhile to see whether "neatness" can fit these criteria.

Neatness is certainly related to non-aesthetic properties, for instance the actual physical properties of the neatened room. We sometimes say "The room

---

21 Sibley, "Concepts."

is messy because there are socks on the floor," or "In order to be neat the clothes need to be lined up straight." (Whether the reasons given really refer to something non-aesthetic is, as I argued earlier, open to question.) Neatness is also perceptual. We *see* that the room is neat. It is not perceptual in the straightforward way that "red" is but in the way that "elegant" is: it is somewhat similar to "taste" in Sibley's sense of that term. Some people are able to notice neatness in ways that others cannot. They often *appreciate* it in ways that others cannot. True, people often disagree strongly about whether or not a room is neat. However, this need not lead to total relativism. We generally distinguish between mere personal preference (whether you *like* to live in a neat house) and matters of fact (whether the house *really* is neat). We will often, to use Kant's term, *demand* that others see the room as we see it: neat or messy.

As with elegance, some people are good judges of neatness. There is an interesting connection between neatness and elegance in English. In slang "neat" is often used to refer to something like "elegant" or "stylish." This points to the possibility that neatness is a primitive cousin to elegance. "Neat" actually comes from the Latin word *nitidus*, for which one translation is "elegant." We agree that there are good judges of the elegant, but what of the neat? Good judges of neatness can point out features that allow us to see the neatness or messiness that we did not see before. Others seem to be neatness-blind. In any cooperative household there is a house-mate who is messier than others. That person may nonetheless insist that he/she *is* neat. The others may say that this person lacks a certain perceptiveness—that he/she is insensitive to mess or clutter. Someone could also lack sensitivity to dirt, filth, and grime. Such a person would be cleanness-blind. Moreover, neatness and cleanness, or cleanliness (the disposition to clean up), are often used as gauges of taste. Persons who care about neatness and cleanness often see persons who do not as tasteless. Ironically, people who maintain a certain level of clutter in their homes, offices, desks, and attire often see obsessive neatness or cleanliness in others as a sign of lack of taste.

Sibley also notes that there are degrees of taste, from rudimentary to refined, and that most people learn easily how to make rudimentary aesthetic attributions.[22] He considers refined attributions as more deserving to be called aesthetic, although he doesn't say why. Two examples of rudimentary attributions are "warm" colours and "gay" pictures. "Neat" and "clean," although not

---

22 Sibley, "Concepts," 560.

clearly metaphorical like "warm" and "gay," may be rudimentary in his sense.

Finally, there are no absolute rules by which we can resolve disputes over the application of everyday surface aesthetic quality terms. There are no necessary and sufficient conditions for determining that something is neat, nor any set of relevant features some sub-set of which is sufficient for application of the concept. One thing is neat for one set of reasons, another for another set. Of course we can give specific stipulative definitions of neatness for specific contexts. A parent may say: "By neat I mean that everything is off the floor." There are also standard dictionary definitions with their separate numbered meanings all of which may be useful under some circumstances to determine correct application of the term.

It might be argued that neatness, messiness, cleanness and dirtiness are non-aesthetic qualities since their main domain is the merely practical, and the aesthetic is non-practical. True, our concern for neatness, cleanness and the unblemished is often not aesthetically motivated. Neatness in our desks, files, computer files, and rooms often helps us to accomplish our goals more effectively. Cleanliness prevents disease. However, as we have seen, not all cases of application of the term "neatness" or "cleanness" are oriented to practical goals. Moreover, practical goals are often entwined with aesthetic matters. For example, unblemished fruits sell more readily because they are more aesthetically pleasing. However, note also that what the general populace may find to be a blemish in a piece of fruit may be considered an attraction to others. Thus "blemished" apples might sell better in communities that are sensitive to possible ecological damage caused by processes used to insure the clean appearance of an apple. The apples may even come to *look* better to these people. Thus, moral as well as practical issues enter into our aesthetic discriminations at this level.

We often think of positive aesthetic qualities as perceptual qualities which please us in the apprehension of them, and of negative aesthetic qualities as ones which do the opposite. When someone who values neatness looks at a neat room, particularly after it has been "neatened" or "cleaned up," he or she will experience a certain pleasure in apprehending that neatness. On this definition, at least, the qualities of "neat," "messy," etc. are aesthetic qualities.

It might be said that in the case of cleanness what is appreciated is not the cleanness itself but the aesthetic qualities of the object cleaned. It is true that when a painting by Monet is cleaned we are better able to appreciate the underlying structure and the brilliance of the colours. However, often when something is cleaned, we simply appreciate the cleanness of it, particularly if *we* have just cleaned it. There can be considerable pleasure in contemplating something cleaned with great effort. What is appreciated is not simply the object cleaned but that plus a combination of process and product: the cleaning up, and the cleaned nature of the object cleaned.

CLEANING ONE'S ROOM AS AESTHETIC EXPERIENCE

Beardsley describes five symptoms of aesthetic experience.[23] These include object directedness, felt freedom, detached affect, active discovery, and a sense of wholeness. He thinks that the first is a necessary condition, and that three of the others must be present if we are to have aesthetic experience. Presumably, aesthetic qualities are qualities which produce at least some of these symptoms.

Let us look at cleaning one's room and contemplating the cleaned nature of the room (or the room-as-cleaned) in terms of these symptoms. (I will assume that the two acts are aspects of one overall experience.) *Object directedness*: The object of the aesthetic experience is the room-as-cleaned. *Felt freedom*: Whereas cleaning one's room is usually thought of as a chore, there is often a felt sense of freedom when we contemplate the cleaned room. *Detached affect*: Someone who contemplates the neatness of a room might well do this in a disinterested way so that the room is "set at a distance." *Active discovery*: Beardsley describes this as "[a] sense of actively exercising constructive powers of the mind, of being challenged by a variety of potentially conflicting stimuli to try to make them cohere ... a sense of achieving intelligibility."[24] Although we sometimes discover things in the process of cleaning our rooms ("There is the library book I failed to turn in!"), this is probably not what Beardsley intended. Nonetheless, the process of cleaning one's room may include a low-level sense of active discovery insofar as one is challenged by choices concerning what is to go where. Certainly the room becomes more intelligible as a result of the process. *Sense of wholeness*: Beardsley defines this as "[a] sense of integration as a person." Many people report an increased level of integration after they have cleaned their rooms, desks, or files. There is a sense of being ready for the next task. The level of sense of personal integration may not be very great, but

---

23 Monroe Beardsley, "In Defense of Aesthetic Value," *Proceedings and Addresses of the American Philosophical Association* 52 (1979): 723-49.
24 Beardsley, "Defense," 741.

it might be greater than what we get from seeing some good paintings, movies, or dances. Beardsley elsewhere describes the aesthetic way of seeing as one in which "there is a relaxation, an absence of strain, but also a kind of visual fulfillment."[25] Contemplating a neatened and cleaned room has this effect.

Objections may be raised against some of these points (for instance, the one about active discovery). However, Beardsley requires only that three out of the four symptoms be present, including the first one, for us to have an aesthetic experience. It follows that cleaning one's room and contemplating it as cleaned counts as an aesthetic experience on Beardsley's definition, although probably not a profound one. And aesthetic experiences are experiences of aesthetic qualities.

In another of his articles Beardsley asserts that aesthetic qualities must be "regional qualities" which may serve as a basis for aesthetic evaluation.[26] A regional quality is defined as a quality that a complex object has as a result of the relation between its parts. For example, a complex colour design can be cheerful, the various colour tones contributing to the cheerfulness of the whole.[27] This may pose a problem for my position since I argued that unlike gestalt qualities everyday surface aesthetic properties are not perceptually complex. However, although cleanness, for example, may be a quality of a complex object it is generally not seen as a matter of relation between the object's parts. This is true even though cleaning sometimes *clarifies* relations between parts.

However, perhaps everyday surface aesthetic quality terms refer to complex properties when they are applied to works of art. Up to now I have assumed that everyday surface aesthetic quality terms refer to the same kinds of qualities when they are used in art contexts as when they are used in non-art everyday contexts. Someone might say, however, that in the context of artworld discourse when someone says that a line is "clean" this claim comes with a number of connotative reverberations, suggesting perhaps that the work in which the line occurs, or at least a significant part of that work, is harmonious and integrated. I accept this modification of my thesis, with the understanding that everyday surface aesthetic quality terms still refer primarily to non-complex properties. It follows then that if these terms *can* refer to complex perceptual qualities in art contexts then they *would*, in these instances, refer to complex regional qualities, which would also be, on Beardsley's view, aesthetic qualities.

---

25 Beardsley, "What is an Aesthetic Quality?," 100.
26 Beardsley, "Quality."
27 Beardsley, "Quality," 94.

THE VALUE OF EVERYDAY SURFACE AESTHETIC QUALITIES

We often assume that "neat," "clean," "uncluttered," and "unblemished," are always positive; and that "messy," "dirty," "cluttered," and "blemished" are always negative aesthetic qualities. However, people hold differing views concerning the value of everyday surface aesthetic qualities. Some value neatness highly. Others, not necessarily the same people, value cleanness highly. Others again do not value either of these very much. These people may actually value messiness and clutter. Kevin Melchionne, for example speaks of pulling off a cluttered look in home decoration.[28] I know artists who revel in the messiness of the creative process, who literally enjoy the messiness of paint. Few adults value dirtiness, although sometimes "dirty" is valued metaphorically, as when the music gets "down and dirty." Children, however, seem sometimes to value dirtiness aesthetically: sometimes it *looks* good to them.

"Clutter," in particular, can to be taken in a positive sense. Many people like to temper neatness with some clutter. They take pleasure in their clutter. Some take pleasure in considerably more clutter than others. Front yards in the California Sierra foothill country are generally much more cluttered than front yards in the suburbs, containing perhaps a junked car, some old farm machinery, or a selection of lawn ornaments. People there prefer this life-style, and may have even moved to that part of the state in part so that they can be free to have a yard full of clutter.

Debates between advocates of neatness and advocates of clutter often take the form: natural vs. artificial. Advocates of clutter and messiness often claim that these properties are more natural and hence more valuable. The hippies of the 1960s argued that messiness and even dirtiness were more natural than neatness and cleanness. However, advocates of neatness and cleanness may also refer to these qualities as more natural. They might refer to the way cats lick themselves and chimps engage in grooming. It all depends on how one sees nature.

THREE NON-WESTERN DIFFERENCES

As with all discussions of aesthetics today, we need to pay attention to non-Western cultures. Some points of difference should be noted. In China, children tend not to draw in the messy ways of their Western counterparts;

---

28 Melchionne, 195.

this challenges our developmental theories about drawing.[29] Psychologist Ellen Winner writes, "Instead of the large, messy, semi-expressionist paintings seen in American preschools and elementary schools, in which children reveal their own invented ways of representing, one sees in China small, neat paintings in which children display their precocious ability to master adult ways of representing the world."[30] She believes this is true because Chinese children are willing to comply and concentrate, and this is because of Chinese child-rearing practices.

Jun'ichiro Tanizaki's *In Praise of Shadows* makes us aware that cleanliness is not a valued property for all people in all cultures in all contexts. He says, "[a]nd of silver and copperware: we [Easterners] love them for the burnish and patina, which they [Westerners] consider unclean, unsanitary, and polish to glittering brilliance."[31] He goes so far as to argue that the "sheen of antiquity" admired by the Chinese and the Japanese "is in fact the glow of grime,"[32] as it is produced by oils that permeate the object over years of handling. In short, "Westerners attempt to expose every speck of grime and eradicate it, while we Orientals carefully preserve and even idealize it."

Cleanliness may also play a powerful positive role in Japanese aesthetics. Kakuzo Okakura observes that in the Japanese tea-room everything is kept absolutely clean.[33] Tea-masters are expected to know how to clean. However, the standards of cleanliness may be quite different from the West. Okakura tells a story of Rikyu (sixteenth-century Japanese tea-master) who asked his son to clean the garden path to the tea-room and when the son claimed there was nothing left to do he exclaimed that this is not the way to sweep a garden path, at which point he shook a tree, spreading leaves. By contrast, in San Jose, California, a middle-class district was once declared blighted because there were wet leaves on a tennis court![34]

---

29 Ellen Winner, "How Can Chinese Children Draw so Well?" *Journal of Aesthetic Education* 23, no. 1, Special Issue: Arts Education in China (Spring, 1989): 41-63.
30 Winner, 41.
31 Tanizaki, *Shadows*, 30.
32 Tanizaki, *Shadows*, 11.
33 Kakuzo Okakura, *The Book of Tea*, ed. Everett F. Bleiler (New York: Dover, 1964).
34 Carol Lloyd, "Are California Bay Area Cities Abusing Eminent Domain as a Redevelopment Tool?" *The San Francisco Chronicle* (March 7, 2005), reprinted in *Knowledgplex*, accessed July 1, 2011, http://www.des.ucdavis.edu/faculty/handy/ESP171/KnowledgePlex%20Article%20Are%20California%20Bay%20Area%20Cities%20Abusing%20Eminent%20Domain%20as%20a%20Redevelopment%20Tool.htm.

PURITY/IMPURITY, POLLUTED, FOULED

Whether "pure" and "purity" are best associated with the aesthetic or the moral is open to question. Jonathan Haidt and Fredrik Björklund have listed purity/sanctity as one of five evolutionary foundations of ethics.[35] They include the concept of "cleanliness" under this. The other four foundations are clearly non-aesthetic, i.e., harm/care, fairness/reciprocity, and authority/respect. (Of course, all of these could have an aesthetic side or be mixed in some way with aesthetics. For example, authority could be gained or exhibited through a certain style of clothing.)

So, is purity basically a moral matter and not an aesthetic one? Haidt and Björklund recognize that whether purity is a moral matter is controversial. For example, liberal moral theorists often see it as a matter of social convention or of prejudice and not of morality. Still, such moral theorists would probably not see purity as a matter of aesthetics, either. I think that Haidt and Björklund are right that matters of purity are sometimes parts of the moral domain and, therefore, are not always aesthetic.[36] If one takes pride in the "purity" of one's blood-line, there doesn't seem to be anything aesthetic involved. This does not mean, however, that purity is never a matter of aesthetics. For example, the Japanese emphasis on the value of purity in the tea ceremony is aesthetic. Tadao Ando's modernist architecture has been praised for its purity. For Westerners it may be surprising that in Japan an adult male who fails to gain a job is considered aesthetically impure.[37]

Although purity is seldom mentioned in aesthetics journals, Immanuel Kant emphasized the concept of purity with respect to aesthetic judgments. Clive Bell, Clement Greenberg, and Adolf Loos are among the best known advocates of the importance of purity in art and architecture. Painting, it was thought by Greenberg, was impure if mixed with other art forms. Purity in art is commonly associated with formalism. However, the question of the status of purity as *itself* an aesthetic quality is seldom addressed. If the pleasurable response to purity is directed to the perceptual features of the object qua perceptual then the experience would seem to be aesthetic. Purity can of course be

---

35 J. Haidt and F. Björklund, "Social Intuitionists Answer Six Questions about Morality" in *Moral Psychology, Vol. 2: The Cognitive Science of Morality*, ed. W. Sinnott-Armstrong (Cambridge, MA: MIT Press, 2007), 181-217.
36 Haidt and Björklund, 203.
37 Kenneth G. Henshall, *Dimensions of Japanese Society: Gender, Margins and Mainstream* (Houndsmills, UK: Palgrave Macmillan, 1999), 179.

seen as the extreme of cleanliness. The pure is appreciated for what it is not: the pure object or substance is unadulterated. A pure sound is not discordant. Pure white snow is admired as such, mainly because snow can be so easily dirtied. If a substance or material has characteristic properties, its aesthetical uniqueness will come out more if it is pure. Thus a tie may be advertised as pure silk, or a jacket as pure wool, or a ring as pure gold. If we really like something we will generally like a pure, unmixed, example of that thing.

Purity, then, can be an aesthetic quality. "Pure" is, of course, not always positive. For example, we speak of "pure nonsense" and "pure idiocy." And sometimes "pure" can be neutral: if a colour is pure, that does not necessarily mean that it is aesthetically more or less valuable. I should add that purity is not a surface quality: for something to be pure it must be so throughout. A question remains whether the same word can have both ethical and aesthetic meanings, and whether one of these is primary.

We cannot leave discussion of the pure and the impure without mentioning sex. Sexual purity (as in virginity and chastity) is not an aesthetic quality. This is not to say that someone couldn't find a person more beautiful upon hearing that he/she was a virgin or chaste. Related to this, such terms as "dirty" and "filthy" are strongly associated with the obscene, the lewd and the pornographic. However, is "dirty" in this sexual sense entirely a moral quality, or might it not also sometimes be an aesthetic one?

Haidt and Björklund also associate "purity/sanctity" with the emotion of disgust as an opposite. Again, disgust is not always strictly speaking an aesthetic reaction. However, there is such a thing as aesthetic disgust, something which, as we saw in a previous chapter, has been explored by Carolyn Korsmeyer.[38]

CONCLUDING COMMENTS

What role should everyday surface aesthetic qualities play in a general aesthetics? Examination of the development of an aesthetic sense in children may be relevant here. Many of our first aesthetic experiences are associated with everyday surface aesthetic qualities. Children are taught to be neat, clean, orderly, and not to be messy, sloppy, and unkempt.[39] Perhaps as a form of rebellion, they often value the opposite qualities, although this varies from

---

38 Carolyn Korsmeyer, "Delightful."
39 Sibley, "Concepts," 559.

country to country.[40] These concepts are learned long before such traditionally recognized aesthetic concepts as "grace" and "delicacy." Does that make them distant from such concepts? Not necessarily.

Sibley gives an account of how children learn complex musical terms which can help us here. He argues that parents and teachers begin to teach aesthetic concepts by suggesting that simple pieces of music are "hurrying" or "running." From there they move to concepts like "lively" and "gay." Finally, they teach more complex concepts like "solemn" and "dynamic."[41] He implies that learning the simpler concepts provides the basis for learning the more complex ones. Perhaps "neat," "clean," and "orderly" are simpler concepts which provide a basis for developing more complex notions such as "harmonious," "organized," and "beautiful." Note that young musicians are encouraged to learn how to be neat, clean and ordered first before more complex abilities are developed. Later, a little messiness or disorder might be allowed in order to better show off underlying structure.

Some readers may still balk at the idea of calling the qualities I am discussing aesthetic qualities. They might insist that aesthetic qualities should have complex features which make them accessible only after much training, that something distinctive emerges at the level of such concepts as "elegant," "beautiful," and "sublime," which just is not there in such concepts as "neat," and "clean." Those same readers may be willing to grant the status of aesthetic quality to everyday surface aesthetic quality terms when these terms are applied by critics and other knowledgeable persons to works of art, since at that level, through connoting such gestalt qualities as "harmonious" and "integrated," these terms may take on a degree of complexity which they lack at the everyday level. These points have merit. Perhaps it might be more appropriate to call everyday surface aesthetic qualities pre- or proto-aesthetic qualities when found at the level of everyday life (given that they are taught in childhood and provide some of the basis for more complex aesthetic concepts) whereas at the level of art they may have sufficient complexity to be called aesthetic qualities in the fullest sense of the term.

---

40 Cf. Winner.
41 Sibley, "Concepts," 560.

CHAPTER 8

Everyday Aesthetics and the Sublime

It may be thought that the concept of everyday aesthetics is incompatible with that of the sublime. In aesthetics the sublime is mainly understood in terms of a tradition that goes back to Burke's theory of a delight that comes from a pain or fear that we apprehend from a safe distance, and Kant's notion of that which gives pleasure while being absolutely great, formless and boundless, creating a fearful object about which we are not actually afraid.[1] However, most dictionary meanings of the term do not refer to fear but to exaltation in feeling, elevation in language, and a sense of awe in art. Although the sublime is traditionally associated with certain kinds of natural scenes, for example dramatic mountains and waterfalls, works of art, for example architecture in Burke's and Kant's writings, have also been considered sublime. This raises the question whether the idea of the sublime can also have application in everyday aesthetics. Certainly, some kinds of sublime experience are far from the everyday, for example when John Muir strapped himself to the side of a cliff in Yosemite Valley to experience the thunderstorms more directly. On the other hand, we frequently refer to experiences of cities as sublime.[2]

---

1 Edmund Burke, *A Philosophical Enquiry into the Origin of Our Ideas of the Sublime and Beautiful* (Oxford: Oxford University Press, 1990), Section VII "Of the Sublime" and all of Part Two. Kant, *Judgment*, #23-28.
2 See, for example Elizabeth Wilson, *The Sphinx in the City: Urban Life, the Control of Disorder, and Women* (Berkeley: University of California Press, 1992).

The view of San Francisco from Twin Peaks is sublime when we see the vast cityscape against the backdrop of the San Francisco Bay and under complex lighting effects produced by variable weather. It is also arguable that urban disaster, whether due to natural or human causes, can have a sublime aspect. For example, the events of 9/11 can be seen in terms of the sublime.[3] Similarly, the sublime can be found in certain aspects of the hurricane Katrina disaster.[4]

Yet disasters are not everyday occurrences, and it could be argued that since the sublime has to do with the "terrible" as Burke puts it then it cannot fall under the everyday.[5] Burke requires a sublime experience caused by nature to be one of astonishment in which "all the motions are suspended, with some degree of horror," and the mind is entirely filled with its object.[6] It is hard to imagine an everyday aesthetic experience that would fit this bill, even when we add the element of delight that Burke requires. On the other hand, if the sublime is a main aesthetic concept, and if everyday aesthetics is one of the main aesthetic domains (certainly a contentious point, but one I have argued for in this book), then one would think there is some place for the sublime in everyday aesthetics. Also, finding a place for the sublime in everyday aesthetics would tend to support the idea that it is one of the main aesthetic domains.

In addition to the examples already mentioned some other writers have found the sublime in everyday experience. For example, Makita Brottman notes that the Futurists regarded shopping as sublime. She argues that the mysticism of power that the Futurist artist Marinetti found in the modern city can now be found realized in the contemporary shopping mall. Jane Bennett

---

3   Vernon Hyde Minor, "What Kind of Tears? 9/11 and the Sublime," *Journal of American Studies of Turkey* 14 (2001): 91-96, accessed June 2, 2008, http://www.bilkent.edu.tr/~jast/Number14/Minor.htm. Margaret Weigel also relates the sublime to 9/11 in "Terrorism and the Sublime, or, Why We Keep Watching," 2001, http://www.margaretweigel.com/comment/portSublime.pdf. Another work which discusses 9/11 aesthetically but never mentions the concept of the sublime is Emmanouil Aretoulakis, "Aesthetic Appreciation, Ethics, and 9/11," *Contemporary Aesthetics* (March 31, 2008), http://www.contempaesthetics.org/newvolume/pages/article.php?articleID=510#FN11link.
4   Bonnie Mann, *Women's Liberation and the Sublime: Feminism, Postmodernism, Environment* (New York: Oxford University Press, 2006). See also Dehlia Hannah, "Naturalized Disaster: Seeking Sublimity in Everyday Life and at the Extremes," unpublished paper delivered at the *Everyday Aesthetics—VIII International Summer School of IIAA*, Lahti, Finland, June 15-18, 2008.
5   Burke, 53.
6   Burke, 53.

similarly finds what she calls "enchantment" (which she describes in a way that makes it very much like the sublime) in a GAP commercial.[7]

Arnold Berleant takes a more critical approach to the sublime in our commodified culture. He identifies a "negative sublime" which he believes represents the sublime in our postmodern age.[8] He associates this with Jean-Francois Lyotard's concept of the modernist sublime in which the unpresentable (that which is beyond perception or imagination) is (paradoxically) presented in a nostalgic form that provides solace and comfort.[9] Disney World is his prime example of something that offers us the negative sublime. For Berleant, the actual or true sublime is lost in our postmodern age. He questions whether magnitude without spiritual elevation, as found in an enormous theme park, *could* attain the true sublime. He also suggests that the concept of the sublime is interesting *today* because it compellingly captures the dominant perception of our lived world, a world in which the power of nature has been made insignificant by barely controlled but unbounded human power. Such an environment, he says is sublime because it is unpresentable. This negative sublime, he believes, has "become the dominant aesthetic consciousness of our age."[10] For Berleant, then, the sublime in human environments is mainly a negative thing, at least in our postmodern era.

Elsewhere, Berleant reacts against an exhibit by Lyotard at the Pompidou Center in Paris in which it is implied that infinitely complex networks of meaning undermine our sense of reality and that the only recourse for perception and imagination is to the concept of the sublime.[11] Berleant sees Lyotard's strategy as an anti-aesthetic displacement of perception by the intellect, the sublime being transformed from the Kantian affirmation of human power into "an involuted consciousness overwhelmed by its own inadequacy." He calls instead for a Husserlian return to the things themselves.

Berleant is certainly right that "sublime" can be a negative as well as a positive aesthetic quality and that Disney World, as it is generally experienced, may

---

7   Makita Brottman, "The Last Stop of Desire: The Aesthetics of the Shopping Center," in *The Aesthetics of Human Environments*, 128. Jane Bennett, *The Enchantment of Modern Life: Attachments, Crossings, and Ethics* (Princeton, NJ: Princeton University Press, 2001).
8   Arnold Berleant, *Landscape*, 77-78.
9   Jean-François Lyotard, *The Postmodern Condition: A Report on Knowledge*, trans. Geoff Bennington and Brian Massumi (Minneapolis: University of Minnesota Press, 1984), "Appendix: Answering the Question: What is Postmodernism?" 71-82.
10   Berleant, *Landscape*, 78,
11   Berleant, *Engagement*, 190, next quote, 191.

well be said to present a kind of false sublime. However, there is no reason in principle why Disney World could not render an actual sublime experience, just as arguably the Parisian streets did for Baudelaire. I concur with Berleant in being skeptical of Lyotard's idea that the postmodern sublime is our only recourse in a world of increasing complexity. However I am also skeptical of Berleant's faith that we can somehow return to the things themselves.

In this chapter I will argue that there is an everyday sublime, and I will do so by following a path through a series of thinkers. I will begin by returning to the question of Zen experience. Although Zen satori seems a promising route to understanding the everyday sublime I will argue that it is ultimately uninformative to those unwilling to engage fully in Zen practice. Proust provides an image that also shows promise, but it is unclear whether he is describing an everyday sublime experience or is simply using the everyday as a stimulus for sublime thoughts. Bullough's analysis of a fog at sea will prove valuable in its focus on imaginative perception and creation of a world, but this will prove not sufficiently cognitive for our purposes. Heidegger's discussion of a Van Gogh painting of shoes, not only construes the experience of art as something both cognitive and sublime but also points towards the dialectic between art and everyday life I have stressed in other parts of this book. Finally, Nietzsche's concepts of the Dionysian and the "tragic man" not only allow for an everyday sublime but point the way to a radically different interpretation of avant-garde art's relation to the everyday than that offered by leading philosopher and art critic, Arthur Danto.

Before I proceed however I should mention the relation between the concept of the sublime and that of aura. Earlier I spoke of a continuum that runs from low-level aesthetic experience to the experience of beauty and beyond. A low level of aura accompanies appreciation of the neatness of a room. Sublime experience involves a very high level of aura. Kant's idea of "aesthetic ideas" (discussed in the "Analytic of the Sublime" section of *The Critique of Judgment*) captures this insofar as these objects of sublime experience seem to go on forever. For Kant, aesthetic ideas are representations of the imagination which induce much thought, but without a concept being adequate to them.[12] Kant emphasizes how these ideas "strain at something that lies out beyond the confines of experience."[13] Insofar as they seem to go beyond themselves, they

---

12 Kant, *Judgment*, 175.
13 Kant, *Judgment*, 176.

have what I have called "aura." A similar idea, discussed in Chapter Three, is Dewey's controversial notion of the background as an indefinite whole that stretches out indefinitely. We will also find the notion of the sublime as aura present in the thinking of Heidegger.

ZEN SATORI

Perhaps the Zen Buddhist monk on achieving enlightenment can experience the sublime in the everyday. Guy Sircello references Lao Tzu and Bodhidarma in an article on the sublime.[14] He associates the sublime with the inexpressibility of the Way and "thoughts about the impossibility of thought." His central concern is with the claim that an experience of the sublime presents the object as epistemologically inaccessible. His cautious conclusion is that epistemological transcendence may not presuppose any ontology. In the end, much like Dewey, he rejects sublime ontology while still attempting to incorporate sublime experience into a naturalist worldview.

Although in this article Sircello ignores the fact that the experience is pleasurable he discusses this in an earlier book.[15] There, he argues that the sublime is a species of the beautiful. The sublime, on his view, is the extreme degree of a set of "properties of qualitative degree." That set includes "profundity, powerfulness, grandeur, [and] magnificence." Also, when "sublimity" is attached to any beautiful quality, as in "sublimely vivid," it designates an overwhelmingly high degree of that property. Although Sircello's idea is similar to my own in talking about a continuum of increasing intensity, it excludes the pain and terror aspect of the sublime considered essential by most other writers, e.g., Burke, Kant, and Lyotard.

Is Zen satori an experience of the sublime within the everyday? Certainly, descriptions of satori have focused on the psychologically powerful responses Zen monks have had to such everyday things as a drop of water or a simple human gesture. D.T. Suzuki says that, in satori, your mental activities all work in a different key in that they are more satisfying, peaceful and joyful.[16] He fur-

---

14   Guy Sircello, "How Is a Theory of the Sublime Possible?" *The Journal of Aesthetics and Art Criticism* 51, no. 4 (1993): 541-50, 549.
15   Guy Sircello, *New Theory*, Chapter 28 "Sublimity," 100.
16   Daisetz Teitaro Suzuki, *An Introduction to Zen Buddhism*, ed. Ch. Humphreys (New York: Grove Press, 1991).

ther states that Zen is rejuvenating in that "[t]he spring flowers look prettier, and the mountain stream runs cooler and more transparent." Things in nature take on an aura through intensification of qualities. Based on these comments we could argue that there is a profoundly aesthetic aspect to satori. However, satori also includes a transcendent cognitive dimension, and although sublime aesthetic experience may be cognitive in some way, it is not clear that its object must be transcendent.

It is also arguable that satori, being atemporal and non-sensual, is not even an experience. Unfortunately, the only person who can speak authoritatively of satori is someone who has achieved it, and we can never know for sure whether someone really has done so. Moreover, the pronouncements of those who have been said to have achieved it are often seen as inadequate to the experience. Finally, as with Sircello, it is doubtful that the satori experience (if there is such) contains the element of pain and fear, or even that of astonishment, so closely associated with the sublime in Western thought. Interestingly, Saito has observed that the sublime is absent from Japanese aesthetics.[17] So, contrary to our initial expectation, the idea of satori is of limited use in our search for the everyday sublime.

As with Zen, life in a Christian monastery also poses the possibility of an everyday sublime. The documentary "Into Great Silence" (2006) by German filmmaker Philip Gröning explores the life of monks at the Grande Chartreuse monastery in the French Alps from the perspective of the aesthetics of everyday life. Many of the scenes go beyond beauty to something sublime. The Alpine setting is no small part of this. But the feeling of something sublime also goes indoors. One scene carefully contemplates the repair of a shoe. Of course we are not seeing the sublime experience that the monks seek. Rather we are seeing an interpretation of their lives from the aesthetic perspective of a film-maker. This film also portrays, and to some extent exemplifies, an intensely more intimate aesthetic relation to everyday life than is normal in contemporary society. For example, in the silent monastery even the most ordinary sounds take on deep significance. After seeing the film, one becomes more aware of the simple pleasures of preparing a meal, washing dishes, saying a prayer, and working a vegetable garden.

---

17 Yuriko Saito, "The Japanese Appreciation of Nature," *British Journal of Aesthetics* 25, no. 1 (1985): 238-52.

PROUST

Consider the famous passage from Proust's *Remembrance of Things Past*.

> And soon, mechanically, weary after a dull day with the prospect of a depressing morrow, I raised to my lips a spoonful of the tea in which I had soaked a morsel of the cake. No sooner had the warm liquid and the crumbs with it touched my palate than a shudder ran through my whole body, and I stopped, intent upon the extraordinary changes that were taking place. An exquisite pleasure had invaded my senses, but individual, detached, with no suggestion of its origin. And at once the vicissitudes of life had become indifferent to me, its disasters innocuous, its brevity illusory—this new sensation having had on me the effect which love has of filling me with a precious essence; or rather the essence was not in me, it was myself. I had ceased to feel mediocre, accidental, mortal. Whence could it have come to me, this all-powerful joy? I was conscious that it was connected with the taste of tea and cake, but that it infinitely transcended those savours, could not, indeed, be of the same nature as theirs.[18]

Marcel's experience has the intensity and the infinite reach associated with the sublime. Also it involves the exquisite pleasure often associated with aesthetic experience. Moreover, although there is no explicit reference to terror, considered essential to the sublime by Burke, the idea of death lurks in the background ("shudder," "mortal").

Assuming that Proust's passage describes an actual experience, we can say that sometimes extraordinary aesthetic experiences happen with ordinary things, in this case tasting a small piece of cake and sipping some tea. Such experiences begin with a sensation, but then go beyond it, perhaps even with the sense that they go infinitely beyond. Proust, therefore, may have been describing a sublime experience.

So let us say that Marcel was having such an experience in relation to something everyday. This is not to say that this kind of event happens every day, indeed it is quite rare. What puts it within the everyday is that it is in response to something everyday. The power of Proust's account is based on the fact that

---

18 Marcel Proust, *Swann's Way*, trans. C.K. Scott Moncrieff (London: Chatto & Windus, 1928), 41.

lesser versions of such experiences are familiar to us: we often find that smells, tastes, sights and sounds have an evocative richness, an inexplicable aura of significance mixed with pleasure.

There are of course dimensions to Marcel's experience that might not be present in all aesthetically sublime everyday experiences, for example the feeling that life's problems are illusions, the sense that one is identical with a precious essence, the feeling that one is not mediocre, and the way the experience opens up past memories. Moreover, the experience seems to be more about these things than about the tea and cake. As the passage continues, Marcel finds that the feeling goes away upon repeatedly sipping the tea. He becomes convinced that the truth is to be found in himself rather than in the sensuous object. Subsequently, he recaptures the memory of tea and cakes served to him by his aunt when young, and this in turn allows him to remember the whole of his experience during that time.

Based on this, one could argue that Marcel is not even experiencing the cake and tea aesthetically but rather is merely prompted to experience *something else* (i.e., his memories) aesthetically by way of the cake and tea. However, I doubt that a clear distinction can be made between the cake and tea *as experienced* and the cake and tea as causal source. Moreover, the notion that the experience would bring with it an unending sequence of thoughts is consistent with Kant's notion of the sublime, as when he speaks of aesthetic ideas as representations of the imagination that induce much thought to which no concept is adequate. True, the significance of the experience lies not so much in the madeleine as in Marcel himself, but this does not tell against my point. Kant, when discussing the sublime, also found the significance of the experience to be in the subject rather than in the object that motivated the experience.

Yet it has been argued by A.T. Winterbourne that Proust's aesthetic experience is located not in the tea and cake *or* the scenes they evoke but in the literary expression of this experience.[19] On this view, although the Proust passage is remarkable in the way it employs the experience of the commonplace to create something artistically valuable, it is confusing to say that eating cakes and drinking tea can, as such, be aesthetic. Winterbourne believes that although food and drink may be occasions for aesthetic experience they are not *part* of it.[20]

---

19 A.T. Winterbourne, "Is Oral and Olfactory Art Possible?" *Journal of Aesthetic Education* 15, no. 2, Special Issue: INSEA 1981—Art, Ideology, and Aesthetic Education (1981): 95-102.
20 Winterbourne, 96-97.

It may be agreed that tea and cake are not art forms, and that the tea and cake Marcel consumed were not works of art. But this does not mean that they were, in this case, just stimuli for art. True, they, or something like them, may have stimulated Proust to write the quoted passage. True, the passage appears in a novel, which is an art form. However, within the novel, the tea and cake are part of an experience that, taken as a whole, is intensely aesthetic. When Winterbourne says it was the memories the tastes evoked that made Proust happy, and not the tastes, he fails to see that taste is an integral part of the experience. Yet, because of these problems, the Proust passage does not provide a clear path to an aesthetics of the everyday sublime.

BULLOUGH AND THE FOG AT SEA

Edward Bullough's famous example of a fog at sea will perhaps be more useful for our project.[21] Instead of dealing with disastrous events or small comestibles it concerns a pervasive environment that generates a certain experience, much like the way a city street can be transformed by the quality of light at sunset. Although fog might seem to come under the aesthetics of the natural environment it can equally be seen as part of everyday life. Weather is fundamental to our everyday lives and is certainly not limited to experiences of natural environments.[22]

Bullough places the aesthetic experience of fog squarely within everyday life by imagining the experience of passengers on a ship. A fog at sea was (in earlier days) acutely unpleasant because of the danger of shipwreck. Yet it could also be a source of enjoyment. This required what he calls "Distancing" which, when applied to the fog at sea, is a matter of abstracting or subtracting the feeling of danger with which one normally associated it. Yet would the experience still be aesthetically interesting if the sense of danger was completely gone? It might be better said that the experience of danger is bracketed or sublimated. Interestingly, Bullough himself does not always hold that the feeling of danger is subtracted from such an experience. For example, he recognizes that the danger involved in mountain climbing may actually *add* to its enjoyment.

Bullough says that to perceive aesthetically we should direct our attention to what he calls the "objective" features of the object (e.g., of the fog at sea, or a work

---

21 Bullough.
22 Saito, "Weather."

of art). Yet, since he admits that art cannot be objective in the sense that history or science can be, and since his theory of "Distance" is intended also for art, his so-called objective features of the fog might better be described as imaginative ones, perhaps in the way that Emily Brady uses the term "imagination." For Brady imagination, unlike fancy, is something one can do well or not.[23] Bullough uses imagination in this sense when he speaks of objective features. An example of imagining well comes when he speaks of the fog as a "veil surrounding you with an opaqueness as of transparent milk, blurring the outline of things and distorting their shapes into weird grotesqueness."[24] Here, he is encouraging us to see the fog *as if* it were a veil, *as if* it were milk, and *as* presenting grotesque shapes. All of these imaginings give the fog a special quality of indeterminate but mysterious meaning. He adds to this that in experiencing the fog you may have an "impression as if you could touch some far-off siren by merely putting out your hand and letting it lose itself behind that white wall." In this case the imagination posits a world beyond the metaphorical wall. Think here of Kant's notion that the productive imagination in the experience of the sublime through fine art seems to create another world. Kant writes: "The imagination (as a productive faculty of cognition) is a powerful agent for creating, as it were, a second nature out of the material supplied to it by actual nature."[25] To be sure, Bullough was serious about the idea of objectivity and thought that what was revealed was an aspect of reality, what he called the "usually unnoticed" side of things. However, I think he merely wanted to stress that what he has described metaphorically is not a mere subjective projection of personal emotions.

Aestheticians have often been blind to the beauty of the experience Bullough described, to the qualities of the description itself, and to the implications that both might have for aesthetics. The typical approach has been to see his idea as a variety of aesthetic attitude theory. And yet as we continue reading the passage it becomes deeper and richer still. Bullough calls on us to "note the curious creamy smoothness of the water, hypocritically denying as it were any suggestion of danger." Not only the fog but the water has taken on the pervasive milky quality. Moreover, the element of danger, which previously was supposed to be subtracted, is found to be ambiguously present.

We learn also that what is being described is not just beautiful but sublime. The concept of the sublime is present when Bullough remarks on the fog

---

23 See Emily Brady, "Imagination."
24 This and the next five quotes, Bullough, 759.
25 Kant, *Judgment*, 176.

experience's evocation of a "strange solitude and remoteness from the world, as it can be found only in the highest mountain tops." He then observes that the fog "may acquire, in its uncanny mingling of repose and terror, a flavor of such concentrated poignancy and delight as to contrast sharply with the blind and distempered anxiety of its other aspects," this last point reminiscent of Burke's idea that the sublime requires an element of fear.

In analyzing Bullough's theory, philosophers have tended to focus on the subtraction of the practical, as when Bullough says that Distance is produced at first "by putting the phenomenon, so to speak, out of gear with our practical, actual self." But what is of interest for our purpose is that he characterizes sublime aesthetic experience as a sudden illumination of "the most ordinary and familiar objects" and not necessarily as happening in the face of dramatic natural phenomena.

Psychical Distance, Bullough argues, lies between ourselves and anything that affects us perceptually, emotionally or ideationally. We gain a new outlook from this "putting out of gear." However, Distance also requires an imaginative creation of a world, or a way of seeing the world, by means of a series of metaphors. Bullough notes that following the negative moment of Distancing, in which the practical is cut out, is a positive moment, in which the experience is elaborated and which is exemplified in the imaginative seeing he has described.

In an influential criticism, George Dickie focused on the idea of "putting out of gear" and dismissed the positive aspect of Distance.[26] Dickie defended this dismissal by claiming that Bullough does not discuss it. Yet, the entire description of the fog at sea experience is related to the positive aspect of Distance. Dickie wrongly saw Distance as functioning entirely in terms of inhibition. This was an important wrong turn in the history of twentieth-century aesthetics.

For Bullough, the concept of beauty in relation to such things as the fog at sea has two features: it involves spontaneous imaginative recreation of the sensuously experienced world as now charged with metaphors that intimate mystery and deep meaningfulness. This moves the experience of beauty towards something more sublime involving, as it does, a background of potential pain. At this point ordinary things become quite extraordinary. Of course, fog need not be experienced in this way to be experienced aesthetically. As Saito has observed, we can aesthetically experience a fog from a beach without any notion of anxiety.[27] However, experiencing the fog as sublime requires it.

---

26 George Dickie, "Bullough and the Concept of Psychical Distance," *Philosophy and Phenomenological Research* 22, no. 2 (1961): 233-38.
27 Saito, "Weather," 163.

HEIDEGGER ON VAN GOGH'S SHOES

Still, Bullough's example does not cover ordinary objects of everyday life rendering a sublime experience. Nor does it capture the cognitive dimension in sublime experience, the way in which, as Heidegger puts it, truth comes forth. Heidegger's well-known analysis of a Van Gogh painting of shoes might help us here, even though it may at first seem irrelevant since it is concerned primarily with the nature of art.[28] In his "The Origin of the Work of Art" Heidegger excellently describes what a sublime experience of a work of art might be. Although he does little directly to explicate sublime experiences of ordinary objects, he indirectly does so by way of his discussion of art. There is a way in which fine art can be a deep reflection on the aesthetics of everyday life, and Heidegger suggests this through his idea that we perceive in Van Gogh's painting not only the shoes themselves but their role within the experience and life-world of their supposed wearer. That is, the shoes depicted by Van Gogh are understood not just as items that cover and protect feet but as containing depths of meaning related to the life of the imagined wearer, including such existential aspects of life as what Heidegger refers to as being-towards-death. This suggests that ordinary objects themselves, the shoes Van Gogh observed for example, can be experienced as sublime. For example, much like the Kantian concept of the sublime, the ideas generated by Heidegger in contemplating Van Gogh's painting go on without the possibility of any definite thought being adequate to them.[29] For Kant, fine art is the art of genius and when the genius produces a work of art it has soul, by which Kant means an animating principle which is in fact the faculty of presenting aesthetic ideas.[30] Similarly, for Heidegger, when the art work lets us know what the shoes are in truth it does not simply give some propositional truths about shoes but a series of thoughts. The shoes give us what Kant calls an "aesthetic idea" i.e., a "representation of the imagination which induces much thought, yet without the possibility of any definite thought whatever, i.e., concept being adequate to it...."[31] Kant then speaks of imagination as something which, in cases like this, creates a second nature out of material from actual nature. Although Heidegger does not mention Kant's concept of the sublime I believe he sees Van Gogh as accomplishing something like

---

28 Martin Heidegger, "Origin."
29 Kant, *Judgment*, 156.
30 Kant, *Judgment*, #49, 175.
31 Kant, *Judgment*, 176.

this in his painting of the peasant shoes. The passage which begins "From the dark opening of the worn insides of the shoes the toilsome tread of the worker stares forth"[32] expands until it covers not only the peasant woman's life-experience as a worker but her being-towards-death and generally the way in which she relates both to the earth and to her world. As Heidegger puts it, in contemplating the shoes through the painting, we are "somewhere else than we usually tend to be."

Someone could argue that, although the experience of an artist in perceiving objects (i.e., Van Gogh and the shoes) and in working on a canvas during the creative process may be part of everyday experience *for the artist*, it is not so *for anyone else*; and further that an artist's experience during the creation of art is more properly categorized under the aesthetics of art than under that of the everyday. However, note that the aesthetic properties of the following items are not properties of works of art themselves: (1) the materials used by the artist, (2) the objects represented, (3) the scenes, moments and objects of artist's inspiration, and (4) the artist's art-making experiences prior to completion of a work. If we accept that the experience of an everyday object as sublime can be an important part of the creative experience of an artist then we are a lot closer to a theory of the sublime in the everyday.[33] Perhaps both artists and non-artist appreciators of everyday aesthetics go through life experiencing everyday objects and events with the idea that seeing them as sublime is possible. I suspect that something like this happens to people who believe in God: they see the world as full of God, and ordinary objects and events as His manifestations. Christian philosopher Søren Kierkegaard, for example, believed that "to be able to land in just that way [assume a definite position, like a master dancer, without vacillation] and in the same second to look as though one were up and walking, to transform the lap in life into a gait, to express the sublime in the pedestrian absolutely—that is something only the knight of faith can do...."[34] The "knight of faith" was Kierkegaard's ideal man. Although an atheist, I accept that such experiences can be deeply meaningful. Kierkegaard certainly finds the sublime in the everyday, or the "pedestrian," as he puts it. One of the things I like about Kant's notion of aesthetic ideas is

---

32 Heidegger, "Origin," 33, next quote, 35.
33 This is in accord with John Dewey's theory of creativity in Dewey, which I discuss in "Pragmatist Theory" and in "Dewey's Aesthetics."
34 Søren Kierkegaard, *Fear and Trembling*, ed. and trans. Alastair Hannay (Hamondsworth: Penguin, 1985).

that they do something similar in a world in which God might well be absent. Kant emphasizes the idea that we should look at the world *as if* it were created by God.[35] One can be an atheist and do this too. Kant's concept of aesthetic ideas works as a kind of substitute for the intellectual intuition of God that, according to him, can never happen.

Heidegger also makes us aware that everyday existence happens within the context of a drama, that of a life that is heading for death. Experience of the sublime, both in general and in the everyday, is related in some way to this fact. Although fear of death is not itself pleasurable, the eventuality of death provides a background against which sublime experience, which seems to deny death, is possible. As Burke put it, whatever excites ideas of pain and danger gives rise to the sublime if we can be made safe. This experience, or rather, the aspect of it that reminds us of our death, lends poignancy to beauty and cogency to the sublime. Although it is tempting to think of the sublime as nothing other than beauty in its highest dimensions, the kind of everyday phenomena that might evoke the experience of the sublime should be different from the kind that would evoke the experience of beauty: there needs to be an element of touching the abyss.

Heidegger begins his essay with an attempt to understand the nature of art, which then leads him to trying to understand the artwork itself. Each artwork has, as he put it, a "thingly" quality, for example a work of architecture in stone has the quality of being in stone. His exploration of the thingliness of a thing leads him to consider equipment (i.e., shoes) as a typical example of a thing. What then is the essence of equipment? To answer this question he asks us to focus on a pair of shoes. At this point he somewhat surprisingly shifts attention to a *representation* of a pair of shoes in a painting by Van Gogh. However, we have not lost sight of the actual pair of shoes. Heidegger observes, I think correctly, that in the Western tradition it has been commonly thought that a thing should be understood on the model of matter and form, or matter upon which form is imposed. This Aristotelian idea has been predominant because of the emphasis placed in the West on technical production of artifacts, and specifically of artifacts that have a function. We in the West then think of the nature of a thing in terms of the nature of equipment, the nature of equipment in terms of matter and form, and form in terms of function. As we have seen,

---

35 Immanuel Kant, *Critique of Pure Reason*, trans. N. Kemp Smith (London: Macmillan & Co., 1929), 709.

Carlson and Parsons exemplify this approach to everyday aesthetics. However, Heidegger urges, we should not be too quick to make this jump. We need to go beyond simply talking about the shoes in terms of their use to talking about them in terms of how they are experienced as they are used. The shoes Van Gogh depicts can be seen in a wholly general way (as Plato or Aristotle would), and this would even accord with a certain unimaginative or un-insightful way of looking at Van Gogh's painting but it would not reveal the thingly nature of the shoes, or more deeply, what it is to be a thing.

It is at this point in his essay when Heidegger shifts from a relatively philosophical mode of discourse to one that is much more poetic, describing something he sees staring forth from "the dark opening of the worn insides of the shoes."[36] The life-experience of the peasant woman he presumes to have worn these shoes can be seen through looking at Van Gogh's painting. Let us not get distracted here by questions of whether the shoes actually belonged to a peasant woman or were in fact Van Gogh's own. Heidegger himself says that it is not required that we believe that Van Gogh has depicted a pair of actually existing peasant shoes. Also, let us not think too much about Van Gogh's painting since we are mainly interested here in the experience of the shoes themselves by Van Gogh and by the peasant woman.

It is plausible that Van Gogh *had* to see the shoes in the way Heidegger describes them for the painting to express what it does. One can see in his paintings of peasants and peasant life, and in his biography, that Van Gogh was deeply involved in depicting the world of the peasant. It is arguable, and consistent with Heidegger's position, that Van Gogh did not see the shoes in terms of form, matter and function but rather in terms of the existential experience of their wearer (i.e., as someone who, like us, is thrown into a world, cares about certain things, and will eventually die). This would have been a kind of imaginative seeing, although not in the sense of an arbitrary or merely playful projection, but in terms of hypothesizing a deeply plausible solution to the problems upon which Van Gogh was working, for example that of expressing his vision of the spiritual aspect of reality. In short, he would have seen the shoes in terms of Heidegger's famous paragraph which begins "From the dark opening of the worn insides of the shoes …" This is a somewhat deeper, complex, and more cognitive use of imagination than that of Bullough.

What, then is known through sublime experience? Something ineffable,

---

36 Heidegger, "Origin," 33.

but also something having to do with the essential nature of the world as we experience it, some domain of possibility, something existentially essential, something at the level of feeling and intuition, some tentative solution to a deep problem, something immanent and yet having to do with self-transcendence.

Now, if this happened to Van Gogh then I think he would have been having a sublime experience in relation to the shoes he perceived. Certainly Heidegger is having a sublime experience of the shoes by way of their representation by Van Gogh. I say "sublime" as the experience would not have been just one of either prettiness (or some other surface aesthetic quality), beauty, ugliness, or something non-aesthetic. Moreover, it would have had the unendingness characteristic of aesthetic ideas as described by Kant, and sublimated fear as described by Burke. The Burkean aspect relates to Heidegger's evocation of his existentialist idea of being-towards-death in the passage in which he describes the shoes in this way: "This equipment is pervaded by uncomplaining anxiety as to the certainty of bread, the wordless joy of having once more withstood want, the trembling before the impending childbed and shivering at the surrounding menace of death."[37]

So one could say that Heidegger's approach to the aesthetic nature of these shoes is that although this nature is to be found in their usefulness, which would be in accord with a functionalist approach to the aesthetics of everyday life, it should not be understood in terms of what we normally consider to be functionality. This approach, rather, understands that usefulness "rests in the abundance of an essential being of the equipment."[38]

Finally, it is only through this work of art that the equipmental quality of this equipment and hence the thingly quality of a thing becomes apparent for Heidegger and, through Heidegger's interpretation of the painting, for us. It is important that, as Heidegger observes, this quality cannot be seen through simply observing the shoes in use, any more than it can be seen through observing the painting in a pedestrian way. We see the shoes more deeply, which is to say in terms of their existential meaningfulness, by means of the artwork and its interpretation. But this is just an uncovering or an actualization of something already implicit. The aesthetics of art, then, is not set in opposition to that of everyday life but rather the two are deeply intertwined. It is perhaps the dominance of art in aesthetic theory that has caused writers to ignore this symbiosis.

---

37 Heidegger, "Origin," 33.
38 Heidegger, "Origin," 33.

When Heidegger seeks to overcome the assumption, common among aestheticians of his time, that a work of art has two distinct sides, the physical and the mental, he shows us that the thingliness of a work of art is not just its physical substratum (what Arthur Danto, who still holds this kind of view, calls the "mere thing") but is that very aspect which allows Being to shine forth. This move, in dissolving dualism, reinserts the spiritual into the material substratum from which it has been abstracted.

So, when Heidegger says that "the nature of art [is] the truth of beings setting itself to work" insofar as the pair of peasant shoes come "in the work to stand in the light of its being"[39] he is not just saying something about art but also about the possibility of experiencing such an ordinary object as a pair of peasant shoes *so that* what I would call its "existential essentiality" shines forth. I use the term "existential essentiality" to distinguish Heidegger's idea from the kind of essentiality that Aristotle might see in the shoe, i.e., the shoeness of the shoe as a plan that can be used in the manufacture of shoes, but also to distinguish it from essences as natural kinds in the mode of contemporary analytic philosophy.

NIETZSCHE VS. DANTO

While Heidegger has redirected our attention to the possibility of sublime experience with small-scale ordinary objects, and has also introduced a cognitive dimension to the experience that we did not find in Bullough, Nietzsche in the *Birth of Tragedy* fills out the possibility of an everyday sublime through his concept of the Dionysian as essential to the tragic and through his ideal of the tragic man.[40] On the face of it, Nietzsche was not much concerned in this book with everyday aesthetics. As with Heidegger, the title of his work indicates that it is about the aesthetics of art, with special emphasis on tragedy and music. However, there are significant passages that relate to the everyday. For example, Nietzsche associates the Apollonian with dreams. Dreams happen every day and they are not works of art, although they are much like art in being creatively constructed stories. Also Nietzsche appears to agree with Schopenhauer that only someone who is able to see the world as if it were a dream is capable of being a philosopher.[41] This notion of seeing the world as if it were a dream does not

---

39 Heidegger, "Origin," 35.
40 Friedrich Nietzsche, "Tragedy."
41 Arthur Schopenhauer, *World*, quoted in Nietzsche, "Tragedy," 35-36.

yet bring us to anything sublime, but it does take us partway there by positing a way of seeing the ordinary that goes beyond the ordinary way of seeing. Nietzsche associates dreams with the world of the Olympian Gods, a world of illusion that the ancient Greeks created to give their lives meaning. However, the true sublime only comes in with his discussion of the Dionysian. This is because the Dionysian is a response to the wisdom of Silenus which says that the best thing for man is never to have been born; second best, to die early. That wisdom relates to awareness of the inevitability of human suffering and death, and, as Burke saw, awareness of death is essential to the sublime. For Nietzsche, Greek tragedy, which synthesizes the Apollonian and the Dionysian, is sublime. Bullough had taken us part of the way to the sublime with his talk of the fog at sea. However, both for Schopenhauer and Nietzsche, the experience Bullough describes might be better seen as a metaphor for the whole of life. Nietzsche speaks of the Apollonian type as someone who trusts in his small boat, i.e., his individuality and his rationality, in the midst of the rough seas of life (think of Bullough's ferry and fog). The Dionysian involves a violation of the dualism that so neatly protects us in the Apollonian dream-world. (Kant, by the way, takes an ultimately Apollonian approach to the sublime with his emphasis on the affirmation of human autonomy in the face of natural forces.) The experience of oneness with nature which Nietzsche describes as Dionysian is similar to the Buddhist experience of satori. It is also similar to the experience of the Schopenhauerian artist who becomes one with the object contemplated. Nietzsche's idea is probably taken in part from Schopenhauer's own borrowings from Buddhism, although Nietzsche tended to see Buddhism itself as a kind of negation of life.

Nietzsche posits the tragic man as someone who belongs to a new, tragic, culture inaugurated by the insight of Kant and Schopenhauer that mere phenomena are not the highest reality or the true essence of things. In such a culture, wisdom, which seeks a comprehensive view, and which is deeply sympathetic to suffering, replaces science as the highest goal. Nietzsche describes the tragic man as someone who is intrepid in vision, who has "a heroic penchant for the tremendous," who proudly opposes optimism, who lives resolutely with wholeness and fullness, who self-educates "for seriousness and terror," and who desires a new "art of metaphysical comfort."[42] This last notion of an otherworldly source of comfort Nietzsche later, I think rightly, rejects.[43]

---

42 Nietzsche, "Tragedy," section #18.
43 Friedrich Nietzsche, "Attempt at a Self-Criticism" which he wrote in 1886 as the preface to the second edition of "The Birth of Tragedy."

Now, one of the leading figures of aesthetics over the last forty years has been Arthur Danto. One of Danto's first books was on Nietzsche and he features Nietzsche's term "transfiguration" in his masterpiece *The Transfiguration of the Commonplace*.[44] One of the main motives of my work in everyday aesthetics has been to oppose an implicit dualism in Danto's thinking and in that of many contemporary aestheticians. I am not claiming that Danto is a metaphysical dualist, but rather that he posits two worlds that are radically separate, the world of "mere things" and the artwork.[45] According to Danto, when Andy Warhol constructed and painted visually indiscernible duplicates of Brillo boxes which he then placed in a museum, he, in a sense, transfigured an ordinary "mere" thing into the world of art.

Given this picture, I take Danto to be essentially a naïve philosopher in the same sense that Nietzsche took Raphael to be a naïve artist, and Raphael's "Transfiguration" (1516-20) to exemplify the naïve point of view.[46] For Nietzsche, a naïve artist is one who proposes an Apollonian world as redemption from the pervasiveness of human suffering. He thought that Raphael symbolized this in his painting by portraying two worlds, the world of suffering below (where the apostles are trying to cure an epileptic boy) and the transfigured world of Jesus above. The Dionysian destroys the boundaries between the two worlds and, as Nietzsche later explained, causes us to say "yes" to everything in life, even to suffering, even if eternally repeated.[47]

Now what I want to suggest here is that Warhol's great gesture in its deepest meaning was not to take the everyday Brillo box into another realm but quite the opposite: it was to destroy or at least to problematize the separation between the realm of art and that of everyday life. Rather than being an Apollonian gesture, as Danto interprets it, it was a Dionysian one, or perhaps a tragic one in the sense of combining the Apollonian and the Dionysian. By creating *Brillo Box*, Warhol transformed something, but in transforming he was intensifying, highlighting, and packing with significance. He was affirming our experience of everyday objects themselves. John Cage was even more explicit about this with his *4'33"* which encourages the listener to attend to everyday sounds as transformed. If this is right, then, although the experiences of Proust and Bullough intimate the possibility of sublime experience with

---

44 Danto, *Transfiguration*.
45 Danto, *Transfiguration*, 94.
46 Nietzsche, "Tragedy," 45.
47 Nietzsche, "Thus Spoke."

the ordinary, it is with Van Gogh and Warhol that we get the true sublime of the everyday, a Nietzschean sublime experience. In a strange way, when art becomes indiscernible from ordinary objects, it becomes a medium by which ordinary objects themselves become transformed, becoming experienceable as more than beautiful, as sublime. It might also be suggested that the highest form of this is one in which the being-towards-death of humans, the way in which the experienced world for humans is always bracketed by death as the end-point, so that our own death is always present as an aspect of experience, is made apparent. Moreover, it could be argued, along Nietzschean lines, that when the ordinary object, scene, or event becomes sublime it parallels tragic art, having both the Apollonian dream side that ignores suffering and death and the Dionysian side that affirms and sublimates it.[48]

Nietzsche continued to explore the sublime in later writings. The doctrine of eternal recurrence as it appears in *Thus Spoke Zarathustra* begins with a story in which Zarathustra hears a dog barking and confronts a spider. The idea that one could *will* that the same event occur an infinite number of times is the idea that each event in everyday life is infinitely precious. Eternity is in essence found in the moment. This notion of eternity replaces that of an afterlife: it is a non-dualistic eternity. However, here it seems that Nietzsche's Zarathustra has reached much the same point as the Zen monk who has achieved satori, although through a different method.

The concept of the sublime is, like other philosophical concepts, culturally emergent and has changed over time. That is, the term "sublime" and its attendant examples, sub-concepts, and associations, have been used differently at different times in history. Moreover, theorizing about such a concept, as with theorizing about all essentially contested concepts, is a matter of trying to solve philosophical and related problems of one's own time. Although concepts of the sublime related to a transcendent deity are still relevant for believers, it is the postmodern sublime, closely associated with the now, which does not directly allude to something transcendent, that captures the interest of non-believers.[49] However, in focusing on the now, as Nietzsche also does in

---

48 For similar criticisms of Danto, see Crispin Sartwell, "Aesthetic Dualism and the Transfiguration of the Commonplace," *The Journal of Aesthetics and Art Criticism* 46, no. 4 (1988): 461-67, and Michael A. Principe, "Danto and Baruchello: From Art to the Aesthetics of the Everyday," in *The Aesthetics of Everyday Life*, 56-69.
49 Lyotard; Philip Shaw, *The Sublime* (London: Routledge, 2006), Chapter 6 "The Sublime is Now: Derrida and Lyotard."

his theory of the tragic man and in his later doctrine of eternal recurrence, one also sees it as heaped with meaning, with memory and with anticipation.

MICHAEL FRIED AND THE SUBLIME OF THE ROAD

There can be a sublime of the road. This would seem obvious when the road goes through natural landscapes. But it can also happen in urban and suburban spaces. In a seminal article written in 1967, critic Michael Fried quoted from sculptor Tony Smith who wrote about a car ride on the New Jersey Turnpike before that road's completion: "it was a dark night and there were no lights or shoulder markers, lines, railings, or anything at all except the dark pavement moving through the landscape of the flats, rimmed by hills in the distance, but punctuated by stacks, towers, fumes, and colored lights."[50] Smith then says: "This drive was a revealing experience. The road and much of the landscape was artificial, and yet it couldn't be called a work of art. On the other hand, it did something for me that art had never done. At first I didn't know what it was, but its effect was to liberate me from many of the views I had had about art." In particular it convinced him of the superiority of an experience that cannot be framed, a sublime experience, to that of merely pictorial painting.

This quote reveals not only the possibility of a non-art, non-nature sublime but also one aspect of the dialectic between everyday aesthetics and art aesthetics. In his article, Fried criticizes artists like Smith, whom he calls "literalists" (their more common name was "minimalists") for being anthropomorphic and "incurably theatrical." Smith's experience, for Fried, was one of "theatre." He saw theatre as involving lack of artistic autonomy and as requiring an audience, and he believed that this was detrimental for visual art. Fried's discussion relates to the sublime since he saw being able to go on indefinitely (much like Kant on aesthetic ideas) as essential to Smith's turnpike experience. He thought that, for the minimalist, this endlessness replaced the object in the gallery. He then wrote that "[w]hat Smith's remarks seem to suggest is that the more effective—meaning effective as theatre—the setting is made, the more superfluous the works themselves become."[51] In a sense, Fried thinks, Smith's is a vision of aesthetic experience after the end of art. Fried goes on to call on modernist painting to defeat theatre. Thus, for Fried, art and the everyday

---

50 Michael Fried, "Art and Objecthood," in *Aesthetics: A Critical Anthology*, 449 [orig. 1967].
51 Fried, 451.

sublime are deeply in conflict, and the success of art depends on the defeat of the latter. Yet, looking back, Fried's article seems nothing more than a rearguard action, the leading artists of his time being ones like Rauschenberg and Warhol who embraced the disintegration of boundaries between the various arts and between the arts and the everyday. Moreover, Smith's passage seems a prophecy of later developments, including Earth Art, and of contemporary environmentalist art in which art continues after the end of the hegemony of autonomous painting of the sort advocated by Fried. Thus, it is somewhat bizarre today to think that the kind of experience Smith describes would somehow be a threat to art. Fried's article is strangely like Danto's in its insistence on a radical separation between art and everyday life, and anti-Nietzsche in its attack on "theatre."

Conclusion

As I read through what I have written in this book the term "neglected" often comes up, not simply in the idea that everyday aesthetics itself has been neglected but also in the idea that certain terms, and thus the experiences to which they refer, have been neglected. The overall thrust of my arguments has been towards a greater inclusiveness, both for aesthetics, insofar as it should include everyday aesthetics as a legitimate field, but also within everyday aesthetics itself. I have often engaged in arguments not only with classical philosophers but also with my colleagues in everyday aesthetics. Often I have argued that they have wrongly excluded certain sorts of things. Carlson and Parsons exclude what does not "look fit for function." Berleant excludes telephone poles and shopping malls. Haapala excludes the extraordinary and the strange. The cute, the pleasant, the pretty, and the nice have all been excluded by various philosophers. Aesthetic qualities associated with smell, taste and touch have been traditionally excluded as well.

My expansion of the field of everyday aesthetics can be seen in my approach to Kant. Although one might think that the everyday would be limited to what he called "the agreeable" I found that it included also much of what he referred to as beautiful, and even, in the last chapter, much that he would have included under the sublime. I have argued for inclusion not only of major league aesthetic concepts such as harmony and balance, but also minor league ones such as neatness and messiness. I have also argued aesthetic qualities exist on a continuum from low-level pre- or proto-aesthetic qualities, through mid-level ones, to highly intense and complex qualities, such as the sublime. In alliance with feminists, I have argued for inclusion of aesthetic phenomena that might be more familiar to women than to men, and which may have been neglected because of that. I have similarly argued for inclusion of more phenomena from non-Western cultures. Finally, I have sought to include the aesthetic experiences both of children and of non-human animals, either as proto-aesthetic or as aesthetic in a full-fledged sense.

The second main thrust of my book has also been directed against fellow explorers of the aesthetics of the everyday, who, in an understandable attempt to free everyday aesthetics from the domination of art aesthetics, have shortchanged the way in which artists have contributed to understanding and experiencing everyday aesthetic phenomena. In these same efforts they have often wanted to emphasize the ordinariness of the ordinary. By contrast, I have sought to show how aesthetics can be a unified field in which the dialectic between art and everyday aesthetics is recognized as central. Art itself, as I argued, has often been defined in such a way as to isolate it from our everyday aesthetic experience. And yet this poses many problems even for our understanding of art. Art can only be fully understood if we consider how it responds to the aesthetic phenomena of everyday life. I have sought to go into the artist's mind, and into her workplace, placing emphasis on how the artist sees her subject-matter and her art materials in the process of creation. The non-artist who appreciates everyday aesthetic phenomena has been called many things, although "aesthete" and "flâneur" have stood out. Such a person seeks to see the world with the eyes of an artist. In both the experience of the artist and of the artist-like perceiver it is not the ordinariness of the ordinary that is important, but the way in which the ordinary can be made extraordinary. The ordinariness of the ordinary is not thereby neglected, however, since it too can be given heightened significance.

To sum up this idea and to show how we are to distinguish aesthetic from non-aesthetic uses of a term I developed the concept of aesthetic experience as experience of objects as having "aura." This concept, applicable to the entire field of aesthetics, solves a particular problem in everyday aesthetics. It allows for expansion of the field of aesthetic qualities, and it allows us to talk about a wide range of terms that may be used aesthetically. Many of these terms have been neglected because of their association with the everyday, for example "pleasant" and "looks nice." This expansion has an admittedly democratic, even populist, tone, insofar as, drawing from Dewey, it emphasizes the pervasiveness of the aesthetic and the continuity between aesthetics of everyday life and aesthetics of art. I have also affirmed the Deweyan call for social changes that would make for broader and more fulfilling aesthetic experience in all aspects of life. I even carried this democratic impulse into the writing of this book insofar as I incorporated ideas of my college students from all levels: lower division, upper division, and graduate. It was easy for them to participate since everyday life is not the sole domain of experts. Everyone lives in everyday life.

Finally, as I suggested in the Introduction, I have indicated wider metaphysical implications for the aesthetics of everyday life. Although, as an atheist, I reject transcendent entities, I affirm Dewey's concept of "background" which had made some of his followers so nervous when reading *Art as Experience*, as well as Nietzsche's affirmation of life, including its tragic dimension. I also argued the notion that aesthetic experience of everyday phenomena can be sublime, and that such sublime experience can be a high point in human experience taking on a religious-like feel.

Index

Absolute, 33, 84–85
"absorbing," 177
abstract expressionism, 221
Adorno, Theodor, 154
advertising, 10, 37, 50, 210–11
aesthete, the, 43–44, 60, 260
aesthetic, 45
"aesthetic"
  confusion with pleasant, 201
  definitions, 64, 204
  evolving meaning, 202–03
  socially derived, 47
aesthetic appreciation. *See* appreciation
aesthetic attitude, 131–32, 194–97, 201
aesthetic attitude theory, 120, 246
aesthetic attributions, cultural influences on, 145
aesthetic deprivation
  underlying dissatisfaction in American society, 45 (*See also* alienation)
"Aesthetic Dualism and the Transfiguration of the Commonplace" (Sartwell), 256n48
aesthetic emotion, 143
aesthetic evaluation. *See* evaluation
aesthetic experience, 30, 57–62, 127–28, 132, 138
  complexity, 136
  content-oriented theories of, 138
  democratizing, 213–14, 260–61
  Dewey on, 182
  evolutionary roots, 10
  as experience of objects as having "aura," 127–49, 260
  nature of, 78
  need for unity (*See* unity)
  pervasiveness of, 201–07
  phenomenological view of, 129
  place and, 111, 184
  sense of wonder aspect of, 141
  as subordinate to moral demands of environmentalism, 96
  theories of, 135–41
  vividness, 134
"aesthetic experience" (term), 58
aesthetic ideas, 142, 240, 244, 248–50, 252
"The Aesthetic Impulse" (Hofstadter), 66n24
aesthetic in ordinary experience
  pervasiveness of, 201–07
aesthetic perception of the nude, 197
aesthetic phenomena of prehistoric humans, 44
"aesthetic poisoning," 215
aesthetic properties, 55, 112, 116, 138–39, 181–82
  Aquinas's view of, 63
  theories of, 127–28

aesthetic qualities, 101, 231
  to everyday non-music sounds, 53
  relevant to both everyday aesthetics
    and to aesthetics of art, 67
aesthetic qualities of rightness and fit, 66
aesthetic terms, 134, 140, 179–85
  canonical aesthetic terms, 64
  for everyday contexts, 64, 151–85, 229
  expansion of the field of, 148, 179, 260
  non-aesthetic uses, 147
  range of, 144
aestheticization, 207–14
  of cruelty, 212
  of everyday life, 210–11
  of politics, 208
  of violence, 209, 215
"aestheticize" (definition), 208
aesthetic/non-aesthetic, 64, 206, 216
aesthetics, 18, 26
  definitions, 17–18
  levels of, 155
  neglected properties in, 9
  new approaches to, 10
  no longer limited to art and high art, 20
  not necessarily a remedy for violence, 215
  role in everyday choices, 13
  as unified field, 260
Aesthetics (Hegel), 32
aesthetics of architecture, 26, 46, 162, 171–72
aesthetics of art, 9, 21, 23, 44, 88–89, 253
  dominance in aesthetics as a whole, 121
  elite aesthetics of, 50
  intertwined with aesthetics of everyday, 252
  limited to the fine arts, 17
  surprise, wonder, and shock, 108
aesthetics of art and the aesthetics of everyday life
  conflict between, 185
  continuities between, 84, 90, 164, 182, 224–25, 260
  dialectic between, 33–35

  dynamic relationship between, 121
  symbiosis between, 252
"The Aesthetics of Daily Life" (Dowling), 27n23
aesthetics of death, 45
aesthetics of decision-making, 45
aesthetics of engagement, 199
aesthetics of environmental buildings and architecture, 162
aesthetics of everyday life. *See* everyday aesthetics
The Aesthetics of Everyday Life (Smith), 208
aesthetics of grooming, friendship, and character, 45–46. *See also* aesthetics of the person
aesthetics of human environments, 93
"The Aesthetics of Living Form in Schiller and Marx" (Wessell), 37n46
aesthetics of man-made environments, 99
aesthetics of nature, 9, 17, 23, 36, 48, 60, 89, 93, 97–99
  as aspect of everyday experience, 98
  cognitivist aesthetics of nature, 106
  lacks the equivalent of art critics, 188
"The Aesthetics of Smelly Art" (Shiner), 68n30
aesthetics of sport, 45
aesthetics of "the day," 169
aesthetics of the home, 75, 99–100, 112. *See also* aesthetics of human environments
aesthetics of the person, 169
aesthetics of the tasteful, 166
affective qualities (funny, glaring), 225
affect-oriented theories of aesthetic experience, 137–40
agreeable, the, 27, 31, 90, 168
  imaginative or cognitive element, 30–31
  Kant on, 27–31, 168, 207, 259
  may be experienced by irrational animals, 28
agreeable arts, 30–31

agricultural roots of contemporary
  culture, 42–43
alienated labour, 36, 212, 216
alienation, 37, 40, 45, 88, 216
amateur photography, 10
"amazing," 174
"amazingly," 111
American Beauty (2001), 96
American Heritage Dictionary, 171
American Philosophy, 10
American pragmatism, 11
American Society for Aesthetics, 11
American vernacular arthitecture, 154
analytic aesthetics, 10–11, 45, 121, 143–44
  reaction against Dewey, 84
analytic philosophy, 85, 253
analytic theories of art, 81
Anderson, Richard L., 68
Ando, Tadao, 43, 234
animal life below the human scale 28, 13
  everyday aesthetics and, 13, 260
  sources of aesthetic experience, 44
anthropocentrism, 184
anthropologists, 10, 42
anthropomorphism, 257
anxiety, 247, 252
Apollonian world, 254–56
"appetizing," 159
applied philosophy, 10
appreciating the ordinary
  need for artist's eye, 114, 260
appreciation, 139
  appropriateness of, 104
  design appreciation, 139
  of designed objects, 114
  mediated through the arts, 105, 210–11
  unethical forms of, 213
appreciation of everyday aesthetics
  through the arts, 105
appreciation of everyday phenomena, 22,
  97, 105, 114, 260
appreciation of nature, 23, 97–99, 180
appreciation of works of art, 22–23

"apprehension," 63–65, 154
"Aquinas" in "Medieval Aesthetics"
  (Margolis), 63n21
architects, 50, 226
architecture, 39, 65
  California arts and crafts architecture, 171
  church architecture, 46
  deconstructivist architecture, 153, 172
  everyone participates in, 46
  fun as a topic or motif, 155
  neatness and messiness, 222
  new interest in everyday life, 52
Aristotle, 70, 104, 190, 216, 250–51
  concept of tragedy, 156
  theory of catharsis, 218
Aristotle's notion of spectacle, 157
art, 21, 74, 82, 111, 195
  arises out of ordinary life and is
    continuous with it, 86
  attention to everyday, 211
  "central art forms," 22
  closeness of art and ritual, 74
  conquering nature, 34
  contemporary art, 109
  contemporary environmentalist art,
    258
  continuity between art and the
    everyday, 10, 41, 44, 79
  definition of, 21–22, 78–79, 81, 83, 91
  dialectic between art and everyday
    life, 35, 78, 240
  dialectical relationship with everyday
    experience, 43
  difference between art and kitsch,
    211–12
  distinction between art and craft, 37
  distinction between art and everyday
    life, 20, 195, 207, 212–13
  distinction between popular and fine
    art, 37
  dynamic interaction of art and
    perception, 87
  essentially contested concept, 91

exclusion of the pretty and the pleasant, 162
intensification of ordinary experience, 33, 83, 110, 112, 120
as interaction between artist, developing artwork, and audience, 81
ontology of, 78
as "significant form," 82–83
taking meaning from context of life in general (not just from artworld), 78
value of art in society, 78
Art (Bell), 41
art and non-art, 22
boundaries between, 10
defining, 21–22
Art and the Aesthetic (Dickie), 131n8
"Art as an Essentially Contested Concept" (Gallie), 91n90
Art as Experience (Dewey), 77, 182–83
Art Deco architecture, 155
art education, 49–50
art history, 10
"The Art of the Science of T'ai Chi Ch'uan" (Delza), 174n73
art photography, 108
art surface aesthetic qualities, 219–20
artifacts, 18, 22, 49, 82, 94, 100–01, 106, 109, 250
"artistic," 166
artistic process, 81, 249, 260
artistic roots of contemporary culture, 42–43
"The Artistry of Ritual Aesthetics of Urban Korean Shamans" (Choi), 74n55
artists, 42, 60, 99, 107, 113, 118, 121, 201, 254
see the extraordinary in the ordinary, 121
artist in his / her studio, experiences of, 121–22
contemporary installation artists, 51
experts in the aesthetics of everyday life, 41, 99, 114, 121, 260
help us "compose" and frame experience, 99
intentions, 23
manic-depression and, 200
propriety and, 105
Schopenhauerian, 254
super-realist artists of the 1970s, 51
who enjoy the messiness of the creative process, 232
artist's eye needed for appreciating the ordinary, 114, 260
Arts and Crafts movement, 37, 117
"Asian Ars Eroica and the Question of Sexual Aesthetics" (Shusterman), 72n47
Asilomar Conference Grounds, Pacific Grove, California, 171–72
assemblage, 95
"attractive," 111, 162
"attractive/unattractive," 217
aura, 11–12, 35, 55, 87, 90, 116, 122–23, 136, 151, 156, 170, 177, 206–07, 214, 241
applies to "beauty" and the sublime, 142–43
attended by an affect, 137
for "beauty" to be applicable the object must be perceived as with aura, 134, 194
Benjamin's usage, 129–30, 133
a characteristic of the object-as-experienced, 139
characterizations of, 132–35
closely associated with beauty, 134
continuum of intensity, 142–43
definitions, 128
false aura, 209
"fascination" and "interest," 137
Greek origin, 133
heightened significance and, 132
Leddy's adaptation of, 129
Leddy's usage, 132–33
levels of aura, 142–43
loss of in the age of mechanical reproduction, 129, 177

meaning "valence," 132
Medieval notion of "claritas" and, 135
"natural aura," 129–30
in the object-as-I-experience-it, 132, 139, 143, 204
as phenomenological characteristic, 128
phenomenological quality common to all aesthetic experiences, 148
power or potentiality and, 134
release from the mundane or boring aspects of the everyday, 140
something to be greater than itself, 133
what aesthetic properties have in common, 135
aura theory, 140–41
advantages, 140, 142–43, 149
Austin, J.L., 62–63
Austin, John, *How To Do Things with Words*, 158n13
Australian Aborigines, 74
authority/respect, 234
automobiles, 52
avant-garde, 36, 83, 109, 196, 210, 240
Away from the Flock (1994), 139
"awe-inspiring," 174

Babylon (Skeel and Skriver), 68
Bahm, Archie J., 195
balance, 67, 226, 259
"balanced," 66, 178, 225
"banal," 163, 215
Banes, Sally, 54n103, 83
"A Bank Executive and His Secretary" (1960), 110
Baudelaire, Charles, 39, 240
The Painter of Modern Life, 39
Baudrillard, Jean, 209–10
Baumgarten, Alexander, 18, 204
Beardsley, Monroe, 54, 59–61, 87–88, 170, 194, 196
emphasized discontinuity between art and life, 78
idea of intensity, 135–37

on LSD experiences, 197
symptoms of aesthetic experience, 229–31
Beat poetry, 51
"beautiful," 64, 66, 111, 155, 163, 236
negative correlate "ugly," 151
beautiful, the, 27, 70, 72, 143, 161, 169
beautiful/pretty distinction, 161–62
beauty, 23, 29, 54, 64, 66, 90–91, 130, 142, 174
from the application of cosmetics, 49
associating the "lower" senses with, 70
in aura conception of aesthetic experience, 134, 195 (*See also* aura)
claritas as essential to, 135
essentially contested concept, 188
exclusion from everyday aesthetics, 29
in the experience not in the object, 207
historical efforts to define, 189
Kant's definition, 29, 32
laws of, 36–37
of nature, 71
Navajo concept of, 42
only available to humans, 28
paradigmatic aesthetic property, 63
from the perspective of "the Whole," 25
theories of, 188
tragic dimensions, 38
universal, 28
Beauty (Scruton), 97n67
"Beauty and the War" (Chapman), 153n3
Bechtle, Robert, 51
Bed (Rauschenberg), 221
Bedroom in Arles (1888) (Van Gogh), 197
Beethoven, *Eroica*, 197
behaviour qualities (bold, nervous), 225
Beigel, Hugo G., "Sex and Human Beauty," 158n14
Being (Heidegger), 109
"being true to the materials," 118
being-suchness, 119
being-towards-death, 183–84, 248–49, 252, 256

Bell, Clive, 42, 131, 143, 152, 158, 234
  Art, 41
  art is significant form, 83
  definition of art, 82
Bell, Julian, 152–53, 155
Benjamin, Walter, 40–41, 131, 208, 210
  loss of aura in the age of mechanical reproduction, 129, 177
Bennett, Jane, 209, 238
Berger, Harris M., *Identity and Everyday Life*, 47n88
Berleant, Arnold, 9, 93–97, 99, 115, 122, 158, 177, 210, 215, 240, 259
  "aesthetics of engagement," 199
  holism, 103
  on "negative sublime," 239
  "The Sensuous and the Sensual in Aesthetics," 159n17
Beuys, Joseph, 72
Bharata, 173
bicycle decoration in Northern Nigeria, 164
biologically-oriented aestheticians, 185
birdsong, 184
Birth of Tragedy (Nietzsche), 253
Fredrik Björklund. 234–35
"blemished," 232
"blemished/unblemished," 217
Bodhidarma, 241
body decoration, 225
Bois, Yve-Alain, "User's Guide to Entropy," 222n8
Bonnard, Pierre, 51, 100, 113
"boring," 152, 178
Boudu Saved from Drowning (1932), 52
Bouguereau's paintings, 160, 193
The Boundaries of Art (Novitz), 45
bourgeois class, 40
Brady, Emily, 68, 71, 246
  "Imagination and the Aesthetic Appreciation of Nature," 120n54
Brand, Peggy, 114, 197–98, 201
Braque, Georges, 51
"bright" and "sombre," 151

Brillo Boxes (Warhol), 84, 195–96, 255
Brottman, Makita, 238
Brown, Denise Scott, 52
Buddhism, 119–20, 254
  notion of "forgetting oneself," 118
Bullough, Edward, 130–31, 240, 254–55
  and the fog at sea, 245–47
  idea of objectivity, 246
Burchfield, Charles, 51
Burke, Edmund, 237–38, 241
  on the sublime, 247, 252, 254
Butterfield, Deborah, 138
"Bye Bye Kitty!!!" (New York City art show), 164

Cage, John, 53, 196, 212–13
  4'33," 195, 255
California arts and crafts architecture, 171
California Sierra foothill country, 232
Candide (Voltaire), 215
capitalist production, 36–38, 88
capitalist system, 40, 50, 212
  suppression and limitation of esthetic quality, 88
Carlson, Allen, 9, 60–61, 66, 72–73, 90, 93, 98–107, 115, 121–22, 193, 198, 210, 251, 259
  to appreciate nature we must compose it, 102
  appreciation should be centred on the thing itself, 100
  discussion of roadside clutter, 218
  exclusion of the pretty and the pleasant, 162
  functional beauty, 100, 106
  naturalism, 117
  Nature and Landscape, 99
Carlyle, Thomas, 213
Carroll, Noël, 82, 137n24, 139–42, 149
  art-identifying narratives, 83
  content-oriented theory, 138
  "Working and Dancing," 54n103
Cartesian dualism, 72
Cartier-Bresson, Henri, 110

Cézanne, Paul, 41, 79, 173
"chaotic," 225–26
Chapman, Emmanuel, "Beauty and the War," 153n3
"charming," 162–63
Chaudhury, Pravas, 174
"Cheap and Tasteful Dwellings in Popular Architecture" (Jennings), 166n45
children, 13, 49, 51, 155, 162, 220, 260
   Chinese vs. American, 233
   contemporary culture of childhood, 170
   prettiness in aesthetic life of, 161
   may sometimes value dirtiness aesthetically, 232, 235
"Children's Reactions as a Basis for Teaching Picture Appreciation" (Waymack), 161n25
children's toys, 21
China, 88
Chinese aesthetics of food, 72–73
Chinese factory floors, 216
Chinese language, 72
Chinese philosophy of Daoism, 102
Choi, Chungmoo, "The Artistry of Ritual Aesthetics of Urban Korean Shamans," 74n55
choreographers, 50, 99
Christian monastery, life in, 242
Christianity, 72
church architecture, Christian meanings expressed in, 46
city streetscapes, 49
class, 40, 47
working class, 36, 39, 51, 88, 216
Classicism, 173
classism, 162
"clean," 67, 111, 155, 228, 232
"clean" and "unclean," 217–18, 221
cleaning one's room as aesthetic experience, 230–31
cleaning up composition of painting or musical work, 220

cleanliness, 67, 166, 220, 233–34
cleanness, 229, 231
   concept learned as children, 220–21
"clear," 111
"cleared/not cleared," 217
clothes and other adornments, 10, 18
   costume, 177
clutter and messiness, 232
"cluttered," 232
"cluttered/uncluttered," 217
coarse, the, 215
cognition, 28, 106, 122
cognitive content, 201
cognitive science, 10
Cohen, Marshall, 60
"coherent," 178, 225
Coleman, Elizabeth Burns, 223
   "Appreciating 'Traditional' Aboriginal Painting Aesthetically," 74n54
"colourful," 163
comfort, 112, 170–72
"comfortable," 107, 111, 170, 212
"comforting," 110
comic, 155
commercial strips, 96
commercialization, 210–12
commodities, 37, 40–41
"common sense," 28
commonplace, 42–43, 195
"complete," 178, 225
"The Completion of Old Work" (McCracken), 215n62
complexity, 136, 155
computer screens, 49
Confucius, 72
connoisseurs, 190–93, 199, 208
"consonant," 225
consumerism, 40, 50
contemplation, 96–97, 115
contemporary aesthetic theory, 9
contemporary painting and photography, 96
contemporary painting and sculpture, 173

INDEX   269

contemporary video art, 120
continental philosophy, 10
convenience, 26–27
cookery, 9, 18, 21, 24, 46, 89. *See also* food
Cornell, Joseph, 51
Cottom, Daniel, "Taste and the Civilized Imagination," 165n44
Courbet, Gustave, 51
courtship, 111
Coyote Creek, 98, 175
"cozy," 171, 185
crafts and craft objects, 27, 39, 66, 73–74, 175, 189
craftsmen, 118
"creative," 166
creative process, 11, 78–80, 91, 121
    Dewey's view of, 86
creator's intentions, 23
The Critique of Judgment (Kant), 240
Crowley, John E., 171
cruelty as
    aesthetic category, 215
Cubist collages from newsprint, 155
Cubist paintings, 139–40
"cuddly," 163
cultivated flower, 179
cultural studies approach to everyday aesthetics, 50
cultural theorists, 182
culture, 82
    visual turn, 48–49
culture critics, 212
culture theorists, 209–10
culture-world, 83
"cute," 162–63, 212
cuteness
    associated with kitsch, 163
    associated with the insignificant, 163
    in contemporary Japanese culture, 164
    defense of, 163

Dadaists' appropriations, 155, 210
Daguerre, Louis, 52

dance, 22
    postmodern, 54, 79, 83
danger, 245–46
Danto, Arthur, 63, 76, 83–84, 195, 224, 240, 253, 255
    on the importance of messiness in aesthetics, 221
    The Transfiguration of the Commonplace, 254
"Danto and Baruchello" (Principe), 256n48
Daoism, 102
Darwin, Charles, 184
death, 45, 213, 256
    awareness of death essential to the sublime, 250, 254
    being-towards-death, 183–84, 248–49, 252, 256
    life that is heading for death, 250
    suffering and death, 183, 254
Debord, Guy-Ernest, 40
"decay," 218–19
deconstructivist architecture, 153, 172
decoration, 111–12, 165
    example of "making special," 164
decoration of our living spaces, 18, 46, 89, 99, 190, 232
"decorative," 165
"deeper reality" of our world of ordinary experience, 87
"deeply moving," 175
Del Negro, Giovanna P., 47n88
delicacy of sentiment, 12, 26, 190–92, 207
delicacy of taste, 188
"delicate," 178
"delicious," 159
Delza, Sophia, "The Art of the Science of T'ai Chi Ch'uan," 174n73
de-materialization, 212
democratizing aesthetic experience, 213–14, 260–61
Demoiselles d'Avignon, 178
"dependent beauty," 28, 32

"depressing," 178
"depressing" day, 169
"dérive," 40
design appreciation, 139
design of everyday objects, 225
design qualities, 138
Dewey, John, 11, 37–38, 41, 54–55, 91, 103, 112, 120, 127–28, 164–65, 184, 212, 216
   aesthetics and art both have to do with animation of everyday experience, 87
   an originator of the aesthetics of everyday life, 44, 77, 204
   art arises out of ordinary life, 86
   Art as Experience, 77, 80, 182–83, 261
   on artistic experience, 81
   challenge to contemporary aesthetic theory, 78
   charge of Hegelianism, 84
   "disorder" gives aesthetic pleasure, 221
   "an experience," 45, 58–59, 61, 77–78, 80, 85, 87, 90, 113, 127, 203–05, 207
   goal to restore continuity between art and the everyday, 44
   idea of pervasive quality, 85–86, 88, 90, 203–05, 207
   idea of social improvement, 88, 212, 260
   no separation of the semiotic from the aesthetic dimension of everyday aesthetics, 183
   not acceptable to analytic philosophy, 84–85
   pragmatic aesthetics, 10–11
   on role of functionality in everyday aesthetics, 101–02
   situating art within a larger context than the artworld, 82
Deweyan notion of expression, 81
Dewey's concept of background, 261
Dewey's effort at democratizing aesthetic experience, 213–14
Dewey's theory of creativity, 249n33
dialectic between everyday life aesthetics and the aesthetics of art, 33–35, 113, 128, 257
Dickie, George, 81–82, 247
   Art and the Aesthetic, 131n8
Dimensions of Japanese Society (Henshall), 234n37
Dionysian as essential to the tragic, 253
Dionysian side that affirms and sublimates suffering and death, 240, 254–56
direct intuitions, 85
dirt in modern art, 221–22
"dirty," 217–18, 232
"dirty" in the sexual sense, 235
"dirty" players (music), 222–23
disaster, 238
"discomfort," 171
disgust, 137, 139, 235
disgusting, the, 215
"disinterested," 27–28
disinterested beauty, 194
disinterestedness, 142, 197, 199, 201
   Berleant's attack on, 96–97
   and feminist needs, 198
   theories of, 120
Disney World, 239–40
displeasure, 64, 112
Dissanayake, Ellen, 76, 83, 164–65, 204
Distance, 246–47
distancing, 130–31, 142, 198, 245
doctrine of eternal recurrence, 257
Don Quixote, 25
Dorter, Kenneth, 161
Dowling, Christopher, "The Aesthetics of Daily Life," 27n23
dreams, 253–54
"dreary" day, 169
"drift," 40
drugs, 111, 134
   psychedelic drug user, 194, 196–97, 199, 201
dualism, 253–55

of artworld vs. real world, 83
Cartesian dualism, 72
Dubuffet, Jean, 221–22
Duchamp, Marcel, 76, 212–13
   In Advance of the Broken Arm, 80
   Fountain, 51
"dull" colour, 64, 152
Duncum, Paul, 48–50
Dutch painters, 32, 34–35, 51
Dutch spirit, 35
Dutton, Denis, 83
dynamic interaction of art and perception, 87
dynamic interaction of subject, object, and surrounding contexts, 105

Earth Art, 79, 258
Eastern traditions, 173–74
Eaton, Marcia, 140, 145
eclectic approach to evaluation in everyday aesthetics, 188, 194
ecstasy, 38
1844 Manuscripts (Marx), 36
Eisenman, Peter, 172
electronic media, 50
electronic screen image, 49
elegance, 20, 91, 158, 228
"elegant," 64, 155, 178
elevator music, 53
Emerson, Ralph Waldo, 36
emotion, 78, 172
emotional qualities, 173, 225
"emotionally intuited," 85
"empty embellishment," 165
Encyclopedia of Aesthetics, 170
engagement, 122, 199
"engaging," 177
environmental aesthetics, 93–96, 98–107
environmental determinism, 116
environmentalism, 93–94, 116
Epicureanism, 38
Epicurus, 24
Eroica (Beethoven), 197

"erotic," 158
essentialism, 117
essentially contested concepts, 91, 188, 203
ethics, 104, 116, 209, 213, 234. *See also* morality
ethics of environmentalism, 116
evaluation, 54, 91. *See also* good judge; taste
   theory of, 89
evaluation of art, 78
evaluation of everyday aesthetics, 12, 187–94
everyday, 91
   artists' attention to, 33, 113
everyday aesthetic experience, 57
   coloured by place, 184
   interaction with experience of art, 62
   neglect of, 110
   sublime, 70
everyday aesthetic properties, 62–69
everyday aesthetic qualities of transience, 21–219
everyday aesthetic quality terms, 64, 151–85, 229
everyday aesthetics, 9–10, 18, 23, 99, 106
   appropriateness of name, 48
   branch of aesthetics, 19, 23, 54, 88, 103
   challenges assumptions within aesthetics generally, 13
   cultural studies approach to, 50
   definitions, 19–21
   domain of minor arts, 21
   and the environment, 93–123
   evaluation of (*See* evaluation of everyday aesthetics)
   familiarity, 108
   feminine experience and, 13
   fit into a philosophy of social improvement, 44
   functionalist approach to, 24, 101
   history, 23–25
   lacks the equivalent of art critics, 188

landscape appreciation as, 95
"looks right" in, 67
moral dimension, 120
neglected, 112
new discipline, 88
normative dimension, 37
relation with aesthetics of art, 23, 84, 90, 120–21, 164, 182, 185, 224–25, 252, 260
science-based approach, 99
similarities to art aesthetics, 23
social, cultural and historical context, 20
in the various art traditions, 50–54
what falls within, 11, 13, 32, 72, 90, 101
when the ordinary becomes extraordinary (*See* ordinary made extraordinary)
Everyday Aesthetics (Saito), 112, 218
everyday aesthetics and religious ritual, 73–77
everyday aesthetics and the aesthetics of popular art, 20
everyday aesthetics and the sublime. *See* everyday sublime
everyday artifacts, 18
Everyday Life (Sherringham), 107n31
everyday phenomena, 20
everyday sublime, 151, 237–58, 261
everyday surface aesthetic qualities, 217–36
  application in the arts, 219, 222, 227, 236
  gender socialization and stereotyping and, 223–25
  neglect of, 218–19, 223–25
  as pre- or proto-aesthetic qualities, 236
  role in general aesthetics, 222, 235
  taught in childhood, 235–36
  value of, 232
everyday surface aesthetic quality terms, 220, 231
everydayness of the everyday, 112, 114–15

everything coming to be seen as art, 196, 209
evolution, theory of, 184
evolutionary aesthetics, 164
exemplification, 202, 207
existential essentiality, 253
existential experience, 251
existentialism, 183, 252
existentialists, 185
exotic, 49
"an experience," 45, 58–59, 61, 77–78, 80, 85, 87, 90, 113, 127, 203–05, 207
"The Experiential Aspects of Consumption" (Holbrook), 153n5
exploitation and alienation, 37, 212
expression, Dewey's notion of, 81
"expressive," 166
expressive culture, 47
expressive properties, 138, 159
expressive qualities, 172
expressive significance, 48
"exquisite," 174
"extraordinary," 174
extraordinary in the ordinary, 42, 120–21, 216. *See also* ordinary made extraordinary

"fabulous," 174
factories, 52
fairness/reciprocity, 234
false aura, 209
false consciousness, 37
familiarity, 107–08
"fantastic," 175
"fascinates," 177
"fascinating," 112, 177
fashion, 39, 166
fashion industry, 193
"fast," 179
Featherstone, Mike, 209–10
feeling-tones, 139
"feels erotic," 158
"feels good," 68

"feels nice," 167
"feels right," 65
"feels sexy," 157
Feldenkrais method, 47
feminist aesthetics, 9, 224
feminist art and artists, 51, 197
feminist needs, 198
feminists, 259
festivals and rituals, 48, 111–12
film and film-makers, 22, 52, 99, 109
"filthy," 217, 235
"fine," 111
fine art, 74
    in art education, 49–50
    as the art of genius, 248
    modes of cognition, 31
    as reflection on the aesthetics of everyday life, 248
fine art museums, 74
Fisher, John, 53–54
"fit," concept of, 66
fitness, 65
"fits," 65
flâneur, 39–41, 44, 260
"The flâneur in social theory" (Frisby), 40n57
flower-arranging, 21, 177
fog at sea, 240, 245–47, 254
folklorists, 10, 47
food and drink, 244. *See also* smell, taste, and touch
    aesthetics of, 72–73, 159
food preparation. *See* cookery
Forest, Roy De, 155
formalism, 28, 83, 131, 143, 234
Fountain (Duchamp), 51
4'33" (Cage), 195, 255
Fowler Museum of Anthropology, 109
framing, 103, 108, 112
freedom, 214, 230
"freedom and gaiety," 34
French Quarter of New Orleans, 115
Freud, Sigmund, 158

Fried, Michael, 213, 257–58
"friendly," 107
"frightening," 157
Frisby, David, "The flâneur in social theory," 40n57
fualah, 68
fun, 152–55
function, 250, 259
functional beauty, 98, 100–01
Functional Beauty (Parsons), 100
functionalism, 24–27, 66, 106, 122, 252
functionality, 54, 90, 108–10, 193
"funny," 155
"The Future of Folklore Studies in America" (Kirschenblatt-Gimblett), 47n88
Futurists, 52, 209, 212, 238

Gadamer, Hans-Georg, 105, 176
Gallie, W.B., 188
    "Art as an Essentially Contested Concept," 91n90
gardens, 10, 18, 50, 99, 117, 178, 222
"Gardens, Nature, Pleasure" (Ross), 222n11
"gay," 159, 228–29
gender, 47
gender socialization and stereotyping, 223–25
genius artist, 41, 142
"gentle," 158
"gentle manners," 158
"gentle movements," 158
Germinal (Zola), 140
gestalt qualities, 225–27, 236
"get dirty," 219
"get old," 218–19
Gilmour, John, 173
"gleam," 134
"glisten," 134
God, 213, 249–50
Godlovitch, Stan, 175, 222–23
Goldblatt, David, 172

good judge, 12, 103, 188, 190–93, 207–08, 228. *See also* taste
good life, 38
good sense, 207
"Good Work and Aesthetic Education" (Petts), 37n47
"good-looking," 111
Goodman, Nelson, 65, 201–02, 207
Gorelick, Kenneth, 168
Gorgias (Plato), 23
grace, 20, 54, 91, 102, 158
"graceful," 64, 178, 206
"graceful" and "graceless," 151
Gracyk, Ted, 179, 198, 201
graduation ceremonies, 75
"great," 68
"great colour," 182
"great shape," 182
Greater Hippias (Plato), 24
Greek tragedy, 254
Greenberg, Clement, 63, 234
Gröning, Philip, 242
Grooms, Red
  Ruckus Manhattan, 60
  "Subway," 60
grunge, 221
Gumbrecht, Hans, 74n53, 108
Guys, Constantin, 39

Haapala, Arto, 93–94, 108, 111, 114, 123, 175
Haidt, Jonathan, 234–35
haiku, 200
"handsome," 160
Hannah, Dehlia, "Naturalized Disaster," 238n4
Hansson, Sven Ove, 24
happiness, 37, 69, 182
harm/care, 234
"harmonious," 66, 225, 236
harmony, 54, 67, 188, 207, 226, 259
  Pythagorean idea of, 189–90
"harsh" sound, 64
Hartshorne, Charles, 184

Hegel, G.W.F., 32–35, 50, 70, 82
  Aesthetics, 32
  use of the term "shining," 134
Heidegger, Martin, 108, 110, 177, 194, 240, 248–53
  Being, 109
  "The Origins of the Work of Art," 248
  sublime as aura, 241
  on Van Gogh's shoes, 248–53
Hein, Hilde, 11
  "Play as an Aesthetic Concept," 153n4
Helsinki, 68, 109
Hendrickson, Gordon, 161n25
Henshall, Kenneth G., *Dimensions of Japanese Society*, 234n37
Hepburn, Ronald, 176
Hermerén, Göran, 155, 159, 172, 226–27
  The Nature of Aesthetic Qualities, 225
Herring, Frances W., "Touch," 71n43
Hertz, Rachel, 69
high art. *See* art
Hippias Major (Plato), 70
Hirschman, Elizabeth C., 153n5
Hirst, Damien, 139–40
Hofstadter, Albert, 65
  "The Aesthetic Impulse," 66n24
Holbrook, Morris B., "The Experiential Aspects of Consumption," 153n5
holism, 94–95, 103
"holy," 176
home decoration, 18, 46, 89, 99, 190, 232. *See also* interior decoration
"the homely," 112
"homey," 107
Homlong, Siri, *The Language of Textiles*, 222n12
Homo Ludens (Huizinga), 153n4
homophobia, 162
Hopper, Edward, 51
horror films, 52
How To Do Things with Words (Austin), 158n13
hózhó, 42

Huizinga, Johan, *Homo Ludens*, 153n4
human and non-human aesthetics
   continuities between, 184
human flourishing, 116, 211
human movement, 20
human sciences, 10
Hume, David, 25–27, 29, 54, 90, 100, 189, 207
   functionalist with respect to the
      aesthetics of everyday life, 26-27
   idea of the good judge, 12, 103, 188,
      190–93, 207–08, 228
   idea that we cannot derive "ought"
      from "is," 146
   on resemblance between mental and
      bodily taste, 192
   A Treatise of Human Nature, 26
Humean approach to everyday
   aesthetics, 190–91
Hummel figurines, 192–93, 207–08, 212
"Hummingbirds, Shells, Picture-
   Frames" (Menninghaus), 32n29
humour, aesthetic importance of, 152
Husserl, Edmund, 128–29, 141, 149
Husserlian return to the things
   themselves, 239

ideal, 34, 59, 84
Identity and Everyday Life (Berger), 47n88
Ikebana, 117
"illuminate," 134
imagination, 28, 31–33, 98, 118, 121–22,
   142, 180, 188, 246, 248, 251
   free play of, 188, 194, 207
"Imagination and the Aesthetic
   Appreciation of Nature" (Brady), 120n54
"imaginative," 166
imaginative perception, 121, 131, 247, 251
Impressionists, 39
In Advance of the Broken Arm
   (Duchamp), 80
In Praise of Shadows (Tanizaki), 233
"In Search of the Aesthetic" (Scruton),
   23n10

India, 72
Ingarden, Roman, 122
insignificant, the, 215
inspiration, 42, 52–53, 80–81, 85, 91, 111,
   121, 193, 249
"integrated," 66, 225, 236
"integration," 226
intensity, 135–36
intentionality, 141
interdisciplinary studies, 10–11
interestedness approach, 199
"interesting," 177
interior decoration, 18, 226. *See also*
   home decoration
interpretation
   theory of, 89
interpretation, nature of, 78
"Into Great Silence" (2006), 242
intrinsic value, 137–38
Ion (Plato), 161
Irvin, Sherri, 58–59, 90, 202, 205–06, 210
   "The Pervasiveness of the Aesthetic in
      Ordinary Experience," 23n10
Iseminger, Gary, 141–42, 149
itches and scratches, 205–06

Japanese, 178–79
Japanese aesthetics, 42, 116, 242
   cleanliness in, 233
   flower arrangement, haiku, and
      packaging, 117
   poignancy of the impermanent, 183
   stresses the essence of the object, 117
Japanese architecture, 43
Japanese art forms
   influenced by Zen sensibility, 199
Japanese concept of *wabi-sabi*, 120
Japanese craftsmen, 116
Japanese gardens, 174
Japanese packages, 154
Japanese Tea Ceremony, 74, 120, 199–200
Japanese woodworking, 43, 66
Jastrow Duck-Rabbit figure, 198

Jay, Martin, 212
jazz, 9, 155
Jennings, Jan, "Cheap and Tasteful Dwellings in Popular Architecture," 166n45
jewellery, 21
joy, 34
Joyce, James, 63
"joyous," 159, 163

kaiwasa, 164
kami, 43
Kant, Immanuel, 27–32, 63, 70, 90, 97, 189, 228, 2626
   aesthetic ideas, 142, 240, 249–50, 252
   on the agreeable (*See* Kant's "agreeable")
   "Analytic of the Sublime," 240
   concept of purity, 234
   The Critique of Judgment, 240
   exclusion of the sensory from the beautiful, 29, 31
   formalist, 28
   idea of disinterested beauty, 194
   notion of a free play of imagination and understanding, 188, 194, 207
   notion of taste, 12
   notion of the sublime, 237, 241, 244, 246, 248, 254
   skeptical about experiencing a thing-in-itself, 119
   view on beauty, 27–28
Kantian affirmation of human power, 239
Kant's "agreeable," 168, 207, 259
   as distinct from the beautiful, 29, 31
   relevance to everyday aesthetics, 27, 29
Katrina disaster, 2238
Katz, Alex, 51
Kaufman, Daniel, 173
Kaufmann, Vincent, "The Poetics of the Dérive," 40n60
Keane, Walter and Margaret, 163
Keats, John, 174

Kelly, Mary, *Post-Partum document 1973-1979*, 51
Kienholtz, Ed, 113
Kierkegaard, Søren, 249
Kirshenblatt-Gimblett, Barbara, "The Future of Folklore Studies in America," 47n88
kitsch, 160, 163, 168, 172–73, 192, 207, 212, 225
   and fine art, 193
Kivy, Peter, 75, 173
knowledge, theory of, 89
Kohák, Erazim, 11
koinos topos, 42
Koons, Jeff, "Michael Jackson and Bubbles" (1988), 193
Korsmeyer, Carolyn, 137, 201–02, 207, 235
Krauss, Rosalind, 222n8
Kriskovets, Yulia, 68n30, 69, 70n39
Kupfer, Joseph H., 45

La Guardiola House, 172
Lalo, Charles, "A Structural Classification of the Fine Arts," 69n34
landscape
   composing natural landscape, 60–61
   "landscape" (Berleant's use of term), 95
landscape appreciation, 95
landscape gardening, 46
landscape painting, 99
landscaping, 99
The Language of Textiles (Homlong), 222n12
Late Spring (1949), 52
laws of beauty, 36–37
Le Corbusier, 52
Leddy, Thomas, 210
   "Sparkle and Shine," 33n32, 134n17, 167n48
Leonard, George J., 195
   Into the Light of Things, 51n95
Levinson, Jerrold, 53, 137–38, 149

Levitt, Helen, 52
Lichtenstein, Roy, 155
Light of Things (Leonard), 51n95
"literalists," 257
London Symphony, 173
"looks amazing," 174
"looks clean," 68
"looks fun," 153
"looks good," 68, 185
"looks great," 174–75
"looks like it fits its function," 100–01, 122, 198
"looks nice," 111, 169, 260
"looks right," 46, 65–67
"looks sad," 157
"looks sexy," 157
Loos, Adolf, 234
Lorand, Ruth, 163, 165
Lorenz, Konrad, 163
Lorrain, Claude, 173
lounger. *See* flâneur
love, 23, 112, 158
"lovely" day, 169
low-level aesthetic experience, 40, 57, 216, 240, 259
low-level aesthetic properties, 207
low-level aesthetic qualities, 160
low-level and high-level aesthetic experience
 continuum between, 216, 259
low-level pleasure, 112
low-level to high-level aesthetic experience
 continuum between, 204–05, 240
Loy, Jessica, 163
LSD taker, 194, 196–97, 199, 201
luminosity, 35
Lyotard, Jean-François, 239–41
 The Sublime, 256n49

"making special," 76–77, 83, 164
Mandoki, Katya, 198, 201, 215–16
manic-depression, 194, 200–01

Mann, Bonnie, *Women's Liberation and the Sublime*, 238n4
Marcus Aurelius, 24–25
Margolis, Joseph, 10
 "Aquinas" in "Medieval Aesthetics," 63n21
Marinetti, Filippo Tommaso, 238
Marsh, Reginald, 51
"marvellous," 174
Marx, Karl, 37–38, 44, 50, 212, 216
 1844 Manuscripts, 36
Marxism, 11, 88
mathematical aesthetics, 30, 48
"maturing," 218
Maybeck, Bernard, 171
McCracken, Scott, "The Completion of Old Work," 215n62
mechanical reproduction, 129, 131, 177, 214
mei-shi, 73
"melancholy," 159
Melchionne, Kevin, 232
Menninghaus, Winfied,
 "Hummingbirds, Shells, Picture-Frames," 32n29
"mere things," 254
"merely pleasant," 72, 180
messiness, 9, 54, 65, 216, 221, 259
 aesthetics of, 151, 221
 appropriate balance with neatness, 219
messiness/disorder, 219, 221, 224
"messy," 65, 185, 217–18, 229, 232
metaphor, 11, 119, 246–47, 254
metaphysical aura, 132
Mexican home altars, 75
Mexican maquiladoras, 216
"Michael Jackson and Bubbles" (1988), 193
middle class, 171
"minimal beauty," 179, 204
"minimalists," 257
Minor, Vernon Hyde, "What Kind of Tears?", 238n3
minor arts, 21
Mister Clean, 166–67

modern architecture, 234
modernism, 51–52
Mona Lisa, 161
Monet, Claude, 51, 105, 229
monuments, 209
Moore, Jared, 160
Moore, Ronald, 61, 141, 162, 180, 184
morality, 118, 120. *See also* ethics
Morgan, Julia, 171–72
Morreall, John, 152, 162–63
Morris, William, 37–38, 44–45, 212, 216
"mouth-watering," 159
moving, 155
Muir, John, 237
Mullis, Eric C., 99
multiculturalism, 9
murder and death, 213
    aestheticization of, 209
Murillo, Bartolomé Esteban, 35
Musak, 168
Museum of Modern Art in San Francisco, 69
museums, 68
music, 49, 53, 62, 75, 113, 175, 179, 236, 253
    aesthetics of, 175
    cleanliness, 222
    "dirty" playing, 222
    emotional qualities such as sadness and serenity, 173
musical terms, 236
musicians, 50
Muslim ascetics, 35
Mussolini, Vittorio, 153
mystical experience, 86

naïve point of view, 255
"nasty," 167
natural aesthetics, 49
natural landscape, composing, 60–61. *See also* framing
natural object removed from its environment
    not appreciated as itself, 105–06

natural supernaturalism, 213
natural vs. artificial, 232
naturalism, 86, 117
naturalist worldview, 241
"Naturalized Disaster" (Hannah), 238n4
nature, 25. *See also* aesthetics of nature
Nature and Landscape (Carlson), 99
nature as culturally-determined concept, 98
The Nature of Aesthetic Qualities (Hermerén), 225
Naukkarinen, Ossi, 48, 169, 208
Navajo, 20, 76
"Navajo Art and Education" (Saville-Troike), 76n60
Navajo concept of beauty, 42
Nazis, 208, 212
"neat," 65, 184, 217, 228, 232, 236
    aesthetic quality, 229
    early training makes us value over messy, 221
neatness, 9, 54, 65, 216, 226–27, 259
    aesthetics of, 151
    not always oriented to practical goals, 229
    perceptual, 228
neatness, prettiness, niceness, cuteness etc.
    differing notions of what counts for, 188
neatness and cleanness, 232
neatness and messiness, 219, 222–23
neatness/order, 219
negative aesthetic experience, 140
negative aesthetic properties, 65, 115, 216
negative aesthetic qualities, 142, 229, 232
negative aesthetic responses, 113
negative aesthetic terms, 152
negative aesthetic values, 96
negative sublime, 239
New Jersey Turnpike, 257
"nice," 167–68, 180
"nice feeling," 167
"nice night," 167
"nice tie," 167
"nice walk," 167
"nicely written," 167

niceness, 169, 192
Niépce, Nicéphore, 52
Nietzsche, Friedrich, 121, 183, 210, 253–56
    affirmation of life including its tragic dimension, 261
    associates dreams with world of Olympic Gods, 254
    Birth of Tragedy, 253
    concepts of the Dionysian, 240, 253
    doctrine of eternal recurrence, 256–57
    theory of the tragic man, 240, 253–54, 257
    Thus Spoke Zarathustra, 256
Nietzschean sublime experience, 256
Night Watch (Rembrandt), 34, 193
9/11 seen in terms of the sublime, 238
"No Fun" (Weitzman), 154
"noema," 129
noematic aspect of intentionality, 141
"noesis," 129
noetic and the noematic aspect of experience, 142
noise, 53–54, 195
non-aesthetic dependence theories, 143–48, 188, 206–07. *See also* supervenience theory
non-aesthetic features, 62, 144, 227
non-aesthetic fun, 154
non-aesthetic properties, 144
non-aesthetic terms
    aesthetic uses, 147
non-musical sounds, 53
non-Western cultures, 42–43, 72, 164, 260
    aesthetic interests, 9–10, 12–13
    Eastern traditions, 173–74
    neatness and messiness, 232–33, 236
"not enough," 68
novelists, 50, 99
Novitz, David, 45, 169, 218
    The Boundaries of Art, 45
now
    focusing on the, 256

object, essence of, 117
object-as-experienced, 129
object-centred approaches, 105
object-directedness, 230
"objective" features of the object, 245
objectivity, 144, 187, 205–06, 246
    in evaluation of everyday aesthetics, 187–88
obscene, 215
Of Birds, Beasts, and Other Artists (Scharstein), 184
Okakura, Kakuzo, 233
"old," 179
Oldenburg, Claes, "Ray Guns," 222
online "places" of experience, 12
ontology of art, 78
order, 189–90
order and disorder, 224
"ordered," 155
"ordered/disordered," 217
"orderly," 236
ordinariness of the ordinary, 120, 260
ordinary, 48, 152
ordinary experience
    essentially contested, 203
ordinary language, 72, 203
ordinary made extraordinary, 76, 108, 111, 115, 176, 247, 260
ordinary objects
    experienced as the sublime (*See* everyday sublime)
ordinary people in photography, 52
"organizes," 236
"The Origin of the Work of Art" (Heidegger), 248
Osborne, Harold, 75
Osmothèque in Versailles, 69
otherworldliness, 57
Ozu, Yasujirō, 52

pain and terror aspect of the sublime, 241–42
The Painter of Modern Life (Baudelaire), 39

painters, 50, 113
painting, 22, 96, 173, 234
Pan, Da'an, 72–73
Panglossian problem, 215–16
"paradox of tragedy," 216
Paris street-life, 52
Parisian intellectuals, 38–40
Parsons, Glenn, 66, 72–73, 90, 93, 101–03, 105, 109, 122, 193, 198, 251, 259
    functionalism, 100, 106
Parsons, Michael J., 161n25
Pass, Joe, 222–23
Pater, Walter, 24, 38
peacefulness, 172
Pepper, Stephen, 84
perception, 87
perceptual complexity, 227
"perfect," 174
perfumery as art form, 69
personal appearance, 18, 190
personal attire, 223
personal autonomy, 212
personal grooming, 224. *See also* aesthetics of grooming, friendship, and character
persons' faces, 145
pervasive quality, 85–86, 88, 90, 203–05, 207
pervasiveness of aesthetic in ordinary experience, 201–07
"The Pervasiveness of the Aesthetic in Ordinary Experience" (Irvin), 23n10
"Peter Pans," 164
petting one's cat, 203, 205
Petts, Jeffrey, 37
phenomenological account of aura, 129–30, 132
phenomenological approach to aesthetics, 11
phenomenological method, 128–29
phenomenology, 129, 141, 149
philosophers, 89, 113, 151, 253
philosophical aesthetics, 11, 45
philosophy, 82

philosophy of art, 17
photographers, 94–95
photographs, 78, 131
photography, 22, 52, 95–96, 99, 110, 114
    amateur photography, 10
    art photography, 108
physical aesthetic experience, 61
Picasso, 51, 178
Pillow Book (Sei Shōnagon), 43
"Piss Christ" (1987), 109
place-settings, 52
plastic bag example, 96–97, 174, 179
Plato, 65, 100, 251
    Gorgias, 23
    Greater Hippias, 24, 70
    Ion, 161
    Republic, 24
    Symposium, 23, 158
Platonic Form, 41
play, 18
    aesthetics of, 66
"Play as an Aesthetic Concept" (Hein), 153n4
"pleasant," 111, 180, 185, 204, 260
    not everything that is pleasant is aesthetic, 207
    relevance to aesthetics of everyday life, 162
"pleasant" day, 169
"pleasing," 163
pleasure, 38, 113, 138–39
    aesthetic vs. non-aesthetic pleasure, 64
    confusion with pleasant, 139–40, 162
"poetic," 166
"The Poetics of the Dérive" (Kaufmann), 40n60
poetry, 51, 62, 180
poets, 50, 60, 99, 113
Pole, D.L., 134
political art, 114
Pop Art, 51, 76, 155
popular art, 9, 17, 20–21
    aesthetics of, 20

positive aesthetic qualities, 232
postmodern age, 239
postmodern architects, 52
postmodern architecture, 155
postmodern dance, 54, 79, 83
postmodern sublime, 240
postmodernism, 49, 52, 210
Post-Partum document 1973-1979 (Kelly), 51
Postrel, Virginia, *The Substance of Style*, 100
post-structuralism, 48
"powerful," 175
pragmatic aesthetics, 10
Pragmatist Aesthetics (Shusterman), 47
Prall, David W., 70–72
pre-aesthetic experiences, 204–05, 260
prettiness in aesthetic life of children, 161
"pretty," 111, 153, 155, 162–64, 204
   applied only to feminine and pettable things, 160
   associated with kitsch, 160
   distinguishing from the beautiful, 161
"pretty" day, 169
Principe, Michael A., "Danto and Baruchello," 256n48
private ownership, 37–38
property terms, 64, 90
proportion, 189–90
"proportional," 66
propriety, 104–05
"proto-aesthetic," 204, 260
Proust, Marcel, 240, 243–45, 255
   Remembrance of Things Past, 243
Proust's madeleine, 142, 244
psychedelic drug user, 194, 196–97, 199, 201
"pulsations," 38
"pure," 235
"pure shining of appearance," 32–33
"pure/impure," 217
purity, 234–35
"purity" and "impurity"
   entire substance, not just surface, 218
purity/sanctity, 234

purpose, consideration of, 28
purposefulness, objects that have the appearance of, 29
purposiveness, look of, 207
Pythagorean aesthetic theory, 189–90, 207
Pythagorean idea of harmony, 190
Pythagorean notion of beauty, 188–89

Quacchia, Russell, 171
"quiet," 172
quilts, 9, 89
"quintessential," 123
"quite," 111

race, class and gender, 47
Rainer, Yvonne, *Room Service* (1964), 79
rap music, 9
Raphael, *Transfiguration* (1516-20), 255
rasa tradition in India, 173
Rauschenberg, Robert, 51, 72, 105, 258
   Bed, 221
   use of junk-yard materials, 155
Rautio, Pauliina, 40
"Ray Guns" (Oldenburg), 222
reaction qualities, 155–56, 177–78
"real artist," 41
reductionism, 144
refined attributions, 228
refinement, 46
regional qualities, 231
relational properties, 147
relativism, 12, 103, 228
"relaxing," 172
religion, 82, 111
   aesthetics of, 75
religious art, 21
religious feeling, 87
religious rites, 74. *See also* ritual
"remarkably," 111
Rembrandt, *Night Watch*, 34, 193
Remembrance of Things Past (Proust), 243

Renne, Elisha, 164
Rennie, Nicholas, 209n46
Renoir, Jean, 51–52
repair, impulse to, 113–15
Republic (Plato), 24
"restful," 172
"Revising Aesthetics' Place Amongst the Disciplines" (Stevens), 212n52
Reynolds, Joshua, 51
rightness, intuitive sense of, 119
rightness as an aesthetic quality, 65–66
Rikyu (Japanese tea-master), 233
ritual, 75, 90, 112, 183
   aesthetics of, 74
   closeness of art and ritual, 74
   institutional nature of, 74
   as part of everyday aesthetics, 73
Robinson, Jenefer, 173
rock music, 9
Roemer, Michael, 52
"romantic," 158
Romantics, 213
Room Service (Rainer), 79
Rorty, Richard, 10
Ross, Stephanie, "Gardens, Nature, Pleasure," 222n11
Rostankowski, Cynthia, 170
Ruckus Manhattan (1975) (Grooms), 60
rudimentary aesthetic attributions, 228–29
Rudrauf, Lucien, 166
Ruscha, Ed, *Twentysix Gasoline Stations* (1963), 114
Ruskin, John, 37, 45, 213, 216
Rybczynski, Witold, 172

Sacks, Oliver, 200
sacred, 76
sacred, the, 74–75
   in the aesthetics of everyday life, 176
   in contexts of high arts and pristine nature, 177
   as a definer of everyday aesthetics, 74

"sacred" and "spiritual"
   used metaphorically for everyday aesthetic phenomena, 177
sacred aura, 176–77
"sad," 157, 159
"sad-looking," 163
sadness, 173
Saito, Yuriko, 25, 57, 90, 93–94, 103, 114–15, 121, 123, 154, 175, 199, 210, 223, 226, 242, 247
   advocacy of "being true to the materials," 118
   emphasizes "negative" aesthetic responses, 113
   essentialism, 117
   Everyday Aesthetics, 112, 218
   "Packaging," 155n9
Sakuteiki, 117
San Francisco, 238
Sandrisser, Barbara, 42–43, 179
Santayana, George, 70
   The Sense of Beauty, 61
Sartwell, Crispin, 54, 73–74, 90, 167
   "Aesthetic Dualism and the Transfiguration of the Commonplace," 256n48
   theory of everyday aesthetics, 176
satori. *See* Zen satori
Saville-Troike, Muriel, "Navajo Art and Education," 76n60
Schafer, R. Murray, 53
Scharfstein, Ben-Ami, *Of Birds, Beasts and Other Artists*, 184
Schopenhauer, Arthur, 41–42, 173, 253–54
science, 82, 132, 254
science-based approach to appreciation, 99
science-based understanding of aesthetics, 10
science-centered aesthetics of nature, 106
scientific or practical knowledge, 105, 180
Scruton, Roger, 45–46, 170, 179, 204, 210
   Beauty, 97n67

"In Search of the Aesthetic," 23n10
  use of "looks right," 65
sculpture, 22, 173
Searle, John, 146
"Second Life" (Internet virtual world), 12n2
second-class aesthetic properties, 162
Sei Shōnagon, 43, 178
  list of "Things That give a Clean Feeling," 67
  Pillow Book, 43
semiotic approach, 48
semiotic change, 224
semioticians, 182, 184
sensation (agreeable sensory experience), 28
The Sense of Beauty (Santayana), 61
senses, 24, 30, 33
"sensual," 158–59
sensual pleasures of the body, 24
"sensuous," 158
"The Sensuous and the Sensual in Aesthetics" (Berleant), 159n17
sensuous cognition, 204
sensuous dimension, 63
"sentimental," 159, 163
"serene," 159
"sereneness," 172
serenity, 172–74
Serrano, Andres, 109
"Sex and Human Beauty" (Beigel), 158n14
sexism, 162, 224
sexual experience, 18, 72
sexual love, 158
sexual purity, 235
sexuality
  aesthetics of, 45, 158
sexy, 157–58
shadows, 90, 101, 130–32, 142, 145, 188
Shaw, Philip, 256n49
Sheeler, Charles, 109
Sheringham, Michael, *Everyday Life*, 107n31
"shimmer," 134
"shine," 134
Shiner, Larry, 69, 70n39
"The Aesthetics of Smelly Art," 68n30
"shining," 35, 122, 135
Shinkei (Zen monk and poet), 199
shock, 108–09
"shocking," 155–57
shopping malls, 12, 49–50, 69, 96, 104, 238, 259
Shusterman, Richard, 10–11, 20, 57, 90, 162, 173
  "Asian Ars Erotica and the Question of Sexual Aesthetics," 72n47
  Pragmatist Aesthetics, 47
  "Somaesthetics," 71n44
Sibley, Frank, 144, 146–48, 160, 227, 236
  taste, requirement for, 181
  "Tastes, Smells, and Aesthetics," 68n29
"Significant Form," 41, 131
"simple," 180, 225
Sircello, Guy, 241–42
Situationists, 40
Skeel, Christian, *Babylon*, 68
Skriver, Morten, 68
Slam poetry, 51
"sloppy," 217
smell
  aesthetic experience related to, 68–69, 72
  emotional connection, 69
smell, taste, and touch, 68–73
smell and taste
  aesthetics of, 68–69, 72
"smells clean," 68
"smells delicious," 68
"smells good," 68
"smells nice," 68, 185
"smells sexy," 157
Smith, Jonathan, 210–11
  The Aesthetics of Everyday Life, 208
Smith, Tony, 213, 257
"smoothness," 181

"snug," 171
social concern, 47
social democracy, 212
social revolution, 214
"solemn," 159
Solomon, Robert, 163, 165, 172
somaesthetics, 47
"Somaesthetics" (Shusterman), 71n44
"sombre," 159
"soothing," 172
sordid, the, 215
Soucek, Brian, 205–06
soul, 43, 134, 189, 248
"sounds fantastic," 174
"sounds fun," 153
"sounds good," 68
"sounds nice," 167
"sounds right," 65
"sounds romantic," 158
"sounds sexy," 157
"sounds wonderful," 174
soundscapes, 53
"sparkle," 134
sparkle and shine, 35, 166–67
　of Dutch painting, 34
"Sparkle and Shine" (Leddy), 33n32, 134n17, 167n48
Sparshott, Francis, 160–61
"species-being," 36–37
spectacle, 41, 156–57
Spencer, Herbert, 102
The Sphinx in the City (Wilson), 237n2
spirit, 32–34, 82
spirit of a work of art, 85
spirit of the artist or the age, 33, 35
"spiritual," 176
sports, 10, 19
Stecker, Robert, 18, 22, 180–82, 184
Steichen, Edward, 78
Steiner, Rudolf, 132
Stevens, Christopher, "Revising Aesthetics' Place Amongst the Disciplines," 212n52

"still," 172
still-lives, 52
"stillness," 172
stoic philosophers, 24
Stolnitz, Jerome, 195–96, 198
Strand, Paul, 52
strangeness, 57, 107, 112
"strikingly," 111
stroller. *See* flâneur
"A Structural Classification of the Fine Arts" (Lalo), 69n34
Stuhr, John, 11
sublime, 27, 142, 151, 155, 161, 189, 213, 248, 259
　as aura, 242
　culturally emergent, 256
　element of touching the abyss, 250
　everyday aesthetics and, 90, 237–58
　Greek tragedy as, 254
　important role in Dewey's aesthetics, 183
　pain and terror aspect of the, 241–42
　postmodern, 240, 256
　very high level of aura, 240
The Sublime (Lyotard), 256n49
sublime aesthetic experience, 247
sublime experience, 35, 70, 213, 251
　religious-like feel, 261
sublime in a naturalist worldview, 241
sublime in postmodern age, 239
sublime in the everyday. *See* everyday sublime
sublime of the road, 257–58
sublime ontology, 241
The Substance of Style (Postrel), 100
"Subway" (Grooms), 60
suchness, 119–20
suffering and death, 183, 254–55
supervenience theory, 144–45, 147–49, 188
surface messiness with underlying order, 221
surface-oriented aesthetic concepts, 155
surprise, 108–09
Surrealists, 51, 107, 210

Suzuki, Daisetz Teitaro, 195, 241
"symmetrical," 178
symmetry, 190, 207
Symposium (Plato), 23, 158

table-settings, 20, 46, 67, 104
Tai Chi Chuan, 174
Taj Mahal, 161
Tanizaki, Jun'ichiro, *In Praise of Shadows*, 233
Taoism, 35
taste, 27–28, 181, 207, 227, 245
   aesthetics of the tasteful, 166
   degrees, 228
   Hume on, 12, 188, 191–92 (*See also* delicacy of sentiment)
   Sibley's sense of, 228–29
   smell, taste and touch, 68–73
   standards of, 187
"Taste and the Civilized Imagination" (Cottom), 165n44
taste qualities (elegant, delightful), 225
"tasteful," 111
tasteful, the
   adult-oriented nature of, 166
   central to home decoration, clothing, and food preparation, 165
   culturally emergent and constantly changing, 165
   often associated with wealth, 165
"Tastes, Smells, and Aesthetics" (Sibley), 68n29
"tastes good," 68, 159
"tasty," 159
tea ceremony. *See* Japanese Tea Ceremony
telephone poles, 96, 259
Temko, Allan, 171
terror, 243
"Terrorism and the Sublime" (Weigel), 238n3
textile arts, 222
textiles, 21

theatre, 24
theme parks, 49–50
Theosophists, 132
Thiebaud, Wayne, 155
thingliness of a thing, 250–52
thingliness of a work of art, 253
things-in-themselves, 119, 239–40
Thomas, Aquinas, Saint, 63, 70, 138, 154, 166, 204
Thoreau, Henry David, 97
3D art, 95
"thrilling," 163
Thus Spoke Zarathustra (Nietzsche), 256
"tightly knit," 225
toggling theory, 198–99, 201
Tolstoy, Leo, *What is Art?*, 41
"too," 68
"total seizure," 85
"Touch" (Herring), 71n43
tourist attractions, 49, 107
tragedy, 216, 253
   Aristotle's conception of, 156
   as a fine art, 184
tragic, 155–56
tragic dimension of human existence, 183
tragic man, 240, 253–54, 257
tranquility, 172
transcendence, 57, 224–25, 241–42
transcendent realm, 86–87
transfiguration, 76, 84, 255
The Transfiguration of the Commonplace (Danto), 254
transformations, 77, 79, 108, 112, 194, 214
A Treatise of Human Nature (Hume), 26
tribal societies, 44, 74, 109, 165
"truth to materials," 117–18
Tsubaki, Andrew, 199
Tuan, Yi-Fu, 43–44, 61, 102–03, 112–13, 118, 154, 215
Turkish language, 72
turning life into a work of art, 210
Tzu, Lao, 241

ugliness, 115, 216
ugly, the, 64, 151, 215
"unblemished," 232
"uncluttered," 232
understanding, 28, 31–32, 188
"undisturbed," 172
"unified," 178
unity, 60, 87, 174, 178, 189–90, 203–04
    helpful in understanding aura, 136
universals, 28, 36, 41
urban aesthetics, 95
urban landscapes, 101
    aesthetics of, 96
urbanized space
    experience of nature in, 97
"User's Guide to Entropy" (Bois), 222n8
Usman, Dakyes, 164
utopia, Wordsworth's idea of, 195

valence, 132–33
Van Gogh, Vincent
    Bedroom in Arles (1888), 197
    peasant woman's shoes (painting), 110, 240, 248–49, 251–52
    true sublime of everyday, 256
Vincent's Chair with his Pipe (1888), 81
Vaughan Williams, Ralph, 173
Venturi, Robert, 52
Venus de Milo, 101
vernacular, 42–43, 52
"very," 111
Vincent's Chair with his Pipe (1888) (Van Gogh), 81
violence, 45, 209, 215
virtual worlds, 49–50
visual arts
    cleanliness (clean lines), 220
    surface aesthetic qualities, 219–20
visual culture theorists, 47
vitality, 182
vividness, 134
Voltaire, *Candide*, 215

Wall, Jeff, 52
Walton, Kendall, 104, 117
Warhol, Andy, 51, 83–84, 109, 113, 254–55, 258
    Brillo Boxes, 195–96, 255
    problematized the separation between art and everyday life, 255
    true sublime of everyday, 256
"warm," 228–29, 171
"warmth," 171
Wartofsky, Marx, 11
Waymack, Eunice Hammer, "Children's Reactions as a Basis for Teaching Picture Appreciation," 161n25
wedding ceremonies, 175
weddings and festivals, 18, 75
Weigel, Margaret, "Terrorism and the Sublime," 238n3
Weitz, Morris, 19, 91
Weitzman, Erica, "No Fun," 154
"well thought-out," 68
"well-laid fire," 177
"well-ordered," 111
"well-planned," 68
Welsch, Wolfgang, 184
Wessell, Leonard P., "The Aesthetics of Living Form in Schiller and Marx," 37n46
Western technological tradition, 120, 250
Weston, Edward, 52
What is Art? (Tolstoy), 41
"what is?" question, 89
"What Kind of Tears?" (Minor), 238n3
Whitman, Walt, 51
Wilson, Elizabeth, *The Sphinx in the City*, 237n2
Winterbourne, A.T., 244–45
wisdom, 254
Witherspoon, Gary, 42
Wittgenstein, Ludwig, 19, 62
women and women's work, 39, 51, 224
Women's Liberation and the Sublime (Mann), 238n4

wonder, 108–10
"wonderful," 174–75
wood-working, 43
Wordsworth, William, 51, 97–98, 195
"The Work of Art" (Benjamin), 214
"Working and Dancing" (Carroll), 54n103
working class, 36, 39, 51, 88, 216
Wright, Frank Lloyd, 176

Yoga, 47
yugen (Japanese concept), 199, 207

"yummy," 159

Zangwill, Nick, 147–48, 168, 191–92
Zen, 119
Zen aesthetics, 199–201
Zen Buddhist monks, 194–96, 199, 201, 241
Zen commitment to egalitarianism, 199
Zen enlightenment, 199
Zen satori, 194–95, 199, 201, 240–42, 254
Zenzen, M.J., 57, 90
Ziff, Paul, 106, 197
Zola, *Germinal*, 140